# Jordan & Syria
## a travel survival kit

Hugh Finlay

**Jordan & Syria – a travel survival kit**
  1st edition

**Published by**
  Lonely Planet Publications
  Head Office: PO Box 88, South Yarra, Victoria 3141, Australia
  Also: PO Box 2001A, Berkeley, CA 94702, USA

**Printed by**
  Colorcraft, Hong Kong

**Photographs by**
  Hugh Finlay

**Published**
  October 1987

Although the author and publisher have tried to make the information as accurate as possible, they accept no responsibility for any loss, injury or damage sustained by any traveller using this book.

National Library of Australia
Cataloguing in Publication Data

Finlay, Hugh
  Jordan & Syria

  Includes index.
  ISBN 0 86442 016 1.

  1. Jordan – Description and travel – Guide-books.
  2. Syria – Description and travel – Guide-books. I. Title.

918.5'04633

## Hugh Finlay

After deciding there must be more to life than civil engineering, Hugh took off around Australia, working in everything from spray painting to diamond prospecting, before hitting the overland trail. He spent three years travelling and working in three continents, including a stint on an irrigation project in Saudi Arabia, before joining Lonely Planet in 1985. The last we saw of him he was heading for North Africa to research our new guide to that area.

| | |
|---|---|
| **Editor** | Peter Turner |
| **Maps & Cover Design** | Vicki Beale |
| **Design & Illustrations** | Valerie Tellini |
| **Typesetting** | Ann Jeffree |

Thanks must also go to Debbie Lustig and Richard Nebesky for proof reading.

### Acknowledgements

Special thanks to Andy Murphy in Amman for his great hospitality and dedication to the task of having a good time all the time, and to the following people for their help along the way: Gerald Fontaine, Christian Springer, Chris Baldensperger, Dorothee Laarmann, Ghislaine Perrier, Greg Wood, Mal Dean, Patrick Crolly and Barbara McCabe, Peter Cape, Tony Howard and Di Taylor, Bernhard the Biker from Germany and David Kennedy.

### The Next Edition

All travel guides rely on new information to stay up to date and one of the best sources of this information is travellers on the road. At Lonely Planet we get a constant stream of letters and postcards that help us keep in contact with the latest travel developments. So if you find that things have changed write to us and let us know. Corrections, suggestions, improvements and additions are greatly appreciated and the best letters will get a free copy of the next edition or another Lonely Planet guide of your choice.

# Contents

# Introduction

If Jordan and Syria were elsewhere in the world they would be crawling with tourists, but because they are in the heart of the volatile Middle East they are low on most people's list of places to visit. Given it's unflattering media profile – that of a region of barren desert and fanatics bent on revolution – it is a surprise to many that not only is it safe to travel here, but that the local Arab inhabitants are among the most hospitable in the world. The closest you'll come to being hijacked is to be dragged off to a café to drink tea and chat for a while with the locals.

Certainly, things aren't the same as at home – in many cases they are a whole lot better. Where else can you leave your belongings unattended for hours, safe in the knowledge that they will be there on your return, and where can you wander the streets any time of the day or night without fear for your safety.

With a history of permanent settlement going back some 11,000 years, the number of archaeological and historic sites is enough to satiate even the most avid ruin buff. They run the whole gamut from 10th-century-BC Jericho through the well-known civilisations of the Phoenicians, Greeks, Romans and Byzantines to the more contemporary Muslims, Crusaders, Ottoman Turks and even the British and the French – they have all left their mark. Add to this a few lesser-known cultures such as the Nabataeans (builders of the incredible city of Petra) and the Palmyrenes, who at one stage had the audacity to

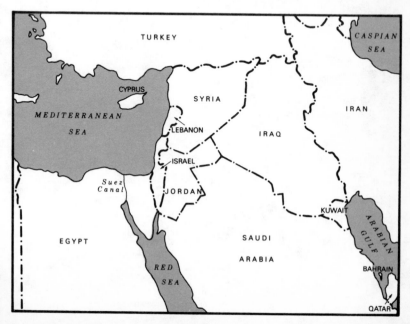

threaten the might of Rome at its peak, and you start to get an idea of the diverse influences which have played a part in shaping this region. Everyone from Tutankhamun to Winston Churchill has been involved at some stage.

When you've had your fill of history, you can take time out to explore some of the natural wonders on offer: take a camel ride through the incredible desert landscapes of Wadi Rum (one of Lawrence of Arabia's old stamping grounds); don a mask and snorkel and head underwater in the Gulf of Aqaba to see some of the finest coral reefs anywhere; or have a swim, or more precisely, a float, in the saline waters of the Dead Sea – the lowest point on earth.

The two countries have developed rapidly this century and both offer the visitor the facilities to make life comfortable at an affordable price. Accommodation ranges from five-star luxury for the well-heeled down to simple but perfectly adequate establishments for the impecunious. Transport is fast and efficient, and modern, air-conditioned buses or trains service all the major centres. And when it comes to food, sit yourself down to a formal banquet, or squat around a communal bowl of rice and meat with a Bedouin family in their goat-hair tent and tuck in by hand.

Fortunately these two countries will never boom as mass tourist destinations, but for those with an open mind, a bit of patience, plenty of time and a taste for something different, Jordan and Syria offer the more adventurous traveller a rare chance to really get off the beaten track.

# Facts about the Region

### HISTORY

The history of Syria and Jordan is one of invasion and conquest. The region was never strong enough to form an empire itself, and it was for the most part a collection of city-states, but its strategic position ensured that all the great early civilisations passed through here. The Egyptians, Assyrians, Babylonians, Hittites, Greeks, Romans, Saracens and Crusaders all helped to shape the history of the region. They traded, built cities and fought their wars here, leaving behind rich cultural influences.

The modern states of Jordan and Syria are creations of the 20th century, however, the region they encompass can lay claim to having one of the oldest civilisations in the world. Archaeological finds from Jericho on the west bank of the Jordan River have been positively dated at around 9000 BC. They have revealed an extensive village where the inhabitants lived in mud and stone houses and there is evidence of agriculture and animal domestication. Major finds in Syria at Ras Shamra (Ugarit, *circa* 6600 BC) on the Mediterranean coast and at Mari (*circa* 4500 BC) on the Euphrates River, show more advanced settlements, that would later become sophisticated city-states.

From 3000 BC, the region was settled by the Amorites, a warlike semitic tribe, and the Canaanites who mostly inhabited the coastal lowlands. It was around this time that the villages of Syria and Palestine came to the attention of Egypt to the south-west, and the expanding Euphrates Valley empires to the east.

Sargon of Akkad, a powerful ruler of Mesopotamia from 2334 to 2279 BC, marched to the Mediterranean in search of conquest and natural resources to supply his growing empire. From humble beginnings, he had become the greatest ruler in Mesopotamia. It is said that as a baby he was fished from the Euphrates River by a gardener who found him floating in a basket. He was raised as a gardener, but Sargon obviously had greater things in mind. After becoming cup-bearer for the ruler of the city of Kish in northern Sumer, he gathered an army and with his great military prowess and ability to organise, he set about conquering the cities of the south. He went on to become king, and the world's first great empire builder.

Sargon of Akkad

Sargon's ascendancy in the Mediterranean area led to the growth of many towns with strong Mesopotamian influence. Trade with Egypt flourished as it too needed wood, stone and metal to supply the needs of its rapidly expanding empire. Cities like Jericho and Byblos (in present-day Lebanon) became well established and prospered with this trade.

By about 1700 BC, Palestine was part of the Hyksos Empire of Egypt. The Hyksos were themselves Asiatic invaders and were therefore despised in Egypt. The revolt and pursuit of the Hyksos across Palestine by the Egyptians under the leadership of Kamose of Thebes led to a period of expansion of the Egyptian empire. By 1520 BC, Thutmose I claims to have reached the banks of the Euphrates River, although he was met by stubborn resistance from the local inhabitants and by no means controlled the entire area.

In 1480 BC, a revolt organised by over 300 Syrian and Palestinian rulers was easily crushed and Egypt was now firmly established in the Palestine and southern Syrian region. They would remain so for over a century. In the north, however, the various principalities coalesced to form the Mitanni Empire. They held off all Egyptian attempts at control, helped in part by their invention of the horse-drawn chariot as a weapon of war.

It was the encroachments of the Hittites from the north in about 1365 BC, under the young ambitious leader Suppiluliumas, which led to the fall of the Mitanni Empire. Despite some half-hearted attempts by the new pharaoh, Tutankhamen, to gain control, by 1330 BC all of Syria was firmly in the hands of the Hittites.

The two powers clashed at the bloody Battle of Kadesh on the Orontes River in Syria around 1300 BC. Militarily it was an indecisive war, but it dealt the Egyptians a strategic defeat and saw them retreat into Palestine. Finally in 1284 BC, the two opposing forces signed a treaty of friendship which ended a long period of clashes between empires for control of Syria. It left the Egyptians with a turbulent Palestine and the Hittites with Syria and the threat from the rising power of Assyria.

This marked the end of three prosperous centuries in the Levant (the early name for the area now occupied by Syria, Lebanon and Israel). The area was well placed to make the most of trade between Egypt to the south, Mesopotamia to the east and Anatolia to the north. Although it was favourably suited to the production of olives, grapes, barley and wheat, as well as livestock-raising, it was the control of the natural resources of the region which really kept the foreign powers interested. The prosperity of the various cities largely depended on the extent to which they controlled the mule-caravan routes.

One of the most important contributions to world history from this period was the development of written scripts. The ancient site of Ugarit in Syria has yielded the oldest alphabet yet known. Until then only Egyptian heiroglyphics and Mesopotamian cuneiform existed. Both required hundreds of symbols that were far too difficult for anyone but the scribes to use. By 1000 BC, linear, rather than pictorial scripts were in general use. It's from these alphabets, developed further in Palestine, that today's alphabets are derived.

From about the 13th century BC, Palestine was threatened by an invasion of 'Peoples from the Sea' – the Philistines. The Egyptian empire was in decline. It had overextended itself and was under threat from Libyan tribes to the west, allowing the raiders from the Aegean to assert themselves and take control of the area. Egyptian influence rapidly dwindled, and the Hittite empire also declined, finally collapsing around 1200 BC. The Philistines settled on the coastal plain of Canaan in an area which came to be known as the Plain of Philistia and from which the name Palestine is derived.

The Philistines' ascendancy owed much to their use of iron for weapons and armour which the Canaanites and Egyptians did not possess. In fact the Iron Age is traditionally given as beginning in the 12th century BC.

At about the same time the east bank of the Jordan River was settled by three

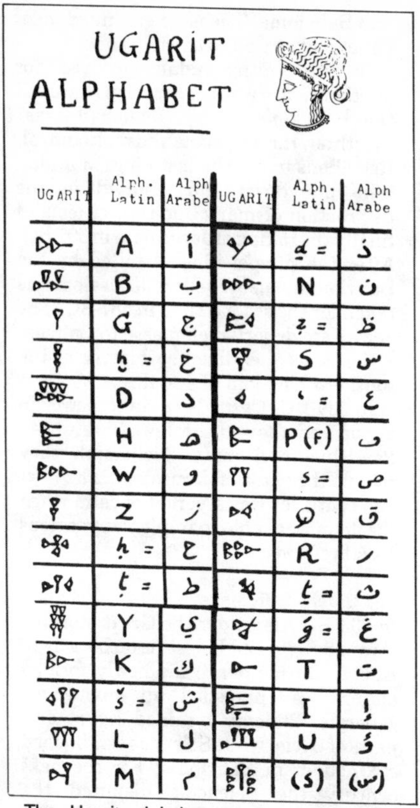

# UGARIT ALPHABET

| UGARIT | Alph. Latin | Alph Arabe | UGARIT | Alph. Latin | Alph Arabe |
|---|---|---|---|---|---|
| ▷▷- | A | ﺍ | ❧ | ḏ = | ﺫ |
| ᵥ̃ᵥ̃ | B | ﺏ | ▷▷▷- | N | ﻥ |
| � | G | ﻉ | ☲◁ | ẓ = | ﻅ |
| ĩ | ḫ = | ﻍ | ᵥ̃ᵥ̃ | S | ﺱ |
| ᵥᵥᵥ | D | ﺩ | ◁ | ' = | ﻉ |
| ☰ | H | ﻫ | ᛒ= | P (F) | ﻑ |
| ᙏᵒᵒ- | W | ﻭ | ᵧᵧ | s = | ﺹ |
| ĩ | Z | ﺯ | ▷◁ | Q | ﻕ |
| ᵒᵍᵒ | ḥ = | ﺡ | ᵦᵦᵒ- | R | ﺭ |
| ▷ᵧ◁ | ṭ = | ﻁ | ᵧ | ṯ = | ﺙ |
| ᵥᵥᵥᵥ | Y | ﻱ | ᵥ◢ | ġ = | ﻍ |
| ᴮ▷- | K | ﻙ | ᵒ- | T | ﺕ |
| ◁ᵧᵧ | š = | ﺵ | ☰ | I | ﺍ |
| ᵧᵧᵧ | L | ﻝ | .ﻡ | U | ﻭ |
| -◁ᵧ | M | ﺭ | ᵦᵧᵦ | (s) | (ﺱ) |

The Ugarit alphabet was carried by the Phoenicians throughout the Mediterranean and was adopted by the Greeks, Etruscans and Romans.

other groups: the Edomites in the south, the Moabites to the east of the Dead Sea, and the Ammonites on the edge of the Arabian Desert with their capital at Rabbath Ammon, present-day Amman.

## Coming of the Israelites
It was not until the late 11th century BC that the Philistines were threatened. Led by Moses, the Israelites had left Egypt around 1270 BC – the Exodus – and after 40 years in the wilderness, they overran the local rulers and settled in the hills of Transjordan (the name used to describe the area east of the Jordan River).

Following the victories of Moses, his successor Joshua led the 12 tribes across the Jordan River and conquered Jericho. The Israelites then suffered a severe defeat at the Battle of Ebenezer in 1050 BC which saw the Philistines capture the ark of the Covenant – the symbol of unity of the 12 tribes of Israel. Further disaster came after another major battle when Saul, who had been made king of Israel in 1020 BC, took his own life and left the Israelites leaderless and at the mercy of the Philistines.

The fortunes of Israel took a turn very much for the better when Saul's successor, David, was proclaimed king in 1000 BC. After defeating the Philistines near Jerusalem, he then set about regaining the territory of his neighbours east of the Jordan. By the end of his reign in 960 BC he ruled the princedoms of Edom, Moab and Ammon, the city-states of southern Syria, and was paid tribute by the Philistine princes and the tribes as far east as the Euphrates.

After the death of David and the ascendancy of his son Solomon to the throne, Israel entered its golden age. This period saw great advancements in trade which extended down the African and Red Sea coasts and into Asia Minor. A visit to Jerusalem by the Queen of Sheba (in present-day Yemen) is evidence that there was also overland trade to the Arabian Peninsula. A great part of the success of Solomon's rule was derived from his administrative skills which, however, led to high tax burdens and forced labour. Resentment of these hardships led to a revolt against Solomon and following his death in 922 BC, the united kingdom was divided into the separate kingdoms of Judah in the south and Israel in the north.

The main threat to Israel was the Aramaen state of Damascus as the two were rivals for the lucrative Syrian and

Transjordanian trade. This rivalry led to an alliance between Israel and the Phoenicians when the sixth king of Israel, Omri, married off his son Ahab to the Phoenician princess Jezebel. The defeat of Ahab by Mesha, the King of Moab, is recorded in the famous Mesha Stele (Moabite Stone) found at Dhiban (near present-day Kerak in Jordan). A short period of relative peace was shattered in 722 BC when the Assyrians under Sargon II devastated Israel and its capital Samaria, deported the citizens and replaced them with settlers from Syria

**Empire of David & Solomon
1000-930 BC**

and Babylonia. The northern kingdom of Israel had ceased to exist.

In the south, Judah survived for another century under Assyrian rule until the Babylonian king Nebuchadnezzar overthrew the Assyrians and took control. Rebellions under the last kings of Judah were put down and resulted in the destruction of many Judaean cities and finally the taking of Jerusalem in 597 BC. After the puppet-king installed by the Babylonians also rebelled, Jerusalem was taken for the second time in 587 BC. The Jews were deported en masse to Babylon – the Exile – ending the history of the southern kingdom of Judah.

In 539 BC, Cyrus II came to power in Persia and allowed the Jews to return to Palestine, and under Nehemiah they rebuilt the walls of Jerusalem. The next two centuries was a period of calm when the Jews were able to implement various social reforms.

### The Greeks & Romans

In 333 BC Alexander the Great stormed through Syria and Palestine on his way to Egypt. On his death his newly formed empire was parcelled up among his generals. Ptolemy I gained Egypt and parts of Syria, while Seleucus established a kingdom in Babylonia. For the next century the Seleucids disputed the Ptolemies' claim to Palestine and tried unsuccessfully to oust the Ptolemies before finally succeeding in 198 BC under the leadership of Antiochus III. He then tried to extend his influence westwards but met with the new power of Rome. His army was defeated by the Romans and in 188 BC he was forced to cede all his territories in Asia Minor.

After attacking Egypt, the Seleucids, under Antiochus IV, sacked Jerusalem and left the Jews with no alternative but to revolt after virtually banning their religion and dedicating the Temple of Jerusalem to Zeus – the supreme god of the ancient Greeks.

Led by Judas Maccabeus of the

Hasmonean family, the Jews gradually re-established themselves and by 141 BC were recognised as an independent territory, occupying a large area east of the Jordan. During the reign of John Hyrcanus and his successors, the boundaries were further extended to cover most of Palestine and Transjordan. On his death a squabble between his sons Aristobolus and Hyrcanus II led to the intervention of the Romans under Pompey who took Damascus in 64 BC and Palestine the following year. The Jewish kingdom was now under Roman control and Hyrcanus II was appointed high priest.

All of western Syria and Palestine became the new Roman province of Syria. The most important cities east of the Jordan were organised into a league of 10. The Decapolis, as it was known, was formed as a commercial and military alliance for the advancement of trade and as protection against the Jews and Nabataeans.

The Parthian kings of Persia and Mesopotamia invaded and occupied most of the province in 40 BC but Mark Antony was able to restore order, albeit with some difficulty. Antipater, minister for Hyrcanus II, was made governor of Judaea and his sons Herod and Phaesal were appointed governors of Jerusalem and Galilee respectively. With the Parthian invasion, the Hasmonean family, now led by Aristobolus' son Antigonus, were able to seize power. Phaesal and Hyrcanus II were captured and Herod escaped to Rome where on appeal to the senate he was named king of Israel and returned to Palestine. With Roman help he expelled the Parthians and took Jerusalem in 37 BC in a bloody conflict. Mark Antony had Antigonus executed.

The period of Herod's rule from 37 BC to 4 AD was a time of relative peace and prosperity for Palestine. What followed after his death was a period of unrest which led to a Jewish revolt in 66 AD.

**Kingdom of Herod the Great 40-4 BC**

Nero entrusted the commander Vespasian with the task of restoring order and he effectively subdued Galilee and Judaea. His son Titus captured (and virtually destroyed) Jerusalem.

The Herodian rulers were a perverse lot. In his later years, Herod the Great suffered from mental instability and became increasingly tyrannical. He murdered his ex-wife Mariamne, and for good measure also murdered many of her family including her mother, brother, grandfather and her two sons. Fearing plots against him, he also disposed of three of his own sons. He tried at least once to commit suicide but finally died of natural causes. His son, Herod Antipas, had John the Baptist put to death; and his sister's grandson, Herod Agrippa I, had St James executed and St Peter imprisoned. The last of the line was Herod Agrippa II, son of Herod Agrippa I, who lived incestuously with his sister Berenice.

It is now widely accepted that a Jew by the name of Jesus lived in Palestine in the 1st century, but there is no evidence to suggest that he saw himself as the Messiah or intended to be the founder of a new church – this was done by those who came after him. They combined his words with elements of Judaism and paganism to form the new religion.

Apart from making the Jewish nation a province, the Romans made remarkable few changes to the Jewish way of life. This leniency led to a second revolt in 132 AD which was put down by Hadrian who then gave Jerusalem the new name of Aelia Capitolina. Captive Jews were sold into slavery and the religious practices of the survivors were strictly curtailed.

In the 3rd century the Sassainians, the successors to the Parthians, invaded northern Syria but were repelled by the Syrian prince Odenathus of Palmyra. He was granted the title *dux orientalis* (commander of the East) for his efforts, but died shortly afterwards. His widow, the ambitious Zenobia, assumed the title Augusta and with her sights set on Rome, invaded western Syria, Palestine and Egypt. In 272, Aurelian destroyed Palmyra and carted Zenobia off to Rome as a prisoner.

With the conversion of the emperor Constantine early in the 4th century, Christianity become the dominant religion. Jerusalem became the site of holy pilgrimage to Christian shrines and this did wonders for the prosperity of the country. During the reign of Justinian from 527 to 565, churches were built in many towns in Palestine and Syria. Meanwhile, the Jews also prospered and continued to build synagogues despite the fact that this was now illegal.

This rosy state of affairs was abruptly shattered in the 7th century when the Persians once again descended from the north, taking Damascus and Jerusalem in 614 and eventually Egypt in 616, although Byzantine fortunes were revived when the emperor Heraclius invaded

Persia and forced the Persians into a peace agreement. In the south however, the borders of the empire were being attacked by Arab invaders – no new thing – but these Arabs were ambitious Muslims, followers of Mohammed.

It was in this period of Greek control that the Nabataean Arabs in Petra and related tribes in Palmyra flourished on the trade which had boomed all the way from the Red Sea in Arabia to the ports of the Mediterranean. Because they controlled the trade routes, they were able to extract hefty protection money and extend their spheres of influence.

## The Coming of Islam

With the Byzantine Empire severely weakened by the Persian invasion, and with the subordinate Aramaen population alienated by Byzantine domination, the Muslims met with little resistance and in some cases were welcomed.

Because of its position on the pilgrims' route to Mecca, Syria became the hub of the new Muslim empire which soon stretched from Spain and west Africa, right across to India. Mu'awiyah, the governor of Damascus, became the first Omayyed caliph and Damascus replaced Medina as the political capital.

The Omayyed period was one of great achievement and saw the building of great monuments such as the Omayyed Mosque in Damascus and the Mosque of Omar and the Dome of the Rock in Jerusalem. Their great love of the desert led to the construction of palaces – the so-called Desert Palaces east of Amman – where the caliphs could indulge their Bedouin past. Omayyed rule was overthrown in 750 when the Abbasid caliphate seized power and transferred the capital to Baghdad. Syria and Jordan went into a rapid decline as a result.

The next important arrivals on the scene were the Crusaders who established four states, the most important being the kingdom of Jerusalem in 1099. Fortresses were built at Kerak, Shobak, Wadi Musa and Jeziret Far'on just offshore from Aqaba. In Syria a string of castles, including the well-preserved Crac des Chevaliers, was constructed along the coast. Their hold on the country was always tenuous as they were a minority and could only survive if the Muslim states were weak and divided. Nureddin, son of a Turkish ruler, was able to unite Syria and annex Egypt. His campaign was completed by Saladin who overthrew the Fatimid rulers of Egypt in 1171 and recaptured Palestine and most of the inland Crusader strongholds. European rule was restored to the coast for another century with the Third Crusade.

Prosperity returned to Syria with the rule of the Ayyubids, members of Saladin's family, who parcelled up his empire on his death. They were succeeded by the Mamelukes in 1250, just in time to repel the onslaught from the invading Mongol tribes from central Asia in 1260. The victorious Mameluke leader, Baybars I, ruled over a reunited Syria and Egypt until his death in 1277. By the end of the 13th century the Mamelukes had finally managed to rid the Levant of the Crusaders by capturing their last stronghold – the fortified island of Ruad (Arwad) – off the coast of Tartus in Syria.

However, more death and destruction was not far off and in 1401 the Mongol invader Timur (Tamerlaine) sacked Aleppo and Damascus, killing thousands and carting off many of the craftsmen to central Asia. His new empire lasted for only a few years but the rout sent Mameluke Syria into a decline for the next century.

## The Ottoman Turks

By 1516, Palestine, Jordan and Syria had been occupied by the Ottoman Turks and would stay that way for the next four centuries.

Up until the early 19th century, Syria prospered under Turkish rule. Damascus and Aleppo were important market towns

for the surrounding desert as well as being stages on the desert trade routes to Persia. Aleppo also became an important trading centre with Europe, and English and French merchants established themselves there.

For almost the whole of the 1830s the Egyptians once again gained control, led by Ibrahim Pasha, son of the Egyptian ruler Mohammed Ali. The high tax burdens and conscription imposed by Ibrahim were unpopular and the Europeans, fearful that the decline of Ottoman power might cause a crisis in Europe, intervened in 1840 and forced the Egyptians to withdraw.

The Muslim Arabs were happy enough under Turkish rule as they saw the Ottoman Empire as the political embodiment of Islam. After the Young Turk movement of 1909, power was in the hands of a military group whose harsh policies encouraged opposition and the growth of Arab nationalism.

## World War I

During WW I, the area of Syria and Jordan was the scene of fierce fighting between the Turks, under German command, and the British based in Suez. By the end of 1917 the British had occupied Jerusalem, followed by the rest of Syria a year later. Their successes in the Levant would not have been possible without the aid of the Arab army which had been formed under the leadership of Emir Faisal, son of Hussein, who was Sherif of Mecca and had taken up the reins of the Arab nationalist movement in 1914. The enigmatic British colonel, T E Lawrence, better known as Lawrence of Arabia, led the British forces under General Allenby's command and played an integral part in channelling the feeling of the Arab Revolt into effective action to drive out the Turks.

Under the Sykes-Picot agreement of 1916, Syria and Lebanon were to be placed under French mandate, while Jordan and Palestine would go to the British, although by the Balfour Declaration of 1917, Britain had already pledged support for a Jewish homeland.

In March 1920, Emir Faisal was proclaimed king of Syria but the Allied powers refused to recognise him. At the Conference of San Remo, the Allied supreme council gave France the mandate over Syria and Lebanon, and the British got Transjordan and Palestine.

Out of this mess emerged the modern-day countries of Syria, Lebanon, Jordan, and later Israel. The histories of the modern states of Syria and Jordan from 1920 on are dealt with under their respective sections.

## RELIGION
### Islam
Islam is the predominant religion in both Jordan and Syria. Muslims are called to prayer five times a day and no matter where you might be, there always seems to be a mosque within earshot.

In the early 7th century in Mecca, Mohammed received the word of Allah (God) and called on the people to turn away from pagan worship and submit to the one true God. His teachings appealed to the poorer levels of society and angered the wealthy merchant class. By 622 life had become sufficiently unpleasant for Mohammed and his followers that they were forced to migrate to Medina, an oasis town some 300 km to the north. This migration – the Hejira – marks the beginning of the Islamic Calendar, year 1 AH or 622 AD. By 630 they had gained a sufficient following to return and take Mecca.

With seemingly unlimited zeal and ambition, the followers of Mohammed spread the word, using force where necessary, and by 644 the Islamic state covered Syria, Persia, Iraq, Egypt and North Africa and in following decades its influence would extend from the Atlantic to the Indian Ocean.

Islam is the Arabic word for submission and underlies the duty of every Muslim to submit himself to Allah. This profession of faith (the *Shahada*) is the first of the Five Pillars of Islam, the five tenets in the Koran which guide Muslims in their daily life:

*Shahada* 'There is no God but Allah and Mohammed is his prophet' – this profession of faith is the fundamental tenet of Islam. It is to Islam what the lord's prayer is to Christianity, and it is often quoted, eg to greet the newborn and farewell the dead.

*Salah* is the call to prayer when five times a day – at dawn, midday, mid-afternoon, sunset and nightfall – Muslims must face Mecca and recite the prescribed prayer.

*Zakat* was originally the act of giving alms to the poor and needy. It has been developed by modern states into an obligatory land tax which goes to help the poor.

*Ramadan* is the ninth month of the Muslim calendar when all Muslims must fast from dawn to dusk. It commemorates the month when Mohammed had the Koran revealed to him.

*Hajj* is the pilgrimage to Mecca, the holiest place in Islam. It is the duty of every Muslim who is fit and can afford it to make the pilgrimage at least once in their life. On the pilgrimage, the pilgrim (*hajji*) wears a white seamless robe and walks around the *Kabbah*, the black stone in the centre of the mosque, seven times.

To Muslims, Allah is the same God that the Christians worship in the Bible and the Jews in the Torah. Adam, Abraham, Noah, Moses and Jesus are all recognised as prophets by Islam. Jesus is not, however, recognised as the son of God. According to Islam, all of these prophets partly received the word of God but only Mohammed received the complete revelation.

In its early days Islam suffered a major

schism that divided the faith into two streams: the *Sunnis* (or *Sunnites*) and the *Shi'ites*. The prophet's son-in-law, Ali, became the fourth Caliph following the murder of Mohammed's third successor, and he in turn was assassinated in 661 by the Governor of Syria who set himself up as Caliph. The Sunnis, who comprise the majority of Muslims today, are followers of the succession from the Caliph, while the Shi'ites follow the descendants of Ali.

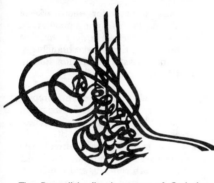

The Basmallah: 'In the name of God the Compassionate the Merciful.'

**Islam & the west** Unfortunately, Islam has been much maligned and misunderstood in the west in recent years. Any mention of it usually brings to mind one of two images: the 'barbarity' of some aspects of Islamic law such as flogging, stoning or the amputation of hands; or the so-called fanatics out to terrorise the west.

For most Muslims, however, and particularly for those in the Middle East, Islam is stability in a very unstable world. They are not aware that they are seen as a threat to the west, and in fact they see the inroads that western culture is making into their society as a threat to them.

While the west is offended by the anti-western rhetoric of the radical minority, the Muslims see the west, especially with its support of Israel, as a direct challenge to their struggle for Islamic rights and political independence.

Meanwhile, in the western media, the political violence of 'fanatics' in Lebanon is condemned, while similar violence in Afghanistan is applauded because it is directed at the Soviet Union. Similarly, political terrorism in the Middle East is emphasised as being motivated by religion, while in similar events in Northern Ireland the religious element barely rates a mention.

Just as the west receives a distorted and exaggerated view of Muslim society, so too are western values distorted in Islamic societies. The glamour of the west has lured those able to compete (usually the young, the rich and the well educated) but for others, the west is the bastion of moral decline and it is easier for them to reassert their faith in Islam, than to seek what they cannot attain. Often what is being accepted or rejected by Muslims is a mish-mash of western values which may bear little relation to life in the west.

As long as these misunderstandings exist, the fact that Islam offers many people a code of religious and political behaviour that they can apply to their daily lives, and makes an often difficult life tolerable, will be overlooked in favour of the view that the majority, rather than an extremely small minority, are extremists or radicals bent on revolution.

**Islamic Customs** When Muslims go to pray, they must follow certain rituals. The first is that they must wash their hands, arms, feet, head and neck in running water before praying. All mosques have a small area set aside for this purpose. If they are not in a mosque and there is no water available, clean sand suffices, and where there is no sand, they must just go through the motions of washing.

Then they must cover the head, face Mecca (all mosques are orientated so that the *mihrab* (prayer niche) faces the right direction) and follow a set pattern of gestures and genuflections – the photos of rows of Muslims kneeling with their heads touching the ground in the direction of Mecca are legion. If a mosque is not nearby, Muslims pray by the side of the road or in the street.

In everyday life, Muslims are prohibited from drinking alcohol, eating pork (as the animal is considered unclean) and must refrain from fraud, usury, slander and gambling.

**Islamic Minorities** In Syria the Shi'ites and other Muslim minorities, such as the Alawite and Druze, account for about 16% of the population.

The Druze religion is an off-shoot of Shi'ite Islam and was spread in the 11th century by missionaries from Egypt who followed the Fatimid caliph, Hakim. Most members of the Druze community now live in the mountains of Lebanon, although there are some small Druze towns in the Hauran, the area around the Syria/Jordan border. Their distinctive faith has survived intact mainly because of the secrecy that surrounds it. Not only is conversion to or from the faith prohibited, but only an elite, known as - *'uqqal* (knowers), have full access to the religious doctrine, the *hikmah*, which preaches *taqiyah* ('caution'). Under this code a believer living among Christians, for example, can outwardly conform to Christian belief while still being a Druze at heart. They believe that God is too sacred to be called by name, is amorphous and will reappear in other incarnations. Although the New Testament and the Koran are revered, they read their own scriptures at *khalwas* (meeting houses) on Thursdays.

In Syria the Alawites, an extreme Shi'ite subsect, are considered by some to be heretics as they worship Ali as a god. They live mostly around Lattakia or in the Hama-Homs area. They are usually found tilling the poorest land or holding down the least skilled jobs in the towns.

Jordan has a 25,000-strong community of non-Arab Sunni Muslims known as Circassians. They fled persecution in Russia in the late 19th century and settled in Turkey, Syria and Jordan. Intermarriage has made them virtually indistinguishable from their Arab neighbours.

The Chechens are another group of Caucasian origin in Jordan and are very similar to the Circassians.

### Christianity

Christians account for about 6% of Jordan's and 13% of Syria's population. There is a bewildering array of churches representing the three major branches of Christianity – Eastern Orthodox, Roman Catholic and Protestant.

**Eastern Orthodox** This branch is represented by the Greek Orthodox, Armenian Orthodox and Syrian Orthodox churches.

Greek Orthodox has its liturgy in Arabic and is the mother church of the Jacobites (Syrian Orthodox), who broke away in the 6th century, and the Greek Catholics who split in the 16th century.

Armenian Orthodox has its liturgy in classical Armenian and is seen by many to be the guardian of the Armenian national identity.

Syrian Orthodox uses Syriac, closely related to the Aramaic spoken by Christ. The patriarch lives in Damascus and the see (where the patriarch lives) has jurisdiction over foreign communities such as the Syrian Malankaras in Kerala, India; and Syrian Orthodox in the USA.

**Roman Catholic** These churches come under the jurisdiction of Rome and are listed from largest to smallest.

Greek Catholics come under the authority of the patriarch who resides in Damascus, but his jurisdiction includes the patriarchates of Jerusalem and Alexandria. The church observes the Byzantine tradition where married clergy are in charge of rural parishes and the diocesan clergy are celibate.

Armenian Catholics form a strong ethnic community. They fled from Turkish massacres in 1894 to 1896, and 1917 to 1921. They have their liturgy in classical Armenian. The patriarch resides in Beirut, and more than half of its members are from Aleppo.

Syrian Catholics have Syriac as the main liturgical language although some services are in Arabic. They are found mainly in the north-east of Syria and in Homs, Aleppo and Damascus.

Maronite Catholics trace their origins to St Maron who lived near Aleppo and under whose leadership the invading Byzantine armies were routed in 684. Their liturgy is in ancient West Syriac although the commonly used language is Arabic. They are found mainly in Lebanon but there are sizeable numbers in Syria in Aleppo. There are also communities in Europe and North and South America.

Latin Catholics live in western Syria and Aleppo where the vicar apostolic lives; and the Chaldean Catholics, who have preserved the ancient East Syrian liturgy which they practise in Syriac, are found mainly in eastern Syria, Aleppo and Damascus.

## LANGUAGE

Arabic is the official language in Jordan and Syria. Although English is widely spoken in Jordan and to a lesser extent French in Syria, any effort you make to communicate with the locals in their own language will be well rewarded. No matter how far off the mark your pronunciation or grammar might be, you'll often get the response (usually with a big smile): 'Ah, you speak Arabic very well!'. Greeting Syrian officials, who are generally less than helpful, with *Salaam wa laykoom* ('peace upon you' – the usual greeting) will often work wonders.

Learning the few basics you'll find useful in day-to-day travelling doesn't take long at all, but to master the horrendous complexities of Arabic would take some years of constant study.

## Greetings

Arabs place great importance on civility and it's rare that you'll see any interaction between people that doesn't begin with profuse greetings and enquiries into the other's health, his family's health and other niceties.

Arabic greetings are more formal than English and there is a reciprocal response to each greeting. These often vary slightly depending on whether you're addressing a man or a woman.

The most common greeting is *Salaam wa laykoom* (peace upon you). The correct reply is *mwalaykoom a salaam* (and on you be peace).

| | |
|---|---|
| Hello | *marhaba* |
| Welcome | *ahlan wa sahlan* |
| | or just *ahlan* |
| How are you? | *shlonak* (m) |
| | *shlonik* (f) |
| Fine (thanks be to God) | *ilhumdalilah* |
| Good morning | *sabah alkhair* |
| (response) | *sabah an-noor* |
| Good evening | *messa alkhair* |
| (response) | *messa an-noor* |
| Good night | *tisbak ala khair* |
| Goodbye | *ma'asalaama* |

### Useful words & phrases

| | |
|---|---|
| please (making a request) | *min fadlak* (to a male) |
| | *min fadlik* (to a female) |
| please (as in: please come in) | *fadha* |
| thank you (very much) | *shukran* |
| | *shukran jazeelan* |
| you are welcome | *afwan* or *ahlan* |
| yes | *aiwa* or *na'am* |
| no | *la* |

| | |
|---|---|
| no problem | *mish mushkila* |
| never mind | *malesh* |
| what is your name? | *sho-ismak* (m) |
| | *sho-ismik* (f) |
| my name is . . . | *ismi . . .* |
| I | *ana* |
| you | *inta* (m) |
| | *inti* (f) |
| he | *huwa* |
| she | *hiya* |
| we | *nahnu* |
| they | *humma* |
| I am . . . | *ana . . .* |
| Australian | *austrahly* |
| American | *amreekahny* |
| Canadian | *kanady* |
| English | *ingleezy* |
| French | *fransaawy* |
| I speak . . . | *ana bikallem . . .* |
| English | *ingleezy* |
| French | *fransaawy* |
| German | *almaany* |
| Do you speak English? | *hal tatakallamy ingleezy* |
| I understand | *ana afham* |
| I don't understand | *ana ma afham* |
| What does this mean? | *yaanee ay?* |
| I need an interpreter | *ana ayzeen mutarjem* |
| Where are you from? | *min wayn inta?* |

## Questions & Comments

| | |
|---|---|
| what is this? | *maa hadha?* |
| how much? | *bikam?* |
| how many? | *kam wahid?* |
| how much money? | *kam lire?* |
| how many kilometres? | *kam kilometre?* |
| is there . . .? | *fi . . .?* |
| there isn't (any) | *maafi* |
| big/small | *kabeer/sagheer* |
| good/bad | *kwayyis/mish kwayyis* |

| | |
|---|---|
| finished | *kalaas* |
| open/closed | *maftooh/mughlaq* |
| cheap/expensive | *rakhees/ghaaly* |
| hot/cold | *harr/baarid* |
| to/from | *ila/min* |

## Travelling & Places

| | |
|---|---|
| where is the . . .? | *wayn . . . ?* |
| post office | *muqtab bareed* |
| tourist office | *muqtab siaha* |
| Foreigners Department | *sho-awn ajaneb* |
| bus station | *mahattah albas* |
| Hotel Orient | *foondooq Orient* |
| bank | *masraf* |
| market | *souq* |
| bus | *albas* |
| train | *alqitaar* |
| plane | *almattar* |
| service taxi | *servees* |
| here/there | *hinna/hinnak* |
| left/right | *yasaar/yameen* |
| straight ahead | *ala tuul* |
| slow/fast | *balee/sareeh* |

## Hotels & Accommodation

| | |
|---|---|
| Do you have . . . ? | *fi . . .?* |
| a room | *ghurfah* |
| a double room | *ghurfah ithneen* |
| a shower | *doosh* |
| hot water | *moi harr* |
| a toilet | *twahlet* |
| soap | *saboon* |
| air-con | *kondishon* |
| electricity | *kahrabaa* |

## Numbers

Arabic numerals are simple enough to learn and, unlike the written language, run from left to right.

| | |
|---|---|
| ¼ | *ruba* |
| ½ | *noos* |
| ¾ | *talata ruba* |

| | | |
|---|---|---|
| 0 | • | *sifre* |
| 1 | ١ | *wahid* |
| 2 | ٢ | *ithneen* |

| | | |
|---|---|---|
| 3 | ٣ | talata |
| 4 | ٤ | arba'a |
| 5 | ٥ | khamsa |
| 6 | ٦ | sitta |
| 7 | ٧ | sabah |
| 8 | ٨ | tamanya |
| 9 | ٩ | tissa'a |
| 10 | ١٠ | ashara |

| | |
|---|---|
| 11 | wahidahsh |
| 12 | ithna'ahsh |
| 13 | talatahsh |
| 14 | arba'atahsh |
| 15 | khamstahsh |
| 16 | sit'tahsh |
| 17 | sabahtahsh |
| 18 | tamantahsh |
| 19 | tissa'atahsh |
| 20 | ashreen |
| 21 | wahid wa ashreen |
| 22 | ithneen wa ashreen |

| | |
|---|---|
| 30 | talateen |
| 40 | arba'een |
| 50 | khamseen |
| 60 | sit'teen |
| 70 | saba'een |
| 80 | tamaneen |
| 90 | tissa'een |
| 100 | mia |
| 101 | mia wa wahid |
| 125 | mia wa khamsa wa ashreen |

| | |
|---|---|
| 200 | miatayn |
| 300 | talata mia |
| 400 | arba'a mia |

| | |
|---|---|
| 1000 | alf |
| 2000 | alftayn |
| 3000 | talat talaf |
| 4000 | arba'a talaf |

**Time**

| | |
|---|---|
| when | mataa |
| tomorrow | bukra |
| today | al-youm |
| day | youm |
| hour | saa |
| week | usbooh |
| month | shahar |

| | |
|---|---|
| year | sanar |
| what is the time? | saa kam? |
| how many hours? | kam saa |
| 5 o'clock | saa khamsa |
| five hours | khamsa saa |

Questions like 'Is the bus coming?' or 'Will the bank be open later?' generally elicit the inevitable response: insh'allah – God willing – an expression you'll hear over and over again.

**Days of the Week**

| | |
|---|---|
| Monday | al-ithneen |
| Tuesday | at-talata |
| Wednesday | al-arbiya |
| Thursday | al-khamees |
| Friday | al-jumah |
| Saturday | al-assabt |
| Sunday | al-ahad |

**Months**

The Islamic year has 12 lunar months and is 11 days shorter than the western calendar, so important Muslim dates will fall 11 days earlier each (western) year.

When the western calendar is being used, which is often the case, the names remain virtually the same; so January becomes yanaayir and October octobar. The Hijra months however, have their own names:

| | |
|---|---|
| 1st | Moharram |
| 2nd | Safar |
| 3rd | Rabei al Awal |
| 4th | Rabei al Tani |
| 5th | Gamada al Awal |
| 6th | Gamada al Taniyya |
| 7th | Ragab |
| 8th | Shaaban |
| 9th | Ramadan |
| 10th | Shawal |
| 11th | Zuu'l Qeda |
| 12th | Zuu'l Hagga |

**ISLAMIC HOLIDAYS**

As the Hijra (Islamic) calendar is 11 days shorter than the Gregorian (western) calendar, Islamic holidays fall 11 days earlier each year. January 1 1988 is 11 Gamada al Awal 1408 AH. (Islamic years are numbered from the Hijra – the flight of Mohammed to Medina in 622 AD.) The actual dates may vary as they depend upon the sighting of the moon.

Ras al Sana
  New Years Day, celebrated on 1 Moharram (13 August 1988, 2 August 1989).
Mulid al Nabi
  The Prophet Mohammed's birthday, celebrated on 12 Rabei El Awal (22-23 October 1988, 13-14 October 1989).
Ramadan
  The ninth month of the Muslim calendar and the second pillar of Islam when pious Muslims fast during daylight hours for the whole month (18 April to 17 May 1988, 7 April to 6 May 1989). There are no public holidays but it is difficult to deal with officialdom because of unusual opening hours.
Eid al Fitr
  The end of the Ramadan fast (17 May 1988, 6 May 1989).
Eid al Adhah
  The time when Muslims fulfill the fifth pillar of Islam – the pilgrimage to Mecca. This period lasts from 10-13 Zuu'l Hagga (25 July 1988, 14 July 1989).

## HEALTH

There are no inoculations needed for entry to Jordan or Syria unless you're coming from a disease-affected area, but it's a good idea to have preventive shots for tetanus, typhoid and cholera. Some border officials may not be aware of which countries are disease affected, so you could save yourself some hassle if you have a duly stamped International Health Card.

The medical services in both countries are well developed in the larger towns and cities and many of the doctors have been trained overseas and speak English. Your embassy will usually be able to recommend a reliable doctor or hospital if the need arises. For minor complaints, pharmacies can usually supply what you need although you will probably have to use sign language in out-of-the-way places. Drugs normally sold only on prescription in the west are available over the counter in Syria, but not in Jordan. The price of antibiotics in Jordan is outrageous (US$20 for a course of tablets) so bring a supply with you.

Any special medication that you take regularly should be brought in with you as it may not be available in Syria or Jordan.

### Medical Kit

It would be an unwise traveller that doesn't carry at least a basic medical kit. Items worth carrying include: bandaids, sterile gauze bandage, antiseptic cream or liquid, cotton wool, thermometer, tweezers, scissors, antibiotic cream, a course of a broad-spectrum antibiotics (check with your doctor), insect repellent, anti-malarial tablets and multi-vitamins.

Some medication for diarrhoea can be handy in emergencies – Lomotil is a popular one – and some paracetamol or codeine for aches and fevers.

### Medical Insurance

Don't leave home without it! Hopefully you'll never need it, but if you do, you'll be glad you've got it. There are many policies around and any good travel agent can put you on the right track. Most travel insurance packages include baggage and life insurance. Read the fine print and find one that suits your needs and covers the countries you will be visiting.

### Food & Water

Tap water in the major towns is safe to drink but if your stomach is a bit delicate, there is bottled water available everywhere. Chances are that if you have just come from Turkey or Egypt and survived you shouldn't have any trouble here. If you

PURE NATURAL
MINERAL WATER

**Kawther**

LITRE
1.5

BOTTLED UNDER THE TECHNICAL SUPERVISION OF
**SPERE FRANCE**
FROM THE HALABAT CASTLE SPRINGS OF AZRAK JORDAN

LABORATORY ASSISTANCE AND CONTROL · HYGIENE INSTITUT, GELSENKIRCHEN, GERMANY
ARAB MINERAL WATER CO. · AMMAN
Tel. 898195 FOR REGISTERING ORDERS 24 HOURS DAILY

الكوثر
من ينبوع قصر الحلبات ـ الأردن

Batch No. 633

are buying bottled water, make sure that the seal is unbroken or you may be paying for plain old tap water. If bottled water is unavailable (there are occasionally shortages in Syria) the locally made soft drinks are fine and have a surprisingly low sugar content.

When it comes to food, there are a few common-sense precautions to take. Never eat unwashed fruit or vegetables and steer clear of stalls where the food doesn't look fresh or the owner looks like a grub.

Milk and cream should be avoided in Syria. Jordan has its own dairy industry and their products are pasteurised. Yoghurt is always OK and some people swear by it if you have a dose of the shits. Ice creams in Syria rarely contain dairy products, so it is OK unless your stomach is having problems coping with the water.

Meat is always alright to eat but make sure it is thoroughly cooked. In stews it's never a problem but when you are buying *shawarmas* – meat cooked on a vertical spit, usually on the street – go for one that looks overdone rather than underdone.

Contaminated food and water can give you all sorts of weird and not-so-wonderful diseases such as hepatitis A, typhoid, cholera, dysentery, giardia and polio but you can minimise the risks of catching any of them by being selective about where and what you eat and by exercising meticulous care with your personal hygiene. Always wash your hands before eating (restaurants always

provide a basin for this purpose) and, needless to say, after using the toilet.

**Diarrhoea**

It's inevitable that at some stage you'll be struck down with diarrhoea, maybe just as a result of a change of food or water, but more often because of a bug of some sort.

Don't go pumping yourself full of antibiotics at the first sign of trouble. This is not a good way to treat your stomach and you can often do more harm than good by destroying all the useful intestinal flora in your gut as well as the nasties that are giving you problems.

The best course of action is to starve the little bastards out. Rest, eat nothing and drink only unsweetened tea, citrus juice and clean water. Make sure you drink plenty of fluids as diarrhoea can dehydrate you very quickly. It is also important to take salt to help your body retain water. If you must eat, stick to simple foods such as boiled vegetables, plain bread or toast, and yoghurt. Keep away from dairy products (other than yoghurt), anything sweet and non-citrus fruits.

If you have to be moving on and it's not practical to stick to this regimen, you may have to take something to block you up for a while. *Lomotil* is effective and handy because the pills are so tiny – take two tabs three times daily. Codeine phosphate tablets or a prescribed tincture of opium are other alternatives. If at the end of all this you are still suffering, you may have dysentery and should see a doctor.

### Dysentery
It's not all that difficult to catch dysentery and the first sign that something is seriously wrong is blood and mucus in stools – indications that the bowel wall has started to break down. There are two types: *bacillary dysentery*, the most common variety, is short, sharp and nasty but rarely persistent and responds well to antibiotics; and *amoebic dysentery* which is caused by amoebic parasites rather than bacteria, is harder to treat, often persistent and can do permanent damage to your intestines if left untreated. The recommended treatments for amoebic dysentery include *Bactrim* and *Flagyl*.

### Hepatitis
This is a liver disease caused by a virus and again there are two types. Infectious hepatitis (type A) is the one you are most likely to catch. It is highly contagious and you pick it up from drinking water, eating food or using utensils contaminated by an infected person. Serum hepatitis (type B) can only be contracted by having sex with a type B carrier or using a needle previously injected into a carrier.

Symptoms start to appear three to five weeks after infection and consist of fever, loss of appetite, nausea, depression, lethargy, and pains around the base of your rib cage (ie the liver). The usual tell-tale sign is when the whites of your eyes start turning yellow and your urine turns a deep orange or brown.

The only cure for hepatitis is complete rest, good food and giving your liver a sporting chance by laying off the alcohol. You should be over the worst in about 10 days but it can last for months, so if you still feel really crook, it might be time to cash in that medical insurance which you took out (you didn't?) and fly home.

If you are going to be away for less than six months, consider getting a gamma globulin shot which will give you some protection from type A for six months but its effectiveness is still debatable.

### Cholera
Cholera usually occurs in epidemics and can be extremely dangerous. Symptoms are bad diarrhoea, vomiting, shallow breathing, wrinkled skin, stomach cramps, dehydration and a fast, faint heartbeat. If you think you have it, see a doctor immediately as you cannot treat it yourself.

Cholera vaccinations are valid for six months and although they are only about 50% effective, any protection is better than none at all. You should have no problem if you are sensible about what you eat and drink.

### Typhoid
This is a dangerous infection that starts in the stomach and spreads throughout the body. The main symptom is high fevers and it can be caught from contaminated food and water. Vaccination is recommended.

### Malaria
Malaria in the desert? Surprising as it may seem, there is a small risk of catching malaria in both Jordan and Syria, particularly if you're going to be in the north-east of Syria by the Euphrates River. If you are just going to be zipping through there is no need to take anti-malarial tablets if you are careful, but for those spending any amount of time in the area, they are recommended.

The disease is spread by mosquitoes which are fortunately few in number and, unlike in many places, the strains of malaria found in this region are not resistant to chloroquine. The period of highest risk is from May to October.

### Other Diseases
You should also make sure you are vaccinated against polio and tetanus. Most people will have been vaccinated as

a child so should only need boosters.
Check with your doctor.

## Coping with the Heat

It gets stinking hot during the summer in
Jordan and Syria and without adequate
protection you'll be a sitting duck for heat
exhaustion – headaches, nausea, dizziness
and other fun things.

Your best insurance against this
happening is wearing a hat and drinking
plenty of fluids other than alcohol and
coffee. Cotton clothes which cover as
much skin as possible are cooler than
brief clothes because the moisture is
trapped against your skin.

Excessive fluid loss through perspiration
(or diarrhoea) results in salt deficiency
and you need to keep up your intake. The
food in this area is usually cooked with
enough salt to maintain a good balance in
your body and you shouldn't have to take
extra.

When it's practical, keep out of the sun
altogether during the real heat of the
day.

## Toilets

Toilets are almost always the hole-in-the-
floor variety and are in fact far more
hygienic than sit-on toilets as only your
covered feet come into contact with
anything.

It takes a little while to master the
squatting technique without losing
everything from your pockets. Always
carry your own toilet paper or adopt the
local habit of using your left hand and
water. There is always a tap at a
convenient height for this purpose –
whether any water actually comes out of
it is something else again!

It is worth noting that toilet paper is
virtually impossible to find in Syria so
either bring some with you or make do
with the paper supplied on the tables in
restaurants.

## FOOD

Food in Syria and Jordan ranges from the
exotic to the mundane and unfortunately
for the budget traveller, exotic food comes
with exotic prices, so it's mostly the
mundane you'll be relying on. The food is
quite tasty as a rule but the lack of variety
can be monotonous.

## Snacks

*Fuul, felafel* and *hummus* are the staple
foods of the region and are eaten for
breakfast, lunch or dinner. *Fuul* is a paste
made from fava beans, garlic and lemon
and is served swimming in oil – a bit hard
to handle first thing in the morning.
*Felafel* is even more widespread and is
deep-fried balls of chickpea paste with
spices and served in a piece of Arabic flat
bread (*khobz*) with pickled vegetables or
tomato. This is one of the cheapest ways
to eat and chances are you'll be
thoroughly sick of felafels by the time you
leave. *Hummus* is cooked chickpeas
ground into a paste and mixed with garlic
and lemon. It is available in virtually
every restaurant and is usually excellent.

*Baba ghanouj* is another of the dips
eaten with bread and is made from
mashed eggplant and *tahini* – sesame-
seed paste.

The meat equivalent of the felafel is the
*shawarma*, and you'll probably be having
your fair share of these as they are cheap
and convenient. Slices of meat are
carefully arranged on a vertical spit and
are topped with a few big chunks of fat,
which drips down the meat as it cooks,
and a tomato for decoration. When you
order a shawarma, more commonly
known as a *sandweech*, the guy will slice
off the meat (usually with a great flourish
and much knife sharpening and waving),
dip a piece of flat bread in the fat that has
dripped off the meat, hold it against the
gas flame so it flares, then fill it with the
meat and either tomato or pickled
vegetables. On the same stall you will
usually find *kibbih*, which are deep fried
balls made of a mixture of meat and
cracked wheat and are stuffed with more
meat fried in onions. Shops selling

shawarma nearly always have the spit set up out by the footpath so you can just pick one up as you are walking along.

In Syria, particularly in Aleppo, you'll come across bakeries selling what look like small pizzas. They are a type of bread topped with spices, cheese and sometimes meat.

Arabic bread (*khobz*) is eaten with absolutely everything and is also called *eish*, which means 'life'. It is round and flat and makes a good filler if you are preparing your own food. On the streets of Amman stalls sell *ka'ik* which are round sesame rings and are tastier than plain old khobz.

Other sandweech stalls specialise in offal of various kinds (liver, kidneys, brains, etc) and they are probably quite OK to eat if you can stomach that sort of thing.

### Main Dishes

For main dishes, you'll be eating either chicken, kebabs or meat-and-vegetable stews most of the time.

Chicken (*farooj*) is usually roasted on spits in large ovens out the front of the restaurant. The usual serving is half a chicken (*noos farooj*) and it will come with bread and a side-dish of raw onion, chillies and sometimes olives. Eaten with the optional extras of salad (*salata*) and hummus, you have a good meal.

*Kebabs* are another favourite available everywhere. These are spicy minced lamb pressed onto skewers and grilled over charcoal. They are usually sold by weight and are also served with bread and a side plate.

Stews are usually meat or vegetable or both and although not available everywhere, make a pleasant change from chicken and kebabs. *Fasooliya* is bean stew, *baseela* is peas and *batatas* potato. They are usually served on rice (*ruz*) or macaroni (*makarone*) which are extra.

In Jordan you can eat the Bedouin speciality *mensaf*. It is traditionally served on special occasions and consists of a whole lamb on a bed of rice and is topped with pine nuts. The fat from the cooking is poured into the rice and is considered by some to be the best part. Everyone sits on the floor around the big dish and digs in, with the right hand only. Traditionally, the delicacy is the eyes which are presented to honoured guests! If you stay with the Bedouin you may be lucky enough to eat mensaf this way, but you can also buy a serve in restaurants in Amman. It is not cheap but should be tried at least once. A tangy sauce of cooked yoghurt mixed with the fat is served with it.

Another Jordanian specialty is *mezze*, which is actually a selection of appetisers but makes a meal in itself. Served on a tray with tea, you get hummus, baba ghanouj, sardines, cucumbers, tomato, liver and kidneys, fried eggs, spice and oil.

Fish (*samakh*) is not widely available and is usually so heavily salted and spiced that it tastes more like a large anchovy.

### Desserts

Arabs love their sugar and their desserts are no exception – they are horrendously sweet. There are pastry shops in every town which sell nothing but these sickly sweets. Just wander in and have a look at the selection. Buy only a small quantity as more than one of anything is too much.

### Soup

| | |
|---|---|
| soups | *shurba* |
| lentil soup | *shurba 'aads* |

### Vegetables

| | |
|---|---|
| vegetables | *khudrawat* |
| potatoes | *batatas* |
| green beans | *fasooliya* |
| lentils | *'aads* |
| peas | *baseela* |
| cauliflower | *anabeet* |
| cabbage | *kharoum* |
| carrot | *gazar* |

| turnip | *lift* |
|---|---|
| okra | *ba'amiyya* |
| eggplant | *badingan* |

**Salad**

| salad | *salata* |
|---|---|
| lettuce | *kahss* |
| tomato | *tamatin* |
| onion | *bassal* |
| garlic | *tum* |
| cucumber | *khiyaar* |

**Meat**

| meat | *al-luhum* |
|---|---|
| lamb | *lahma danee* |
| camel | *lahma gamil* |
| chicken | *farooj* |
| liver | *kibda* |
| kidney | *kelawwi* |

**Desserts**

| *mahalabiyya* | a milk pudding |
|---|---|
| *mahalabiyya wa festa* | same but with pistachio nuts |
| *baklawah* | multi-layered flaky pastry with nuts and drenched in honey |
| *kinaafa* | shredded wheat over goat cheese baked in syrup |
| *zalabiyya* | pastries dipped in rose-water |
| *booza booza* | ice cream |

**Fruit**

| fruit | *fawaka* |
|---|---|
| apricot | *meesh-meesh* |
| apple | *toofa* |
| orange | *burtuaan* |
| lime | *limuun* |
| banana | *mohz* |
| date | *tamr* |
| grape | *einab* |
| fig | *tiin* |
| pomegranate | *ruman* |
| watermelon | *bateeq* |

**Miscellaneous**

| salt | *mahal* |
|---|---|
| pepper | *filfil* |

| bread | *khobz* or *eish* |
|---|---|
| eggs | *bayd* |
| cheese | *gibna* |
| sugar | *sukur* |
| yogurt | *labanee* |
| butter | *zibda* |

## DRINKS
### Tea & Coffee

Tea (*shay*) and coffee (*qahwa*) are the national obsessions and are drunk in copious quantities. They are also extremely strong and when your body is not used to them, drinking either in the evening is usually a recipe for a sleepless night.

The main pastime for men is sitting in a café sipping on a tea or coffee, sucking on a water pipe (*nargileh*) and chatting or playing cards or backgammon. Every town has at least one of these places and they are good for meeting local people. Arab women don't frequent cafés but it is no problem for western women to enter, although in the smaller towns you may get a few strange looks.

Tea is served in small glasses and is incredibly sweet unless you ask for only a little sugar (*shwayya sukur*). If you want no sugar at all, ask for it *bidoon sukur* (without sugar), but it tastes bitter and has a strong tannin aftertaste.

Coffee is usually Turkish coffee in small cups and is also sweet. It is very thick and muddy so let it settle a bit before drinking. Don't try and drink the last mouthful (which in cups this size is usually the second mouthful) because it's like silt. As with tea, it is very sweet.

The traditional Arabic or Bedouin coffee is heavily laced with cardamom and drunk in cups without handles which hold only a mouthful. It is poured from a silver pot and your cup will be refilled until you make the proper gesture that you have had enough – hold the cup out and roll your wrist from side to side a couple of times. It is good etiquette to have at least three cups although you are unlikely to offend if you have less. Coffee is then followed by tea *ad infinitum*.

### Juice (*Aseer*)

All over the place you will find juice stalls selling delicious freshly squeezed fruit juices. In Syria these stalls are instantly recognised by the string bags of fruit hanging out the front.

Popular juices include lemon, orange, banana, pomegranate, and rockmelon, and you can have combinations of any or all of these.

Some stalls put milk in their drinks which you'd be well advised to stay away from.

### Soft Drinks

Syrian soft drinks are cheap and not too sweet. This is one of the few countries where Coca-Cola and Pepsi are not available. If you take a drink away from the stall or shop you will have to pay a small deposit on the bottle.

Jordan has Pepsi and a local product called *Viva* which comes in non-returnable bottles so, apart from being wasteful, it is also more expensive.

### Alcohol

Despite the fact that Islam prohibits the use of alcohol, it is widely drunk and readily available.

**Beer** Both countries brew their own local beers. Syria has *Al Chark* in Aleppo and *Barada* in Damascus and both are quite palatable and cheap. In Damascus the black-marketeers sell cans of *Amstel* smuggled over the border from Lebanon.

Jordan has *Amstel* beer brewed under licence from the parent European company. In Amman and Aqaba you can buy beer imported from all over the world – everything from *Guinness* to *Fosters*.

**Liquor** *Araq* is the indigenous firewater and should be treated with caution. It is similar to Greek *ouzo* and is available in shops and on the streets in Syria. The best *araq* is said to come from Lebanon.

In Jordan you can find all sorts of imported liquor in the big department stores in Amman, but you'll need a fat wallet if you are going to make a habit of it. A good bottle of scotch will set you back JD5 (US$17) or more.

**Wine** Locally made *Latroun* wine from the West Bank is not bad and reasonably priced from about 800 fils (US$2.70) a bottle. It certainly doesn't compare with western wines but is still quite palatable.

# Syria

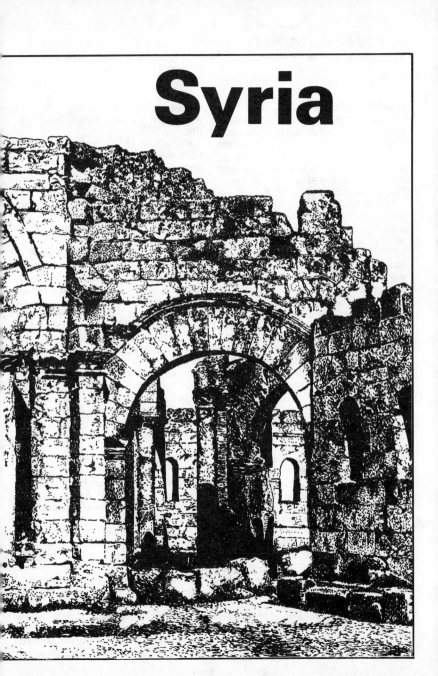

# Facts about the Country

## HISTORY SINCE 1920

In March 1920 the Arab nationalists proclaimed Emir Faisal of the Hashemite family as king of Syria. The French, who had been given the mandate over Syria and Lebanon by the League of Nations, moved against the Arab army and forced Faisal into exile.

In 1932 the first parliamentary elections were held and despite the fact that the majority of moderates elected had been hand picked by the French, they rejected all French terms for a constitution. Finally in 1936 a treaty was signed; the state included the *sanjak* of Alexandretta, the present-day Turkish province of Hatay. After riots by the Turks protesting against becoming part of Syria, the French encouraged the Turks to send in troops to help supervise elections. The outcome favoured the Turks and the sanjak of Alexandretta became part of Turkey. This has never been recognised by the Syrians and any maps printed in Syria will still show the area as Syrian territory.

With the fall of France to the Germans in 1940, Syria and Lebanon were controlled by the Vichy government until July 1941 when the British and Free French forces took over. It was not until 1946 that Syria gained complete independence when the French troops were finally forced to withdraw after continued pressure from Syrian nationalist groups.

In Lebanon meanwhile, what was originally the mainly Christian Turkish province of Mt Lebanon became, with the annexation of some non-Christian (mainly Sunni, Druze and Shi'ite) territories, the state of Greater Lebanon. The French governor was forced to bow to Lebanese demands for self-rule and in 1926 when the new constitution was adopted, Greater Lebanon became the Lebanese Republic. As was the case in Syria, full independence was achieved with the withdrawal of the French troops in 1946.

Civilian rule in Syria was short-lived. In March 1949, the Kouwatli government was overthrown by the army, and successive military coups brought to power officers with nationalist and socialist leanings. By 1954, the Ba'thists in the army, who had won support among the Alawite and Druze minorities, had no serious rival.

The Ba'th party were committed to pan-Arabism which led to Syria forfeiting its sovereignty to become what amounted to the Northern Province of the United Arab Republic in a merger with Egypt under President Nasser in 1958. Despite the popularity of the move within Syria, the Egyptians treated the Syrians as subordinates which led to the restoration of Syrian independence following yet another military coup in September 1961. Although outwardly civilian, the new regime was under military control and it made few concessions to Ba'th and pro-Nasser pan-Arabists, resulting in yet another change of government in March 1963.

A month before the Ba'th takeover in 1963, the Iraqi branch of the party had seized power in Baghdad and attempts were made to unite Iraq, Egypt and Syria but the parties were unable to agree on the tripartite federation. Syria and Iraq then tried to establish bilateral unity but these efforts also came to nothing when the Ba'th party in Iraq was overthrown in November 1963.

Now that Syria was on its own, the Ba'thists were faced with the problem that being pan-Arabist, it had branches in other Arab countries, thereby giving non-Syrians a significant say in Syrian affairs. There followed a party split and in February 1966 the ninth coup saw a new regime set up in the name of the Syrian Ba'th.

The socialist government was severely weakened by loss in two conflicts. The first was the defeat of the Syrians at the hands of the Israelis in the June 1967 war. This war, which came to be known as the Six-Day War, was in retaliation for raids by Syrian guerillas on Israeli settlements. Israel attacked after President Nasser, having pledged support for Syria, closed the straits of Tiran (at the entrance to the Red Sea) to Israeli shipping. The end result was a severe political and psychological defeat for the Arab states and saw vast areas of land fall into Israeli hands. Syria was the target for a furious assault; the Golan Heights were taken and Damascus itself was threatened.

The second conflict was the Black September hostilities in Jordan in 1970. In this clash, the Jordanian army moved against and defeated Syrian-supported Palestinian guerilla groups who were vying for power in Jordan.

At this point, Defence Minister Hafez al-Assad seized power, and ousted the civilian party leadership. He was sworn in as president on 14 March 1971.

Since then Assad has managed to hold power longer than any other Syrian Government since independence with a mixture of ruthless suppression and guile. His success can be attributed to a number of factors: giving disadvantaged and minority groups a better deal; stacking the bureaucracy and internal security organisations with members of his own Alawite faith (which has led to wide-scale repression and silencing of opposition both at home and abroad); and an overall desire, no doubt shared by many Syrians, for political stability. In 1985 he was elected to a third seven-year term with a predictable 99.9% of the vote.

In the last few years, opposition to Assad's regime has been on the increase. The main opposition comes from the extremist militant group, the Muslim Brotherhood, who particularly object to Alawite-dominated rule, as the Alawites account for only 11.5% of the population. Membership of the Brotherhood became a capital offence in 1981, but in 1985 the official attitude softened and exiled members of the group were pardoned and allowed to return to Syria, and it was reported that 500 members were freed from jails within the country.

The Brotherhood's opposition has sometimes taken a violent course. In 1979, 32 Alawite cadets were killed in a raid in Aleppo. Anti-Ba'th demonstrations were held in Aleppo in 1980, and in the most serious threat to Assad yet, as many as 30,000 people were killed when the army, under Assad's brother Rifa'at, moved in to brutally quash a revolt led by Sunnis who ambushed Syrian security forces and staged a general insurrection in February 1982. Since then little has been heard of the opposition but in early 1984 when Assad was recovering from a heart attack, a vigorous internal power struggle ensued when it seems that Rifa'at attempted to seize power and was effectively exiled to France. In 1986 he was allowed back and was re-elected to the Regional Command, the most powerful body in the country.

With no obvious successor for Assad in sight and an opposition that can't be written off, Syria after Hafez al-Assad is likely to be far from stable.

## GOVERNMENT

Actual power resides in the president as leader of the Arab Ba'th Socialist Party. He has the power to appoint ministers, declare war, issue laws and appoint civil servants and military personnel. Under the 1973 constitution approved overwhelmingly by the Syrian electorate, legislative power lies with the people and freedom of expression is guaranteed. With the constant military and political tensions, enforcement of these principles has been less than thorough to say the least.

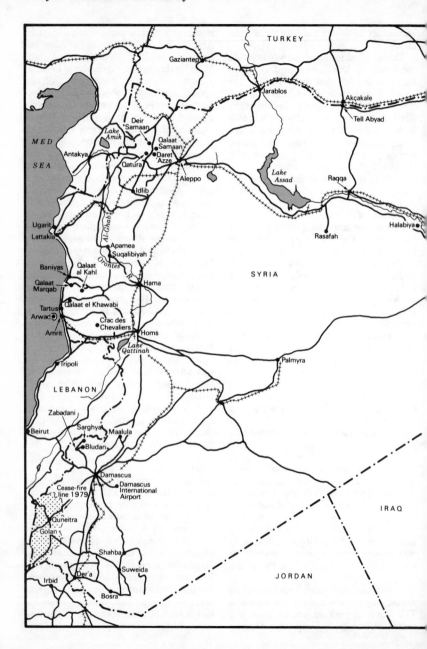

**Syria**

0      50      100 km

Qamishle

Ras al Ain

Hassake

Deir z-Zur

IRAQ

Doura Europos

Mari

Abu Kamal

River

Euphrates

Area under Israeli Military Administration

All political parties are officially affiliated through the National Progressive Front, of which Assad is also the leader. Being dominated by the Ba'th Party, the Front is for all intents ineffective and is little more than a tool by which Assad's regime can influence the non-Ba'th parties.

## ECONOMY

The Syrian economy is virtually bankrupt. It relies heavily on aid from Arab countries but only Saudi Arabia continues to support it. The slump in oil prices only makes the future look worse for Syria. Iran supplies Syria with 20,000 barrels of free oil per day as payment for Syrian support in the Gulf War.

Severe strain is placed on the economy by defence spending which accounts for over 60% of total expenditure, more than four times what is spent on education. The internal security apparatus also soaks up a sizeable chunk.

Agriculture is important not only for the revenue generated, but also because it provides employment for at least 50% of the workforce. For this reason it figures high on the list of government priorities for development spending.

Principal exports include cotton, crude oil, textiles, tobacco, live animals, hides and phosphates with the main destinations being the Eastern Bloc and the European Economic Community.

Despite campaigns to control smuggling, the black market continues to thrive. Corruption within the government is rife and the breakdown of customs control is so widespread that goods smuggled in from Lebanon are sold openly in the street. The despair that many Syrians, particularly the businessmen, feel about the level of corruption is voiced in an Arab saying: 'If he (Assad) knows about it, it's a disaster; if he doesn't know about it, it's a bigger disaster'.

In an attempt to keep valuable tourist revenue in the banking system, the tourist exchange rate has been raised to almost the same level as the black market rate.

## GEOGRAPHY, WEATHER & CLIMATE

There are four geographical regions in Syria: the coastal strip, the mountains, the cultivated steppe and the desert.

### The Coastal Strip

The coastline of Syria stretches for about 180 km between Turkey and Lebanon. The Jebel an-Nusariyah (Ansariyah Mountains) almost front the coast in the north but give way to the Sahl Akkar (Akkar Plain) in the south. The fertile alluvial plains are intensively farmed year-round. The two major ports are Lattakia and Tartus and there's a large oil refining complex at Baniyas.

Average daily temperatures range from 29°C in summer to 10°C in winter and the annual rainfall is about 760 mm.

### The Mountains

The Ansariyah Mountains form a continuous jagged ridge running north-south just inland from the coast. With an average height of 1000 metres, they form a formidable and impenetrable barrier which dominates the whole coast. Snowfalls on the higher peaks are not uncommon in winter. The western side is marked by deep ravines while on the east the mountains fall almost sheer to the Orontes, the fertile valley of the *nahr al-Assi* (the 'rebel river') which flows north into Turkey.

The Jebel Lubnan ash-Sharqiyah (Anti Lebanon Mountains) mark the border between Syria and Lebanon and average 2000 metres in height. Syria's highest mountain, Jebel ash Sheikh (Mt Hermon of the Bible), rises to 2814 metres. The main river to flow from this range is the Barada, which has enabled Damascus to survive in an otherwise arid region for over 2000 years.

Other smaller ranges include the Jebel Druze which rise in the south near the Jordanian border, and the Jebel Abu Rujmayn in the centre of the country north of Palmyra.

### The Cultivated Steppe

As the name suggests, this is Syria's main agricultural region where the major centres of Damascus, Homs, Hama, Aleppo and Qamishle are found. The Euphrates and Orontes Rivers provide enough water for intensive farming, while away from the water sources, dryland wheat and cereal crops are grown.

Temperatures average around 35°C in summer and 12°C in winter. Rainfall varies from about 250 to 500 mm.

Dagon – Philistian/Assyrian god of the earth and agriculture

### The Desert

The Syrian desert occupies the whole south-east of the country. It is a land of endless stony plains. The oasis of Palmyra is on the northern edge of this arid zone and along with other oases used to be an important centre for the trade caravans plying the routes between the Mediterranean and Mesopotamia.

The Bedouin (desert nomads) are at home in this country. During the winter months they graze sheep until water and fodder becomes scarce, and then move west or into the hills.

Temperatures are high and rainfall low. In summer the days average 40°C and highs of 46°C are not uncommon.

## Distances

Syria is not a large country – it has an area of 185,000 square km, a bit over half the size of Italy. It is roughly a 500-km square with Lebanon intruding in the south-west and Jordan and Iraq in the south-east.

## When to Visit

Spring is the best time to visit as temperatures are mild and the winter rains have cleared the haze that obscures views for much of the year. Autumn is the next choice.

If you go in summer, don't be caught without a hat and water bottle, especially if visiting Palmyra or the north-east. A siesta in the heat of the afternoon is a popular habit although when the daily power cuts leave you stranded in a hot room with no fan, you may as well be outside.

Winter can be downright unpleasant on the coast and in the mountains, when temperatures drop and the rains begin.

## What to Wear

Syrians are conservative when it comes to dress and are not accustomed to the bizarre ways some tourists dress. Women should always wear at least knee-length dresses or pants and tops that keep at least the shoulders covered.

Men will have no problem walking around in shorts but will be considered a bit eccentric and should expect to get stared at a lot, particularly in the cities.

When crossing borders or dealing with officials, there's no need to smarten yourself up specially as officials seem more interested in who you are rather than what you look like.

## PEOPLE

Syria has a population of 10.3 million, and it's annual growth rate of 3.8% (one of the highest in the world) is way out of proportion with it's economic growth.

### Ethnic Groups

Ethnic Syrians are of Semitic stock. About 90% of the population are Arabs, which includes some minorities such as the Bedouin.

The remainder is made up of smaller groupings of Kurds, Armenians, Circassians and Turks.

Of the estimated 10 million Kurds, about one million are found in Syria and, along with their counterparts in Turkey, Iran and Iraq, are agitating for an independent Kurdish state – with little success so far. They have been blamed for some acts of terrorism in Syria, which were seen as part of their push for self-government.

### Linguistic Groups

Arabic is the mother tongue of the majority. Kurdish is spoken in the north-east, Armenian in Aleppo and other major cities, and Turkish in the villages east of the Euphrates.

Aramaic, the language of the Bible, is still spoken in two villages.

English is widely understood and French is still quite common, particularly amongst the older people.

### Religious Groups

Islam is practised by about 86% of the population – one-fifth of these are minorities such as the Shi'ite, Druze and Alawite, while the remainder are Sunni Muslims.

Christians account for some 13% and belong to various churches including Greek Orthodox, Greek Catholic, Syrian Orthodox, Armenian Orthodox, Maronite and Protestant.

There are a few thousand Jews although most have emigrated to Israel.

## HOLIDAYS

Most holidays are either religious (Islamic and Christian) or are celebrations of important dates in the formation of the modern Syrian state. For Islamic holidays see that section in the Facts About the Region chapter. Other holidays are:

1 January
    New Years Day
8 March
    Revolution Day
23 July
    Egypt's Revolution Day
1 September
    Union of Syria, Egypt & Libya
25 December
    Christmas

## LOCAL CUSTOMS

Arabic social etiquette is quite formal and a simple encounter can often turn into a major social occasion with flowery and elaborate 'How's the family?' type of questions.

As an *ajnabi* (foreigner) you're not expected to know all the ins and outs but if you can come up with the right expression at the appropriate moment they'll love it.

### Ramadan

During the month of fasting, a faithful Muslim will not allow *anything* to pass his lips during daylight hours. As a foreigner you're not expected to follow suit but it is polite not to eat, drink or smoke in public during Ramadan. This holds true more for the smaller towns than the large cities.

Business hours may change and are usually shorter, and in more out-of-the-way places you may find it hard to find a restaurant that opens before sunset.

### Body Language

Syrians often say 'no' merely by raising the eyebrows and lifting the head up and back. This can be a little off-putting if you're not used to it – don't take it as a snub.

Shaking the head from side to side (as we would to say 'no') means 'I don't understand'.

If an official holds out his hand and draws a line across his palm with the index finger of the other hand, he is not pointing out that he has a long life-line but that he wants to see your passport.

As the left hand is associated with toilet duties it is considered unclean and so you should always use the right hand when giving or receiving something.

# Facts for the Visitor

## VISAS

All foreigners entering Syria must obtain a visa. These are available at Syrian consulates outside the country, or supposedly on arrival at the border, port or airport, although there have been conflicting stories about this. To be on the safe side, get a visa before showing up at the border. If there's any evidence of a visit to Israel in your passport you won't be allowed into Syria. Similarly, if you plan on going to Israel after Syria, don't say so. A passport with a lot of stamps in it may well slow you down at times – at one stage it took two Syrian officials half an hour to decide that my trekking permit from Nepal had nothing to do with Israel!

A tourist visa is valid for 15 days and can be extended for a further 15 days once inside the country. Costs vary depending where you get them but it seems that the closer you get to Syria, the cheaper the visa. In Europe they can cost up to US$20, in Jordan or Turkey US$6, and at the border US$1.

Regardless of where you get your visa, there's no escaping the mandatory changing of US$100 at the border at less than half the usual bank rate. The only exception that I've heard of, is one traveller who crossed at the small Turkey/Syria border post at Akçakale/Tell al Abyad and wasn't asked to change money. The officials always ask for cash but will grudgingly accept travellers' cheques. If you re-enter Syria within two months then officially you are not required to change again, but I wouldn't guarantee it.

Three-day transit visas are also available but there's little advantage in getting one as you still have to change US$100. The cost of the visa itself is not much cheaper than a regular tourist visa and unless you load yourself up with souvenirs, you'd be hard pressed to spend the US$100 in the three days.

If you want to go to Lebanon (not a good idea), get a multiple-entry visa as it's not possible to get back into Syria without one and the only other (cheap) way out of there is by ferry to Cyprus.

### Visa Extensions

If your stay in Syria is going to be more than 15 days you have to get a visa extension. This can be done at any police station although it's likely to be more straightforward at an immigration office which you'll find in all of the cities. Don't believe it if you get told in Damascus that you can only extend your visa there.

Extensions are usually only granted on the 14th or 15th day of your stay, so if you apply earlier expect to be knocked back. If, as sometimes happens, they do extend it earlier, check that they give you 15 days from the last day of your visa and not from the day you get the extension. If your 15th day is a Friday you can extend on either the 14th or 16th day.

The cost, number of passport photos and the time taken to issue the extension all vary from place to place. The cost is never more than US$1; you'll need anything from two (Damascus) to five (Aleppo) photos; and time taken varies from on-the-spot (most places) to 1 pm the following day (Damascus). There's also a form to fill in which is available from the immigration office and is titled 'Request for Identity Card' in French.

## MONEY

US$1 = S£9.75 (border & hotels)
US$1 = S£23 (bank rate)

The currency is the Syrian pound (S£), known locally as the *lire*. Coins in circulation are ¼, ½ and one pound. Notes are S£1, 5, 10, 25, 50, 100 and 500.

The S£500 notes are really too big for everyday use and can be a hassle to change although it's surprising how often the owner of some crummy little street stall will bring out a wad of notes and change it for you.

In an effort to keep the money out of the black economy the bank exchange rate has been raised to a realistic level, so if you change money a second time you'll get S£23 instead of the rip-off S£9.75 that you get at the border.

All hotels require payment in US dollars *cash*, so make sure you carry a supply of small notes for this purpose. The more expensive hotels may insist that you go to the bank, change money (at the low rate of S£9.75!) and get a receipt, which the hotel then keeps. The receipt from the border is not acceptable for use in hotels.

### Currency Declaration Form

All foreigners are supposed to fill in one of these when entering Syria and it is to be handed in when leaving, but the enforcement is very haphazard. If you do get issued with one, it may be noted in your passport. If that's the case, make sure you have it when you leave.

The form itself just lists what foreign currency you are taking into the country and is designed to stop people taking out more than they brought in. You may be asked to show your funds at the border when filling in the form.

No bank receipts or the like are asked for when leaving although you will be asked if you're taking any Syrian money with you. If you are, don't say so or it will be confiscated. If it's any consolation, if you do get any money confiscated the official will write a receipt on a scrap of paper which you can then hand in to the Syrian embassy in your own country for reimbursement.

### Changing Money

The banking system in Syria is entirely state owned. The Commercial Bank of Syria is its public face and there's always at least one branch in every major town. The fun starts when there's more than one branch because the different departments of the bank will be in its different branches, so Branch No 1 might change cheques but not cash and Branch No 2 might take neither or both!

It's not possible to reconvert Syrian pounds to hard currency, so you either spend what you've got or exchange it at a terrible rate in a neighbouring country.

### Blackmarket

Changing money on the blackmarket used to be easy and safe; now it's neither. In late '86 the government, in one of its periodic crackdowns, brought in harsh penalties which allow for up to 15 years jail for Syrians caught dealing in the black economy. Consequently, finding someone willing to change for you is not easy, and with the rate now only about 5% over the bank rate, it's hardly worth the risk.

### COSTS

Even at the tourist exchange rate, Syria is a cheap country. For most travellers, the US$100 changed at the border is enough for seven to 10 days, but this does not include accommodation which must be paid for in *US dollars cash*. If you stay longer it becomes even cheaper because you switch to the higher rate when you change money a second time, so your money goes twice as far.

### INFORMATION

Although Syria is trying to attract more tourists, the country is just not geared for tourism at present. You'd find more tourists in London on any one day in summer than you would in Syria in a whole year. In 1984 Syria received only 86,000 western visitors. This becomes apparent when you visit a site or museum, as often you'll be the only one there.

There is usually a tourist office in major

towns but don't expect too much in the way of information. Printed matter is scarce and what little is available is often only in Arabic or French, although in Aleppo and Damascus they have good handout maps.

Often the museums and archaeological sites will have small booklets on sale but their favourite trick is to have a stock of only one booklet, and it will be about somewhere else. So in Aleppo you will be able to pick up a booklet on Bosra and in Bosra they'll have one for the Crac des Chevaliers and at the Crac they'll have absolutely nothing.

For information before you get to Syria, contact any Syrian diplomatic missions overseas.

## ACCOMMODATION
### Hotels
There's every level of hotel accommodation available in Syria from the five-star, characterless, could-be-anywhere hotels down to the noisy, filthy shitboxes that you can find in virtually any city in the world, all with prices to match.

At the time of researching this book, accommodation in budget hotels could be paid for in Syrian pounds, but as of mid-

1987 it was reported that *all* accommodation now has to be paid for in US dollars. This is not too disastrous as you can still get a bed for US$3, but the crunch comes when the hotel has no change, so prepare yourself by bringing plenty of small bills. Otherwise you will have to go through the rigmarole of going to the bank, changing your money and then presenting the receipt to the hotel. However, the banks themselves are often short of change, so it is much better to make sure you have plenty of small US$ notes. The Syrian pounds prices in the book still apply, but you have to divide them by 9.75 and round them off to get the US dollar rate.

Rooms in most of the cheap hotels are let on a share basis and will have two to four beds. If you want the room to yourself you'll have to pay for all the beds. For solo male travellers these share-rooms are quite OK and your gear is always safe when left unattended. Solo females will have to take a room.

The biggest drawback with cheap hotels is that they're often noisy, both from the street and from guests. A pair of earplugs can mean the difference between a good night's sleep and being kept awake by loud chatter, music and the television. Rooms at the back, away from the street, are usually quieter and sometimes cheaper.

Most hotels will want to keep your passport in the 'safe' overnight; an arrangement which I certainly don't like, especially when the safe is usually only a drawer at the reception desk. The reason for keeping it is that the police very occasionally come around checking in the middle of the night. If you tell the hotel owner that you don't mind being woken at any time he'll let you hang on to it.

The supply of electricity, and therefore water, is erratic all over Syria and if the hotel has no power or water when you check it out, it probably will later on. Hot water is rare, which is no problem in summer but look out in winter.

## Youth Hostels

There are Youth Hostels in Damascus, Bosra and Homs. A student card will usually be enough if you are not a member of the IYH. Membership of the Syrian Youth Hostels Association costs S£100 annually.

## SAFETY

Despite being depicted in the western media as a land full of terrorists and similar nasties, Syria is really a safe country to travel in. It is quite safe to walk around at any time of the day or night, which is more than can be said for most western countries.

People are basically very honest and foreigners are still enough of a novelty that they're not seen as easy targets for a rip-off. There's no such thing as one price for locals and another for foreigners and if you pay someone too much it would be rare indeed that they'd pocket the extra. I even came across one taxi driver who refused to take any money at all!

## Theft

Theft, or more precisely the lack of it, has got to be one of the most refreshing things about travelling in Syria. Your bags will be quite safe left unattended virtually anywhere. This is no excuse for inviting trouble through carelessness, but at least you don't have to keep a hawk-like watch over your stuff like you do in South America, for example.

## Police

You'll see lots of uniforms and guns in Syria, partly because the military make up the police force but also because military service for men is compulsory (the only exemptions are only-sons). Four years is the usual length of service. With all these men in uniform, jobs have to be found for them so public buildings, ministries, embassies, banks and even bus stations are all guarded by armed soldiers.

Due to trouble in the past, the

authorities are fairly touchy about what people carry on public transport. It is not unusual to have a baggage search when boarding a train or entering a bus station although these are usually only cursory. They're only looking for explosives and are not really interested in anything else you may be carrying. Passports are checked time and again but as long as your visa is in order it's never any hassle.

### Secret Police

Syria has several internal intelligence organisations and it's no exaggeration to say that there are secret police all over the place. If a Syrian starts talking politics to you or tries to drag you into a conversation about Assad, don't reciprocate unless it's someone you know well. The official line is that Assad is the best thing since sliced bread and to say anything to the contrary could land you in all sorts of trouble.

The main thing is not to get too worried about it or you'll isolate yourself and miss out on a lot. Most Syrians are very friendly and hospitable. Don't hesitate to take up an offer if someone invites you to their village or home.

Just to give you an idea of the array of security forces, the following is a list of the major ones known to exist by Amnesty International, the international human rights organisation.

*Siraya al-Difa' 'an al-Thawra* (Brigades for the Defence of the Revolution), headed by Rif'at al-Assad. Estimated to number between 15,000 and 25,000. Their main function is to protect the President, the administration and the revolution.

*Al-Wahdat al-Khassa* (Special Units) comprise about 5000 to 8000 para-troopers and commandos.

*Al-Mukhabarat al-'Ama* (General Intelligence) responsible to the Minister of Interior.

*Al-Mukhabarat al'Askariyya* (Military Intelligence). Collects and acts upon intelligence affecting the armed forces; responsible to the Ministry of Defence.

*Mukhabarat al-Quwwa al-Jawiyya* (Airforce Intelligence) Same as military intelligence but with respect to the airforce.

*Al-Amn al-Siyassi* (Political Security) Monitors political activity and acts upon information gathered; responsible to the Ministry of Interior.

*Al-Amn al-Dakhili* (Internal Security). Responsible to Ministry of Interior.

*Maktab al-Amn al-Qawmi* (National Security Bureau) Responsible to the Presidential Security Council.

### Women Alone

Unfortunately Syrian men have a slightly twisted view of western women. Muslims are very conservative when it comes to sex and women, and men have little or no contact with either before marriage. Western movies and television give them the impression that all western women are promiscuous and will jump into bed at the drop of a hat.

Regardless of this, women travelling alone or in pairs should experience few problems if they follow a few tips: avoid eye contact with a man you don't know; ignore any rude remarks and act as if you didn't hear it; dress modestly at all times but particularly in smaller towns which are likely to be more conservative than the cities.

A wedding ring will add to your respectability in Syrian eyes. If you have to say anything to ward off an advance, *imshi* (leave me alone) should do the trick.

### BUSINESS HOURS

Government offices are open from 8 am to 1.30 pm Sunday to Thursday. Other offices and shops are generally open from 8.30 am to 1.30 pm and then again from 4 to 6 or 7 pm Sunday to Thursday. On Fridays only some restaurants and smaller traders are open.

Banks and post offices are open from 8.30 am to 2 pm although in Damascus and Aleppo they stay open until 7 pm and are also open on Fridays.

## ELECTRICITY

A lot of Syria's electricity is generated using thermal power but the biggest source of electricity is the hydro-electric generating station on the Assad Dam on the Euphrates River.

The only problem seems to be that there isn't enough of it. Every town and city is without power for four hours a day but at least it happens at the same time every day so you can plan around it. The main inconvenience is that the hotels will have no fans and usually no water.

Syrians will tell you that the shortage is the fault of the Turks who have just completed their own massive dam on the Euphrates and are holding back the flow into Syria, despite an agreement signed in 1980. Others will tell you that it's because Syria sells power to Jordan to earn much-needed foreign currency. The truth probably lies somewhere between the two.

## MEDIA

The English-language daily newspaper, the *Syria Times*, is published under direct government control and is predict-ably big on anti-Zionist, pro-Arab rhetoric and short on news. It does have a 'What's on today' section which lists exhibitions, lectures and films as well as important telephone numbers and radio programmes.

Foreign newspapers and magazines such as the *International Herald Tribune*, *Le Monde* and *Newsweek* are irregularly available in Damascus, Aleppo and Homs.

The Syrian Broadcasting Service has a foreign-language service operating on 344, 280 and 228 metres medium wave from 10 am to midnight. Programmes are in French, English, Turkish, German and Russian. For times see the *Syria Times*.

If you have a radio, the best way to keep in touch with events both in and outside the country is through the BBC World Service which transmits from Cyprus on 639 khz medium wave from 6 am to midnight.

The Syrian Television service reaches a large audience and programmes range from news and sport to American soaps.

## POST & TELECOMMUNICATIONS
### Post

The Syrian postal service is slow but effective enough. Letters mailed from major cities take about 10 days to Europe, 15 days to Australia or the USA. The cost

Published by Tishreen Press and Publishing Foundation

Monday, September

telephone office in Damascus or through any of the five-star hotels. It's not cheap however, at S£170 for three minutes to Australia and the USA, S£150 to Europe. Calls made from major hotels will cost even more. It usually takes a couple of hours to get a line.

## TIME
Syria is two hours ahead of GMT in winter (November-April) and three hours in summer (May-October).

Time is not taken too seriously in Syria – something that should take five minutes will invariably take an hour. Trying to speed things up will only lead to frustration. It is better to take it philosophically than try to fight it.

## WHAT TO BRING
A hat, sunglasses and water bottle are essential in summer. A few other handy items are: a Swiss army knife, a torch (flashlight), a few metres of nylon cord, a tennis ball cut in half makes a good universal sink plug, earplugs, a medical kit and a sewing kit.

Toilet paper is impossible to find, and tampons are not widely available. You should also bring your own contraceptives or any special medication which you need.

of sending a letter or postcard seems to be different every time. Letters are about S£3.70, postcards S£2.10.

The poste restante counter at the main post office in Damascus is well organised and you can ask to look through any number of piles. There's a charge of S£1 for every letter collected.

### Posting a Parcel
To send a parcel from Damascus, take it (unwrapped) to the parcel post office for inspection. After it's been cleared, it has to be wrapped and then covered with cotton. The wrapping you'll have to do yourself but there's a guy at the parcel office who will cover it in cotton for S£10. There's numerous forms to fill in and the whole process takes a couple of hours. A five-kg parcel to Australia costs S£170.

The parcel office is on the northern side of the main Post Office building.

### Telephone
International calls can be made from the

## THINGS TO BUY
In the souks of Damascus and Aleppo it's possible to pick up anything from silk and cotton to antique silver jewellery, and compared with prices in Europe these are incredibly cheap.

Inlaid backgammon boards and jewellery boxes are popular buys and look great, even though the inlay work is not actually inlay but a thin veneer of readymade wood, plastic and fake mother-of-pearl. A large intricate backgammon board shouldn't cost more than about S£500.

Other good souvenirs include brassware, *nargilehs* (water pipes), embroidered tablecloths and leather sandals.

## Bargaining

Whatever you buy in the way of souvenirs, remember that bargaining is an integral part of the process and listed prices are always inflated to allow for it.

Show only a casual interest if you really want something and name a price well below what you are willing to pay. Take your time, smile and don't feel obliged to go above your intended price just because the shopkeeper is hospitable and serves tea or coffee. If after all this you can't agree on a price, try another shop – there are plenty of them.

## FILM & PHOTOGRAPHY

Kodak and Sakura print film is readily available but a lot of it looks like it has been on the shelf for years. Slide film is only available in Damascus and Aleppo.

Photography is not a problem as long as you avoid taking snaps of military sites. Be discreet if photographing women – show them the camera and make it clear that you want to take a picture of them – some may object and others won't. A powerful lens is helpful for good people pictures.

# Getting There

There are three ways of getting to Syria: by air, overland or by sea. Most travellers will be arriving by the overland routes from either Turkey or Jordan.

## AIR

Syria has two international airports: Damascus and Aleppo. Both have regular connections to Europe, other cities in the Middle East, Africa and Asia.

As it's not a popular destination you won't find much discounting on fares to Syria. Aeroflot and the eastern European airlines such as LOT are considerably cheaper than airlines which are members of IATA.

Aeroflot quotes the IATA fare from London as £357 one-way and £714 return but sells tickets for £215 and £430 respectively. Other airlines serving Damascus include Royal Jordanian, Cyprus Airways, Lufthansa, KLM and Swissair.

## OVERLAND

### To/From Turkey

**Bus** There are at least seven border posts between Syria and Turkey, the most popular and congested being the one that connects Gaziantep and Aleppo. Crossing here can take up to six hours so be prepared for a wait. Other posts may be less crowded but crossing is still a long process.

There are direct buses running daily from Istanbul to Aleppo and Damascus, or you can catch a *dolmuş* from the last Turkish town to the border, cross the border yourself and continue on by *meecro* (micro-bus) on the Syrian side.

For direct buses to Istanbul, book through the Karnak bus offices in Damascus or Aleppo. The trip from Damascus takes about 30 hours, 24 hours from Aleppo.

**Train** Twice a week there's a direct train from Istanbul to Aleppo taking 40 hours. It leaves Aleppo on Sunday and Wednesday at 7 am; S£116. Book at least a day in advance if you want a sleeper.

### To/From Jordan

There's only one border crossing between Syria and Jordan and that's at Der'a/Ramtha. Consequently it's extremely congested at times. You can cross by direct bus, service-taxi or by using a combination of local transport and walking.

**Bus** There are two direct air-conditioned Karnak buses daily in each direction between Amman and Damascus, at 7 am and 3 pm; JD3 from Amman, S£75 from Damascus. It's about a seven-hour trip depending on the border crossing. Book two days in advance as demand for seats is high.

**Service-taxi** The *servees* are faster than the buses but tend to get more thoroughly

47

searched at the border and don't save you any time at all. JD4 from Amman, S£100 from Damascus.

There are also service-taxis running from Damascus to Irbid and vice versa.

**Local Transport** The Der'a border is easy to tackle on your own. For details see the Der'a (Syria) and Irbid (Jordan) sections.

### To/From Lebanon
**Service-taxi** If you're feeling extremely brave there are service-taxis running between Beirut and Damascus and between Homs and Tripoli. Good luck!

### Car & Motorbike
A *carnet de passage* is required and third party insurance has to be bought at the border at the rate of US$25 for 10 days. Make sure that your own insurance company will cover you for Syria because some Middle Eastern countries are considered 'war zones' by insurance companies and you won't be covered.

If you are taking a car to Syria, you'll be better off if it runs on diesel. Super petrol is not always available and even regular is often of dubious quality.

## SEA
### To/From Cyprus & Turkey
Turkish Maritime Lines run a weekly car-ferry from Mersin to Lattakia via Famagusta (Cyprus). It departs Mersin on Friday evenings and Lattakia on Monday mornings and costs US$60.

# Getting Around

Syria has a well-developed road network and public transport is frequent and cheap. Private cars are relatively rare.

Distances are short so journeys are rarely more than four hours. About the longest single bus ride you can take is nine hours from Damascus to Qamishle in the north-east.

Whatever type of transport you use, make sure you are carrying your passport and it's not in your luggage or left in the hotel if you're on a day trip. To get into bus and railway stations you often need to show it and there are usually checks made en route.

## AIR

The internal air services operated by Syrian Arab Airlines are fairly limited but ridiculously cheap.

There are flights from Damascus to Aleppo and return daily except Sunday and the one-way fare is a paltry S£92. Where else can you make a 400-km flight for less than US$10?

Damascus to Deir Ez-Zur costs S£107 and operates on Sunday and Wednesday.

The only other destination is Lattakia with flights on Saturday, Monday and Thursday for S£92.

## ROAD
### Karnak Bus

The orange and white air-conditioned Karnak (government) buses connect every major town and city in Syria. They are cheap, comfortable, fast and reliable and the cost is about double what you would pay for a regular bus.

They are staffed by a two-man crew – a driver, and a conductor who serves passengers with water and bonbons at regular intervals during the trip.

You need to reserve a seat at least a day in advance as they are popular among the well-to-do and the military. One big advantage Karnak buses have over regular buses is that the office/terminal is always well located in the centre of town. Microbus stations are generally on the outskirts and you'll need a taxi to get you there, which often costs more than the bus trip itself.

The regular buses are a more interesting way to travel but if you just want to get from A to B with the minimum of fuss, Karnak is the way to do it.

From Damascus buses go to: Der'a S£10, 1½ hours; Palmyra S£28, 3 hours; Deir Ez-Zur S£47, 5 hours; Hassake S£72, 8 hours; Qamishle S£72, 9 hours; Abu Kamal S£72, 7 hours; Ras el Ain S£72, 9 hours; Homs S£12, 1½ hours; Hama S£12, 2 hours; Aleppo S£50, 6 hours; Tartus S£16, 3 hours; and Lattakia S£30, 5 hours.

### Bus/Microbus

Buses connect all major towns, and microbuses (called *meecro*) serve the smaller places. They have no schedule and just leave when full, so on the less popular routes you may have to wait for an hour or so until it fills up.

From the outside the buses look quite plain but on the inside they are always decorated with an incredible array of gaudy ornaments – plastic fruit and plants, lights and mirrors. The driver usually has enough uncluttered window to see at least some of the road ahead! Then there's the cassette player – no bus would be complete without one. The sound is invariably tinny, the tapes worn out and the volume loud. They are far less comfortable than the Karnak buses but as the distances are short it's no real hardship and it is one of the best ways to meet the local people, who will often invite you to their homes or villages. Try to keep your shedule flexible enough to make the most of Syrian hospitality.

Fares are cheap. From Damascus to Homs for instance (a 160-km, two-hour trip) costs just S£7.

### Service-taxi

The service-taxis (*servees*) in Syria are usually old American limousines from the '50s and '60s. There's a chronic shortage of spare parts but ingenuity and improvisation keep them running. They only operate on the major routes and cost about 50% more than the Karnak buses. Unless you're in a tearing hurry there's really no need to use them.

The advantage of service-taxis is that they are fast and as there are only five seats in each, you never have to wait long for them to fill up.

### TRAIN

Syria has a fleet of fairly modern trains made in East Germany. They are cheap and punctual, but the main disadvantage is that the stations are usually a few km from the town centres.

First class is air-conditioned with aircraft-type seats; 2nd class is the same except it's not air-con. On the Qamishle-Damascus run there are 1st-class sleepers available but unless you're a train buff, the bus is quicker and cheaper.

The main line connects Damascus, Aleppo, Deir Ez-Zur, Hassake and Qamishle. A secondary line runs along the coast from Aleppo to Lattakia, Tartus and on to Homs and Damascus.

In 1908 the French-built Hejaz Railway was opened to take pilgrims from Damascus to Medina (Saudi Arabia). This line no longer carries passenger traffic, despite sporadic efforts by Jordan and Syria to re-open it.

The railway line from Damascus to Beirut is also closed although trains run from Damascus to the (closed) border every Friday taking picnickers out along the Barada Valley. This makes a good day trip – see the Around Damascus section.

### TOURS

If time is important or you're just in Damascus for a couple of days, there are tours run by Karnak Tourism & Transport, but they're not cheap. The tours use four-seater vans and as you have to charter the whole thing it becomes a lot cheaper per head if there are four of you.

All tours start and finish in Damascus and go to places such as:

Around Damascus, half-day, S£140 per person for four people, S£210 per person for two

Bosra, half-day, S£260 per person for four

Maalula, half-day, S£200 per person for four, S£250 per person for two

Crac Des Chevaliers, one day, S£320 per person for four, S£530 per person for two

Palmyra, one day, S£360 per person for four, S£620 per person for two

### LOCAL TRANSPORT
### Bus

All the major cities have a local bus system but as the city centres are compact, you can usually get around on foot. This is just as well because, with the exception of Damascus, the buses have no signs in English (and often nothing in Arabic either) to indicate where they are going.

### Taxis

Taxis in most cities are plentiful and cheap. In Damascus they have meters and drivers use them; anywhere else it's a matter of negotiating the fare when you get in.

It's a real surprise to find taxi drivers who aren't a pack of sharks. In Syria, if you get into a taxi and ask how much it is to the bus station or wherever, nine times out of 10 you'll get told the correct fare and bargaining will get you nowhere.

# Damascus

Damascus (*ash-Sham* in Arabic) is the capital of Syria and with a population of 2.2 million is by far the largest city. It's a fascinating city of contrasts. Veiled women in traditional dress walk alongside women dressed in trendy western clothes and adorned with make-up. Old men in *galabiehs* and *kaffiyehs* pass young men in Michael Jackson T-shirts selling blackmarket Johnny Walker whisky. In the old city you can hear the busy sounds of the craftsmen at work and the cries of the hawkers while the new city assaults the ears with the roar of traffic and the constant wail of Arabic music from the cassette shops.

The city owes its existence to the Barada River which rises high in the Anti Lebanon Mountains. The waters give life to the Ghouta Oasis, which makes settlement possible in what is an otherwise uninhabitable area.

### History

Damascus can lay claim to being the oldest continuously inhabited city in the world. The hieroglyphic tablets of Egypt make reference to 'Dimashqa' as being one of the cities conquered by the Egyptians in the 15th century BC but excavations from the courtyard of the Omayyed mosque have yielded finds dating back to the 3rd millennium BC.

It has been fought over many times and some of the earliest conquerors include King David of Israel, the Assyrians in 732 BC, Nebuchadnezzar (*circa* 600 BC) and then the Persians in 530 BC. In 333 BC it fell to Alexander the Great. Greek influence declined when the Nabataeans occupied Damascus in 85 BC. The Romans soon sent the Nabataeans packing in 64 BC and Syria became a Roman province. It was here that Saul of Tarsus was converted to Christianity and became St Paul the Apostle.

Damascus was an important city under the Romans and it became a military base for the armies fighting the Persians. Hadrian declared it a metropolis in the 2nd century BC and during the reign of Alexander Severus it became a Roman colony.

By the end of the 4th century AD most of the population had adopted Christianity. The Temple of Jupiter became a cathedral dedicated to St John the Baptist, whose head supposedly lies in a tomb inside the Omayyed Mosque.

With the coming of Islam, Damascus became an important centre as the seat of the Omayyed Caliphate from 661 to 750. The city expanded rapidly and the Christian cathedral was turned into a mosque. When the Abbasids took over and moved the Caliphate to Baghdad, Damascus was plundered once again.

After the occupation of Damascus by the Seljuq Turks in 1076, the Crusaders tried unsuccessfully to take it in 1148 before it finally fell to the Egyptian general Nureddin in 1154. Many of the monuments in the city date to the time of his successor, Saladin, when Damascus became the capital of a united Egypt and Syria.

The next to move in were the Mongols who, after only a brief occupation, were ousted by the Mamelukes of Egypt in 1260. During the Mameluke period Damascene goods became famous worldwide and attracted merchants from Europe. This led to the second Mongol invasion under Tamerlaine when the city was flattened and the artisans and scholars were deported to the Mongol capital of Samarkand. The Mamelukes returned soon after and proceeded to rebuild the city.

From the time of the Ottoman Turk occupation in 1516 the fortunes of Damascus started to decline and it was

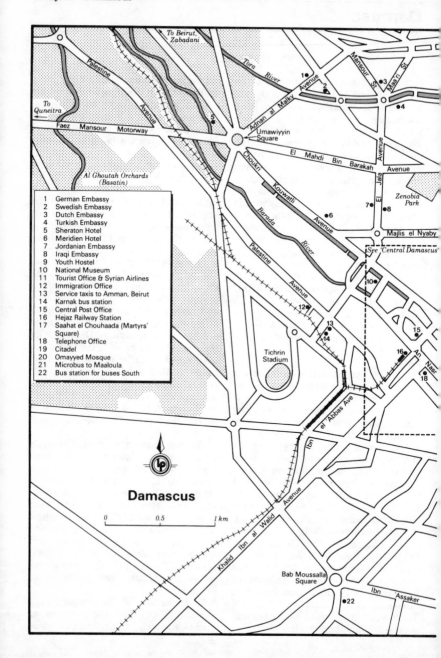

1  German Embassy
2  Swedish Embassy
3  Dutch Embassy
4  Turkish Embassy
5  Sheraton Hotel
6  Meridien Hotel
7  Jordanian Embassy
8  Iraqi Embassy
9  Youth Hostel
10 National Museum
11 Tourist Office & Syrian Airlines
12 Immigration Office
13 Service taxis to Amman, Beirut
14 Karnak bus station
15 Central Post Office
16 Hejaz Railway Station
17 Saahat el Chouhaada (Martyrs' Square)
18 Telephone Office
19 Citadel
20 Omayyed Mosque
21 Microbus to Maaloula
22 Bus station for buses South

**Damascus**

0    0.5    1 km

To Beirut, Zabadani
To Quneitra
Faez Mansour Motorway
Palestine Avenue
Tora River
Adnan al Malky Avenue
Mansour St
Maa'ri St
Umawiyyin Square
El Mahdi Bin Barakah Avenue
Al Ghoutah Orchards (Basatin)
Choukri Kouwatli Avenue
Barada River
El Jala Avenue
Zenobia Park
Majlis el Nyaby
See 'Central Damascus'
Palestine Avenue
Tichrin Stadium
An Nasr
Ibn el Abbas Ave
Khalid Ibn al Walid
Ibn Avenue
Bab Moussalla Square
Ibn Assaker

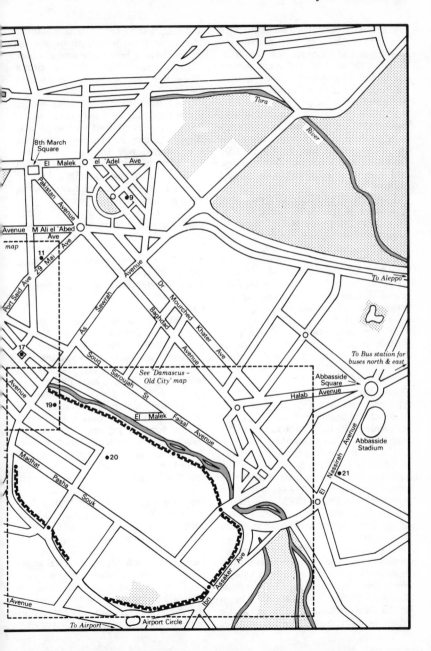

reduced to the capital of a small province in a large empire. The only interruption in 400 years of Ottoman rule was from 1831 to 1840 when it once again became the capital of Syria under the Egyptians, following the rise to power there of Mohammed Ali Pasha.

By 1878 the city's population had grown to 150,000 and great improvements were made in sanitary conditions and a transport system was built. By 1908 Damascus had a network of tramlines, and was connected by rail to Beirut and Medina.

The Turkish and German forces used Damascus as their base during WW I. When they were defeated by the Arab Legion and the Allies, the first Syrian government was set up in 1919.

The French, having been given a mandate by the League of Nations, occupied the city from 1920 to 1945. They met with a lot of resistance and at one stage in 1925 they bombarded the city to suppress rioting.

With the evacuation of the French and British forces in April 1946, Damascus became the capital of an independent Syria.

## Orientation

The city centre of Damascus is fairly compact and finding your way around on foot is no problem, despite the fact that street signs are nonexistent.

The real heart of the city is the Saahat al-Chouhada (Martyrs Square). The rather curious bronze colonnade in the centre commemorates the opening of the first telegraph link in the Middle East – the line from Damascus to Medina. Most of the cheap hotels and restaurants are around here.

The main street, Said el Jabri Avenue, begins at the Hejaz Railway Station and runs north-east, changing its name to Port Said Avenue at the Choukri Kouwatli Avenue flyover, and then again to 29 Mai Avenue at the Peasant's Monument (Mydaan Youssef al Azmeh),

finishing at the Central Bank Building. The whole street is only about one km long and along here you'll find the post office, tourist office, various airline offices and many mid-range restaurants and hotels.

The Barada River is unfortunately not much more than a smelly drain which flows from north-west to south-east through the city. Right in the centre it has been covered over. On its banks to the west of the Martyrs Square is the Takieh es Sulaymanieh Mosque and the National Museum. Close by is the University, Karnak bus station and immigration office.

The old city lies to the south of the river, just east of Martyrs Square. Apart from the old Roman road, now known as Street Called Straight (no need to explain why), it's a tangle of narrow and twisting roads with the old houses often almost touching overhead.

## Information

**Tourist Office** This is in the same office as Syrian Arab Airlines on 29 Mai Avenue just up from the Peasant's Monument. It's open from 9 am to 6 pm and the staff speak English and are very friendly and helpful. They have a good free map of Syria which has plans of Damascus, Aleppo and Palmyra on the back. If you go to the Ministry of Tourism at Martyrs Square you can get some good colour wall-posters of various Syrian scenes. There's also an information booth at the airport staffed by helpful students on vacation but it's not always open.

**Post** This is on Said el Jabri Avenue. You can't miss it – it's a big imposing building with a large picture of Assad on the front. It's open from 8 am to 6 pm seven days a week. It's one of the few buildings in Damascus which doesn't have an emergency generator so when the power goes out from 2 to 6 pm daily, the interior is very dark and gloomy. The poste restante counter is fairly efficient. The parcel post office is outside and around the corner.

**Money** The branch of the Commercial Bank of Syria on the corner of Baroudy Rd and El Jabri Avenue opposite the Hejaz Railway station takes cash and travellers' cheques. There's also a booth at the entrance to the Souk Al Hamadiyeh which is open until 6.30 pm but they will only change cash here.

The American Express agent is Chami Travel (tel 111652), Mouradi Building, Fardous St. The postal address is PO Box 507, Damascus.

**Immigration** For visa extensions, the immigration office is on Palestine Avenue, one block up from the Karnak bus station. As with all government departments it's open from 8.30 am to 2 pm Sunday to Thursday. You need two passport photos which you can get on-the-spot outside the office if necessary. The extension costs S£5 and despite the fact that it takes no time at all to issue, you'll probably be told to pick your passport up at 1 pm the following day.

**Jordanian Visas** are available at the border but if you want to get one here, the embassy is on Avenue el Jala, about five minutes walk over the bridge from the National Museum. One-month tourist visas are issued the same day, require two passport photos and cost anything from nothing (Australians) to S£120 (Germans). The embassy is only open from 8 to 11 am Saturday to Thursday.

**Bookshop** There's a good bookshop, the Libraire Universalle, on the short street next to the Hotel Venise. As well as books on Syria and the Middle East, it stocks magazines such as *Time* and *Newsweek*.

## Things to See
To get a good view of the city, take a No 1 Mouhagrin bus from opposite the Hotel Venise. Ride the bus to the end and then climb the stairs to higher up on Jebel Qassioun. It's best to go in the late afternoon when the sun is behind you.

### Old City
Most of the sights of Damascus are in the old city which is surrounded by a Roman wall. The wall itself has been flattened and rebuilt several times over the past 2000 years. The one which stands today dates from the 13th Century. It is pierced by a number of gates (*Babs*), only one of which (Bab Sharki - East Gate) dates back to Roman times. The best preserved section is between Bab as-Salam (Gate of Peace) and Bab Touma (Thomas Gate - named after a son-in-law of the Emperor Heraclius) in the north-east corner. For most of its length the wall is obscured by new buildings which have been built over and around it. Bab as-Salam is a beautiful example of Ayyubid military architecture but unfortunately it is now draped with electric cables and telegraph wires. The Bab Kisan houses St Paul's Chapel; the front gates are closed but you can enter from the orphanage at the back. This is where tradition has it that the Christians lowered St Paul out of a window in a basket to escape the wrath of the Jews (Acts 9: 25).

### Citadel
The citadel forms part of the western wall at the end of An Nasr Avenue. It used to be the home of the National Guard but is now closed for restoration. No-one seems to mind if you stroll in and take a look around. There's some good views of the old city from the ramparts. In the courtyard the stonemasons can be seen chipping away at the enormous blocks which will eventually form the reconstituted walls.

### Souk al Hamadiyeh
Next to the citadel is the entrance to the covered market, the Souk al Hamadiyeh. The gloomy cobbled souk with its bustling crowds, hawkers and tenacious merchants is worlds away from the traffic jams and chaos of the streets outside. It's also the closest thing to a tourist trap in Syria. Most of the shops sell handicrafts –

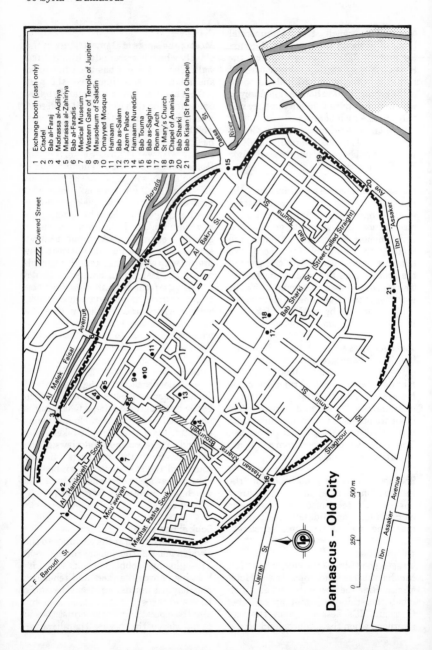

Key (legend):
1 Exchange booth (cash only)
2 Citadel
3 Bab al-Faraj
4 Madrassa al-Adiliya
5 Madrassa al-Zahiriya
6 Bab al-Faradis
7 Medical Museum
8 Western Gate of Temple of Jupiter
9 Mausoleum of Saladin
10 Omayyed Mosque
11 Hamaam
12 Bab as-Salam
13 Azem Palace
14 Hamaam Nureddin
15 Bab Touma
16 Bab as-Saghir
17 Roman Arch
18 St Mary's Church
19 Chapel of Ananias
20 Bab Sharki
21 Bab Kisan (St Paul's Chapel)

ZZZ Covered Street

Damascus – Old City

0   250   500 m

inlay work, brass and copperware, jewellery, silk and carpets – and the shopkeepers stand outside trying their best to entice you in. It's the best place to buy souvenirs but the golden rule when buying anything is to bargain and bargain hard. The mix of people in the souk is wonderful – from Europeans in United Nations uniforms (members of the UNIFIL contingent in Lebanon) to Iranian women tourists covered from head to foot in purdah.

At the far end of the souk the vaulted roof suddenly gives way to two enormous Corinthian columns supporting a decorated lintel – the remains of the western gate of the old Roman Temple of Jupiter dating back to the 3rd century AD. It too is draped with all manner of electric cables, telegraph wires and lights. At the foot of the columns the stalls sell souvenirs for the religious – Korans, pictures of Mecca and wall-hangings with calligraphic messages of the 'One True God' and 'Allah is Great' variety.

## Omayyed Mosque

Opposite the end of the souk is the entrance to the Omayyed Mosque – daunting in size and impressive in its construction. Take your time on a visit. It's a peaceful place and is a respite from the heat and hustle outside. The tourist entrance is 30 metres to the left of the main entrance and here you pay the S£2 entry fee. Men in shorts and all women have to use the black robes supplied. Only Muslims are admitted on Fridays. It's OK to take photos anywhere inside.

The history of the site itself goes back almost 3000 years to the 9th century BC when the Aramaens built a temple to their god, Hadad, mentioned in the Book of Kings in the Old Testament. The enormous Temple of Jupiter, measuring 380 by 310 metres, was built on the site by the Romans in the 3rd century AD. With the rise of Christianity in the 4th century, the temple was converted into a church and was named after St John the Baptist.

When the Muslims entered Damascus in 636 they converted the eastern part of the temple into a mosque and allowed the Christians to continue their worship in the western part.

This arrangement continued until 705 when the sixth Omayyed caliph, Alwalid, decided that he wanted to 'build a mosque the equal of which was never designed by anyone before me or anyone after me'. Consequently all the old Roman and Byzantine constructions within the enclosure were flattened and for the next 10 years more than 1000 stonemasons and artisans were employed in the construction of the grand new mosque.

Most of the interior of the mosque today was reconstructed at the end of the last century when a fire swept through the original building.

The three minarets all date from the time of Alwalid but they have been renovated and restored at later dates by the Ayyubids, Mamelukes and Ottomans. The one on the northern side is the Minaret Al'Arous (Minaret of the Bride) while the one on the south-eastern corner is the Minaret of Jesus, so named because local tradition has it that this is where Jesus will appear on Judgement Day. The northern part of the rectangular mosque is an open courtyard with a beautiful, smooth marble floor – cool to walk over even on hot days, but mind the pigeon shit. The courtyard is flanked on three sides by a double-storeyed portico which used to be covered with veined marble. The two pillars either side of the fountain in the centre used to hold lamps to light the courtyard. The small octagonal structure on the eastern side is the old treasury which used to keep public funds safe from thieves. It is decorated with some fine mosaics.

On the southern side of the court is the prayer hall. It's a rectangular hall of three aisles divided by a transept. High above the transept is the Dome of the Eagle, so called because it represents the eagle's

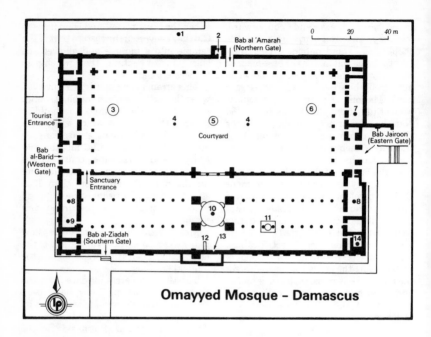

**Omayyed Mosque – Damascus**

| | |
|---|---|
| 1 | Mausoleum of Saladin |
| 2 | Minaret al 'Arous |
| 3 | Treasury dome |
| 4 | Old lighting columns |
| 5 | Ablution fountain |
| 6 | Clocks dome |
| 7 | Mashhad al Hussein (Al Hussein Mausoleum) |
| 8 | Mashhad (ablution hall) |
| 9 | Western minaret |
| 10 | Transept & Eagle Dome |
| 11 | Shrine of St John the Baptist |
| 12 | Minbar (pulpit) |
| 13 | Main mihrab |
| 14 | Minaret of Jesus |

head while the transept represents the body and the aisles are the wings. Looking somewhat out of place in the sanctuary is the structure surrounding the tomb of John the Baptist (the Prophet Yahia to the Muslims). It is believed that his head was buried on this spot. The original

wooden tomb was replaced by the present marble one after the fire of 1893.

### Mausoleum of Saladin

Saladin's mausoleum was originally built in 1193 and restored with funds made available by Kaiser Wilhelm II of Germany during his visit to Damascus in 1898. The walnut-wood cenotaph is richly decorated with motifs of the Ayyubid period and next to it lies the modern tomb in marble, also donated by Kaiser Wilhelm.

The mausoleum is covered by a red dome and is in a pleasant garden setting outside the northern wall of the Omayyed mosque. The old character looking after the place will invite you in and give a guided tour in broken English.

### Azem Palace

The Azem Palace, just to the south of the Omayyed Mosque, is another peaceful haven. It was built in 1749 by the Governor of Damascus, Assad Pacha al-Azem, out of black basalt and limestone and the alternating layers of white and black give a curious effect.

The rooms of the modest palace also house the exhibits of the National Museum of the Arts & Popular Traditions of Syria (see under Museums).

The palace is open from 8 am to 2 pm daily except Tuesday. Entry is S£1.

### Hamaams

Hamaams (Turkish baths) are a great way to spend a couple of hours but unfortunately it is usually a men-only activity. There's a couple of them close to the Omayyed Mosque and the second one may take couples if there is no-one else using it at the time.

The first is very plush and prices are correspondingly high. Called Hamaam Nureddin it is in the covered street that runs between the Omayyed Mosque and Street Called Straight. Here they sting you for everything – S£20 for the bath, S£25 sauna, S£30 massage, S£4 towel and S£2 for soap.

The second hamaam is on the small street which runs from the eastern wall of the Omayyed Mosque. It has no sign in English but it's right opposite the small café. A bath and sauna will cost just S£20 and you'll probably have the place to yourself.

### Churches

About two-thirds of the way along the Street Called Straight are the remains of a Roman arch. This roughly marks the boundary of what might be called the Christian quarter. There are a few churches in this area but the only one of any historical interest is the Chapel of Ananias (Kanissat Hananya), the old cellar of the house of Ananias.

Ananias, an early Christian disciple, was charged to 'go into the street which is called Straight, and inquire in the house of Judas for one called Saul of Tarsus (St

Paul)' (Acts 9: 11) so that he might be able to touch him and restore Saul's sight. The entrance is on the outside of the wall between Bab Sharki and Bab Touma.

The Chapel of St Paul (Bab Kisan) marks the spot where the disciples lowered St Paul out of a window in a basket one night so that he could flee from the Jews, having angered them after preaching in the synagogues.

### Takieh es Sulaymanieh Mosque

This mosque, on the banks of the Barada River just to the west of the post office, was originally built by the famous Turkish architect, Sinan, in 1554. It is a particularly graceful mosque built in alternating layers of black and white stone with two towering minarets and it's very peaceful to sit by the fountain and watch the world go by, away from the

Treasury dome, Omayyed Mosque

traffic outside. The grounds also house the Army Museum.

Next to the mosque is the Artisanat – a handicraft market housed in an old caravanserai built by the Ottoman Sultan Selim in 1516 to accommodate poor pilgrims. The former quarters, kitchens and offices are now workshops where you can see all sorts of crafts practised, from weaving to glass-blowing.

## Museums

**National Museum** This is the most important of the city's four museums and it is next to the Takieh es Sulaymanieh. It is well worth at least one visit and is open from 9 am to 4 pm Saturday to Thursday, and 9 am to 12.30 pm and 2 to 4 pm on Friday. Entry is S£1. All bags and cameras have to be left in the office at the entrance. Unfortunately most of the exhibits are labelled only in French or Arabic and some have no label at all.

The large shady garden in the front of the museum has bits and pieces of statuary from sites all around the country and the small café sells tea and soft drinks. To sit under the large eucalypts and sip a *shay* on a hot afternoon is a good way to recharge your system.

The facade of the museum is imposing – it is the entrance to the old Qasr al-Hir ash-Sharqi (a desert palace/military camp near Palmyra dating to the time of the Omayyed Caliph Hisham in 688) and was transported to Damascus stone by stone and reconstructed. It looks somewhat cramped by the wings of the museum.

Inside is a fantastic array of exhibits: written cylinders from Ugarit using the first known alphabet, dating from the 14th century BC; statuary from Mari, 3rd to 2nd millennium BC; two halls full of marble and terracotta statues from Palmyra; a reconstruction of an underground burial chamber from the Valley of the Tombs, Palmyra; frescoes from Doura Europos; sculptures of black basalt from the Hauran around Bosra; Damascene weapons; old surgical instruments from

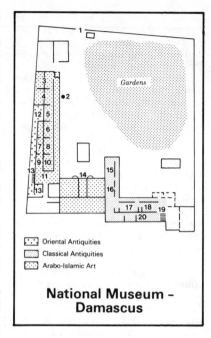

**Oriental Antiquities**

**Classical Antiquities**

**Arabo-Islamic Art**

## National Museum – Damascus

| | |
|---|---|
| 1 | Entrance |
| 2 | Cafe |
| 3 | Room from Azem Palace |
| 4 | Manuscripts, Korans |
| 5 | Hama |
| 6 | Terracotta pottery |
| 7 | Phoenician glass |
| 8 | Ceramics |
| 9 | Metalwork, damascened swords |
| 10 | Architecture & decoration |
| 11 | Raqqa – models, vessels |
| 12 | Mari (Tell Hariri) – statuettes, figurines |
| 13 | Ugarit – alphabet, statuettes |
| 14 | Facade |
| 15 | Hauran (Bosra) – basalt sculptures |
| 16 | Jebel Druze – mosiacs, basalt sculptures |
| 17 | 5th-3rd century BC statuary |
| 18 | Palmyra – mosiacs, frescoes |
| 19 | Reconstructed hypogeum, Palmyra (basement) |
| 20 | Christian art, 1st-7th centuries |

doctors' graves; Phoenician glassware from the 13th century BC; a collection of Korans dating back to the 13th century; and a complete room decorated in the style of the Azem Palace of the 18th century.

**Army Museum** This is in the grounds next to the Takieh es Sulaymanieh mosque. It has a fine collection of weapons and armour. As is often the case in Syrian museums, the descriptions are only in French and Arabic. Outside the museum are various cannons and planes, most are relics of WW II or the Arab-Israeli war of 1967. There's also a pile of the twisted remains of planes shot down in the war in 1973. The museum is open daily from 8 am to 2 pm except Tuesday and entrance is the usual S£1.

**Medical Museum** This is in the old city, just off the Souk al-Hamadiyeh. It is housed in an old 12th-century hospital and is open from 8 am to 2 pm daily except Tuesday; entry is S£1. Descriptions are in French and Arabic.

The collection of old medical and surgical instruments from Roman to Ottoman times look more like implements of torture – there's even an old electric-shock machine. It's easy to see why many patients carried good-luck charms. There's also a display of 100 or so medicinal herbs and spices used in ancient times.

**Museum of the Arts & Popular Traditions of Syria** This impressively titled museum is housed in the Azem Palace. Unfortunately the displays are not quite as impressive but they do manage to give some idea of Syria as it was. It is not well labelled, so try and latch on to one of the attendants to show you around.

**Damascus International Fair**
This is a trade exhibition that takes place annually in the first two weeks of September. Although it is of little interest

to the traveller, during the show there are often cultural events put on by some of the participating countries. Check the *Syria Times* for what's happening.

**Places to Stay – bottom end**
Damascus has a big selection of cheap hotels, most of them grouped around Martyrs Square, but unfortunately a lot of them are suspicious of foreigners and insist that the hotel is full. Many others seem to be permanently reserved for Iranian tourists who come here in droves to visit a holy Shi'ite mausoleum on the southern outskirts of Damascus. The accommodation shortage is particularly bad around the time of the *hajj* when many Turks stop on their way to or from Mecca. Try to arrive in the morning before things fill up.

Note that of mid-1987, the Syrian government now requires all hotels to be paid for in US dollars, at the low rate of S£9.75. So a budget hotel that charges S£25 for locals, will hit foreign visitors with a bill of around US$3.

The *Abdeen Hotel* is right in the centre of things and the manager is very friendly and welcoming. Double rooms with fan cost S£70 and beds in share rooms are S£30. Just a couple of doors away, on the corner, the *Hotel Said* has similar prices.

The *Rida Hotel* has some rooms the size of cupboards and others which are quite OK. Prices are a bit steep at S£50/100/150 for a single/double/triple but it usually seems to have room when all the others are full. The old woman running the place can be abrupt. The entrance is next door to a cinema by the barrier across Fourat St and the hotel is on the 4th floor.

The *Pakistan Hotel* must be a strong contender for the title of 'worst hotel in the world' but because of that, it always has room. It's in a big old bluestone building and has the air of an old insane asylum. The rooms are filthy and even the bed bugs have died (I hate to think

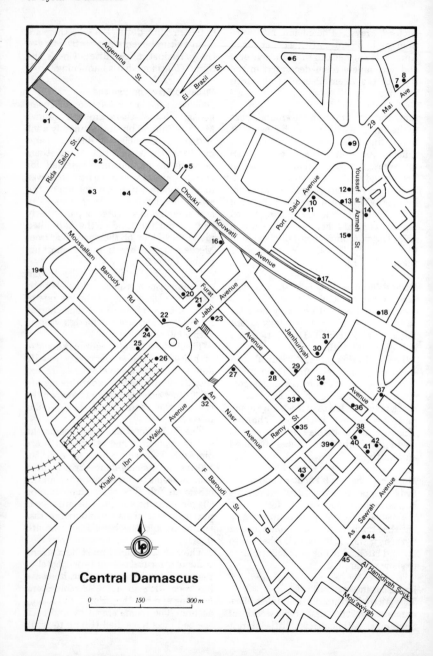

**Central Damascus**

0    150    300 m

| | |
|---|---|
| 1 | National Museum |
| 2 | Military Museum |
| 3 | Takieh es Sulaymanieh Mosque |
| 4 | New Craft Souk (Artisanat) |
| 5 | Turkish bus companies |
| 6 | Sham Palace Hotel |
| 7 | Tourist Office & Syrian Airlines |
| 8 | Al Kamal Restaurant |
| 9 | Mydaan Youssef al Azmeh Monument |
| 10 | Karnak Tours |
| 11 | Commercial Bank of Syria |
| 12 | Hotel Venise |
| 13 | Libraire Universalle bookshop |
| 14 | Bus to Muhagrin |
| 15 | Hotel International de Damas |
| 16 | Hotel Semiramis |
| 17 | Airport bus |
| 18 | Bus to Kaboun & ticket booth |
| 19 | Salam Hotel |
| 20 | Al Afamia Hotel |
| 21 | Central post office |
| 22 | Commercial Bank of Syria (cash & cheques) |
| 23 | Nightclub |
| 24 | Hamburger & juice shop |
| 25 | Loasis Hotel |
| 26 | Hejaz Railway Station |
| 27 | Ministry of Tourism |
| 28 | Rida Hotel |
| 29 | Exchange Office |
| 30 | Omar al Khayyam Hotel |
| 31 | Good felafel shop |
| 32 | Telephone Office |
| 33 | Shawarma shops |
| 34 | Saahat al-Chouhada (Martyrs Square) |
| 35 | Pakistan Hotel |
| 36 | Siaha Hotel |
| 37 | Vegetable souk & kebab stalls |
| 38 | Said Hotel |
| 39 | Restaurant |
| 40 | Abdeen Hotel |
| 41 | Sahloun Restaurant |
| 42 | Restaurant |
| 43 | Juice stall |
| 44 | Citadel |
| 45 | Exchange booth (cash only) |

In the street next to the Hejaz Railway station, the *Loasis Hotel* is quiet and secure and the guys running it are helpful. Rooms with fan and bath are S£90/120 for singles/doubles but try bargaining.

One of the best bargains is the clean, quiet and friendly *Salam Hotel* in a side street just behind the Takieh es Sulaymanieh Mosque. It's well situated halfway between Martyrs Square and the Karnak bus station. There is only a couple of double rooms, the rest are share rooms, and beds cost just S£20.

The *Al Rabie Hotel* (tel 218373) is near the airport bus stop by Martyrs Square. It has a marble courtyard with a fountain and paintings, and it has a friendly staff. It costs S£25 for a bed.

The *Youth Hostel* is a bit out of the way in a small street behind the Central Bank Building, about 20 minutes walk from the centre. You need a youth hostel card but a student card should also be OK, otherwise you can join the Syrian Youth Hostels Association for US$10. One traveller wrote to say he got deported from Syria when the manager of the hostel informed the police when he spotted a stamp from an Israeli youth hostel in his book! It is open from 8 to 10 am and 4 to 10 pm and the curfew is strictly enforced. Beds in dorms cost S£15 per night.

### Places to Stay – middle

If you want to go up-market a bit, you'll have to stay in a one-star hotel where minimum charges are US$8/14 for singles/doubles.

The *Afamia Hotel*, right behind the post office is one of the better one-star hotels. The management are none too friendly but the rooms have baths and are all air-conditioned.

Other similar hotels around Martyrs Square include the *Hotel Siaha, Hotel Semiramis* and the *Hotel Omar al Khayyam*.

what of!) but if you're really stuck late at night it's better than sleeping in the street, but not much. Beds cost S£20 per person.

### Places to Stay – top end

For those who want the best available, there's the *Sheraton, Meridien* and *Sham Palace* hotels where the amount spent on a bed for the night is enough to keep most travellers going for a couple of weeks.

The *Sham Palace Hotel* is the latest show-place in Damascus, complete with revolving restaurant, and is also the most conveniently located of the biggies. It's just one block west of the Mydaan Youssef al Azmeh Monument.

The *Meridien Hotel* is on the north bank of the Barada River, about 10 minutes walk north-west of the centre, and the *Sheraton* has a pleasant situation by the river, a further km west along Choukri Kouwatli Avenue.

### Places to Eat

Martyrs Square is also the focus for cheap eats. There are small stalls and restaurants dotted around selling the usual kebabs, chicken, shawarma and felafels.

The big *Sahloun Restaurant* has all the standard things as well as a variety of meat and vegetable stews, rice and macaroni. It also has fans and an upstairs 'family salon' for families and women. A half chicken, salad and hummus will cost about S£25. Bean stew and rice is S£11. There's a similar place (with no name) a few doors further along – the entrance is also a hotel entrance.

For a good felafel, if you can face another one, try the small shop opposite the building site on the north side of Martyrs Square. They come in McDonalds wrappers, which is hopefully as close to Syria as McDonalds will ever get. If a burger is what you're really after, the juice shop opposite the Commercial Bank of Syria near the Hejaz Railway station does a fair imitation. A burger with egg and pickles is S£3.

There are also excellent juice stalls all over the city. You can't miss them as they have string bags of fruit hanging outside. Apple, orange, banana and pomegranate are favourites and cost from S£4 to S£6. The tiny stall close to the An Nasr Avenue does great rockmelon juices and also has cheese and jam sandwiches.

What is the vegetable market by day becomes the kebab stalls at night. It's just on the edge of Martyrs Square and is interesting in the evening when it throngs with kebab and fruit stalls and black marketeers selling *Amstel* beer from Lebanon (S£15 a can) as well as whisky and *araq* – the local firewater, and you hear the cries of the cigarette sellers: 'Marl-poro, Marl-poro!'.

There's a whole string of more expensive restaurants along 29 Mai Avenue but even at these a basic meal won't cost more than about S£30. The *Al Kamal Restaurant* next to the tourist office is typical.

For a bit of *al fresco* dining in style, the *Al Khater Restaurant* is on the 3rd floor in the Hotel International de Damas. The terrace is pleasant and a meal of kebabs, hummus and salad is S£40; beer is S£12 for a half-litre bottle but is only available with a meal.

On An Nasr Avenue between the Hejaz Railway station and the telephone office are a couple of shawarma stalls and an enormous café with tea, coffee and waterpipes (*nargileh*).

### Getting There

**Air** Syrian Arab Airlines fly to:

Aleppo, Monday to Friday, S£92

Deir Ez Zur, Sunday and Wednesday, S£107

Lattakia, Saturday, Monday and Thursday, S£92

**Karnak Bus** The Karnak Bus station is about a 15-minute walk to the east of Martyrs Square. It's a big bustling place where you need to show your passport to get in and there's often a cursory baggage search as well. The station also has a reasonable restaurant.

Buses go from Damascus to all major

Top: Courtyard of the Omayyed Mosque, Damascus
Left: Water seller, Damascus
Right: Damascus from Jebel Qassioun

towns in Syria as well as Amman and Istanbul. It is essential to book at least one day in advance.

**Amman**, 7 am and 3 pm daily, at least six hours, depending on the border crossing, S£75

**Istanbul**, 8 am daily except Friday, about 30 hours, S£250. It's a Turkish bus and a dozen or so seats are reserved for passengers getting on in Aleppo. A better alternative is to take a Karnak bus to Aleppo, then the Turkish bus from there.

To destinations within Syria, there is at least one departure daily to the following places:

Der'a, 1½ hours, S£10
Palmyra, three hours, S£28
Deir Ez-Zur, five hours, S£47
Hassake, eight hours, S£72
Qamishle, nine hours, S£72
Abu Kamal, seven hours S£72
Ras el Ain, nine hours, S£72
Aleppo, six hours, S£35
Homs, 1½ hours, S£12
Hama, two hours, S£12
Tartus, three hours, S£16
Lattakia, five hours, S£30

**Bus** There are two main bus stations (both known as 'garage') in Damascus for regular buses. Buses run to no set schedule and just leave when full.

For buses north and east (Homs, Palmyra, Aleppo), the station is about three km east of the centre past the traffic circle contrarily called Abbasside Square. To get there catch a green local bus going to Kaboun (the destination is written in English on the side). Get off at the first roundabout after the big football stadium on the right.

The station for buses south (Der'a) is just south of the roundabout Bab Moussala Square, about two km south of the centre. The easiest way to get there is a taxi, S£6 from Martyrs Square.

Other buses to Turkey and Iran leave from a small station on Choukri Kouwatli Avenue, just east of Martyrs Square. Book in advance.

**Service-taxi** The *servees* station is right next to the Karnak station. Taxis leave throughout the day and night for Amman (five hours, S£100) and Beirut.

**Train** The Hejaz Railway Station is right in the centre of town. It's an impressive old building and the ceiling inside is intricately decorated. Trains are infrequent and slower than the buses and run daily to Homs, Hama, Aleppo, Raqqa, Deir-Ez Zur, Hassake, Qamishle and Tartus.

The big disadvantage with the trains is that the station is usually right on the outskirts of the towns and it can be a hassle to get to the centre.

### Getting Around

**Airport Transport** The Damascus International Airport is 35 km south-east of Damascus. Local green buses leave every 20 minutes from next to the Choukri Kouwatli Avenue flyover from 5.30 am to 12.30 am, cost S£3 and take half an hour.

**Bus** Damascus is well served with a local bus network but as the centre is so compact, it's rare that you have to use them. Tickets have to be bought before you get on and there are small booths for this – there's one on Choukri Kouwatli Avenue where the bus to Kaboun leaves from. A book of five tickets costs S£2.50 and each ticket is good for two journeys, or one journey for two people. Each bus has a ticket-punching machine in the entrance but a lot of people seem not to bother with buying tickets.

**Taxi** All the taxis are yellow, there are hundreds of them, and they are cheap but make sure that the driver uses the meter.

## AROUND DAMASCUS
### Maalula

Set in a narrow valley in the foothills of the Anti Lebanon range, Maalula is an interesting little village where the houses cling to the cliff face. They are often plastered in yellow, blue or mauve which makes the village far more attractive than most Syrian villages where the buildings are just drab, grey, concrete block-houses.

Although there are some Muslims, most of the residents are Greek Orthodox Catholics. The village's real claim to fame, however, is that Aramaic is still spoken here. This old dialect dates from the 1st millennium BC and was the language that Jesus spoke. The Lord's Prayer and the Old Testament book of Daniel were first written in Aramaic.

At the main intersection in the village, the road forks. The right fork leads to the Convent of St Thecla, tucked snugly against the cliff. The convent itself is of no particular interest, but carry on past it along a narrow cleft cut through the rock by the waters draining the plateau above the village. Turn back to the left where the cleft opens out and walk along the cliff edge for some spectacular views of the town and valley. The flash building under construction right on the edge is a fancy new hotel. Past the hotel is another convent, dedicated to St Sergius (Mar Sarkis). The low doorway leads into the monastery where there is a small Byzantine church. Take the road leading down from the monastery and it brings you out at the fork in the village.

**Places to Stay** Until the fancy hotel overlooking the town is finished, there is no accommodation in Maalula. Even when it is finished, prices will be way out of the budget traveller's range. This is no problem as it's an easy day-trip from Damascus.

**Getting There** Minibuses run to Maalula every hour or so from a separate station in Damascus. To get to it from the centre, take a Kaboun bus from Choukri Kouwatli Avenue and get off at the Abbasside Square, a big traffic circle with fountains in the centre. It's easy to recognise because you'll see the football stadium (Malaab el Abbasside) on the far side of it. Walk down Nassirah Avenue in front of the stadium to the first main intersection. The minibuses leave when full from a small car park on the left. The trip takes 1¼ hours, S£2.75.

### Zabadani & Ain el Fijah

These two small towns are in the valley of the Barada River as it makes its way down from the Anti Lebanon range to the Ghouta Oasis and Damascus.

The countryside is very pleasant but the main attraction is the narrow-gauge train trip up the valley every Friday. Damascenes flock there on Fridays to escape the city and picnic by the river. The train is loaded with a real variety of people – from elderly veiled women with children and grand-children in tow, to teenage boys sporting their latest western clothes and ghetto-blasters.

The train crawls all the way up to the (closed) border with Lebanon at Sarghya, taking about three hours to cover the 50 km from Damascus. It then stops for about three hours before making the return trip. As there's nothing to see at Sarghya, it's best to get off the train at Zabadani on the way up, catch a minibus down to Ain el Fijah and then either wait for the train or catch another minibus to Damascus.

**Getting There** Trains only run on Fridays, leaving the Hejaz Railway station at 8 and 9 am, returning from Sarghya at 3.15 and 3.45 pm. The fare is S£2 to Zabadani, S£1 to Ain el Fijah.

# Mediterranean Coast

The 183-km-long Syrian coastline is dominated by the rugged mountain range which runs along its entire length. The coastal strip, narrow in the north, widens towards the south and is extremely fertile and heavily cultivated.

The port city of Lattakia (*Al Lathqiya*) with its beach resorts, and the ruined ancient city of Ugarit, lie in the north. From here roads head north to Turkey, east across the mountains to Aleppo, and south to Tartus, Syria's secondary port.

The mountains behind Lattakia contain Syria's only forests and these are easy on the eyes after the often monotonous country in the interior. Excessive clearing of the forests for timber have led to large areas being reduced to scrub, although the government has laid aside some areas for preservation.

The beaches along the coast are certainly nothing to rave about as the water is murky and the sand is littered with garbage, but they are popular with holidaying Syrians.

## LATTAKIA

This busy port city is dominated by the harbour facilities and the freighters anchored just offshore. Most of Syria's imports and exports come through here and car-ferries connect it to Cyprus and Turkey.

It's certainly not a typical Syrian town. It has almost a European feel with its wide tree-lined streets and the occasional café with chairs and tables on the footpath. It's also the one of least conservative cities in Syria. The people are very snappy dressers and it's not often you'll see a veil or traditional Arab dress.

The city itself has no real attractions but the ruins of the ancient city of Ugarit are worth a visit.

## History

Lattakia became a city of importance under the Seleucids in the 2nd century BC and was named Laodicea by Seleucus I. It came under Roman control in the 1st century AD and Mark Antony made it a free town. Many serious earthquakes during the Middle Ages took their toll and with the rebellions of the Alawites against the ruling Muslims in the 1800s it had little chance of regaining its former prosperity. Only recently has it boomed with the development of the port facilities.

## Information

The **tourist office** is in the small building in the middle of the dual-carriageway main street and is open from 8.30 am to 1 pm daily except Friday. It also serves as a small post office. The staff here are very friendly but as usual they have little or no printed information and are vague when giving directions.

The **post office** is south of the centre towards the harbour entrance.

To change **money** the Commercial Bank of Syria is on the main north-south road, five minutes walk from the tourist office and is open from 8.30 am to 1.30 pm.

For visa extensions, the **immigration office** is on the 3rd floor of the police building. The immigration officer is a jovial soul (unusual for a Syrian in uniform) who speaks good English. Before going up to the 3rd floor, buy the form with the revenue stamp on it from the boy just inside the door. Extensions are issued on the spot.

## Museum

There's a small museum down near the waterfront housed in an old Greek fort. All descriptions are in Arabic, although the caretaker is quite helpful. There's

1  Hotel Ramitha
2  Khayyam Hotel
3  Police & Immigration
4  Buses to Ras Shamra, Blue Beach
5  Tourist Office
6  Bus station to Aleppo
7  Micro-bus station for Tartus
   & Turkish border
8  Hotel du Tourisme
9  Karnak Hotel
10 Pizza restaurant
11 Mosque & cafes
12 Nahhas Hotel
13 Afamia Hotel
14 Park & tea stalls
15 Museum
16 Commercial Bank of Syria
17 Restaurant
18 Post Office
19 Karnak bus office

some pottery and written tablets from Ugarit, chain-mail suits and a section of contemporary art. It's open from 9 am to 1 pm daily. Entry is S£1.

### Places to Stay – bottom end

The real cheapies are all in the area around the mosque and on the street leading south from it. It's a very busy area so they are all noisy. The *Nahhas* and *Afamia* hotels are typical and cost S£30 for a bed.

The *Khayyam Hotel* opposite the police station not only gets the 5 am wake-up call from the mosque, but is also on a corner where buses roar around every few minutes. To add to that, the owner has the nerve to try and ask for S£60 a double – and the toilets are filthy. Bargain him down or better still, go somewhere else.

The *Ramitha Hotel* is excellent value and recommended; it's clean and above all, quiet. It's worth the five-minute walk to get away from the noise. Rooms have showers and fans and some have a view of the harbour, although this is becoming obscured by a multi-storey concrete monstrosity which is going up right in front. Doubles cost S£63. The *Karnak Hotel* opposite has similar prices but is not as good.

### Places to Stay - top end
On the waterfront is the old *Hotel du Tourisme* dating back to the days of the French mandate. It must have been quite grand in its day but looks a bit sad now, especially as it no longer looks out onto empty sea but onto the new harbour and freighters. It's officially a two-star establishment and costs US$11/14 for singles/doubles.

About six km north of town is the *Hotel Meridien* with the usual five-star facilities and prices to match.

### Places to Eat
As with hotels, the cheap restaurants and street stalls are around the mosque area. A quick hunt around will turn up the old faithfuls – felafel, chicken, kebabs and shawarma.

For the same food in better surroundings, there's a partly open-air restaurant upstairs on the first corner south of the mosque. Kebabs, hummus and salad for S£25.

The pizza restaurant marked on the map is nothing special but provides a welcome alternative to the standard fare.

All over Lattakia shops sell cheap locally made ice cream which is similar to gelati. If you can handle the lurid colours, the ice cream is quite good.

### Getting There
**Air** Syrian Airlines has flights to Damascus on Saturday, Monday and Thursday for S£92. Buy tickets from any of the travel agents. The airport is a few km out of town and taxis are the only way to get there.

**Bus** The Karnak bus station and office is in the southern end of the town centre. Book one day in advance for the buses which run daily to Aleppo (S£20), Tartus, Homs and Damascus (S£30).

There are two other bus stations on the main street about 300 metres along from the tourist office. The first is for the big buses which leave for Aleppo every half hour or so. The trip takes four hours and costs S£10. The other station, a further 100 metres along, is the microbus (*meecro*) station for buses to all other destinations. To Tartus takes 1½ hours and costs S£5.25. To get to Antakya (Turkey) take a microbus to Kasab (S£5) and from there a *dolmuş* to Antakya (TL 2000).

**Train** There are trains to Aleppo but the station is way out of town. Along the line up in the mountains you can see a railway bridge which was blown up by insurgents. A detour has been built until it is repaired.

**Sea** There is a weekly car-ferry to Cyprus leaving from the northern dock on Monday mornings. The fare to Limasol is US$60 per person. The agent is Lattakia Shipping Agencies (tel 33163) Port Said St, or PO Box 28, Lattakia.

### AROUND LATTAKIA
### Ras Shamra (Ugarit)
Although there's not much to see today, Ugarit was once the most important city on the Mediterranean coast. It first came to prominence in the 3rd millennium BC, when it traded with Cyprus and Mesopotamia. Its golden age however, was from about the 16th to the 13th century BC when it was a centre for trade from Egypt, the Aegean Sea, Cyprus, Syria and Mesopotamia. Offerings were sent by the kings of Egypt to the famous Temple of Baal and Ugarit became a centre of learning. The city fell to the Greeks in about 1500 BC and was finally destroyed by the Philistines when they invaded in about 1190 BC.

In the 13th century BC the royal palace at Ugarit was one of the most imposing

Ivory head, Ugarit

and famous buildings in western Asia. It started out as a modest structure but in time was enlarged to cover more than one hectare and featured courtyards, piped water, drainage and burial chambers. Similar features were also found in the houses of the well-to-do. At its peak Ugarit was a very wealthy city.

The city had a library and it is here that written clay tablets were found. The writing on the tablets is widely accepted as being the earliest known alphabet. It was adopted by the Greeks, then the Romans and it is from this script that all alphabets today are derived. The texts found here are the most important source of information on early religion and life in Syria. They contain various texts and myths of religious significance as well as lists of gods, and dictionaries. The tablets are on display in the museums in Lattakia, Aleppo and Damascus as well as the Louvre in Paris.

### Things to See

On the right of the track up to the ruins is the original entrance to the city, although now it looks more like a large drainage outlet. Once up on top of the small hill the site is laid out before you – a massive jumble of blocks with poorly defined streets and buildings. In the ruins there are vaulted tombs, wells and water channels. Water played an important part in the funerary rites. The dead had to have water near them, hence the elaborate wells and channels.

Two temples once stood on the highest point of the site. One was dedicated to the storm god, Baal, the supreme god for the Canaanites, Phoenicians and Aramaens. The father of all gods (except Baal) is El, the creator of man. The second temple was dedicated to Dagon, the father of Baal and the god associated with the fertility of crops.

The Mediterranean is just visible through the trees to the west. It has receded 100 metres or so since Ugarit's heyday. Don't try and walk to the water as it's a military area and you're likely to get a less than friendly reception.

**Getting There** Local town buses make the 16-km trip to Ras Shamra every hour or so from the bus stop outside the school in the main street of Lattakia. There's a small booth on the footpath which sells tickets (S£2). It's a busy stop and as the buses have no destination displayed, ask the guys in the ticket booth to show you which one to catch, and ask the driver where to get off. It's easy to hitch back to Lattakia or flag down a microbus or service-taxi.

The road goes through some extremely fertile country full of orchards surrounded by high cypress hedges. Fruit stalls along the road sell apples and oranges in season.

### Blue Beach

The road to Ras Shamra also passes Blue Beach, the major coastal resort in Syria. It's between the sports complex built for the 1987 Mediterranean Games and the Meridien Hotel. There are expensive bungalows set up along the beach and some effort is made to keep it cleared of garbage. The murky brown water, however, is none too inviting.

Out on a point, the multi-storey Meridien Hotel sticks out like a sore thumb. Here the beach is a little better but you have to pay S£40 per day for the privilege of using it! They also have peddle boats and sailboards for hire.

There's a very squalid little camping area next to the Meridien but it has absolutely nothing to recommend it.

**Getting There** Catch an orange local bus for Ras Shamra or, from the same stop, buses with a blue stripe on the windscreen, that sometimes have a Blue Beach sign. Get out at the roundabout after the sports complex; you can see the Meridien out to the left.

### BANIYAS

Baniyas is south of Lattakia, half-way to Tartus. It is a busy port town with a large

Gold bowl, Ugarit

oil refinery. The only reason to stop here is to visit the old Crusader fort of Qalaat Marqab, six km south of the town.

It was originally a Saracen stronghold but was extended by the Crusaders in the 12th century. The fortifications are still impressive although not much remains inside the walls. The 12th-century chapel has two fine doorways and frescoes. There are great views of the valley to the east and the sea to the west.

Entrance is S£1 and to get there take a pick-up (S£2) from Baniyas and ask for Qalaat Marqab.

### TARTUS

Tartus, Syria's second port, is an easygoing town with a reasonable beach. The old fortified island of Arwad is just offshore. Like Lattakia it is popular with holidaying Syrians and the road along the foreshore is a pleasant place for an evening stroll, but the complete lack of trees makes it hot and glary in the daytime. The beach is not too bad although women should wear at least a modest one-piece bathing suit – a bikini would be inappropriate, especially when the Muslim women hop into the water fully clothed.

Tartus is also a good base from which to visit the beautifully preserved Crusader castle, the Crac des Chevaliers. It is also possible to see the Crac en route from Tartus to Homs or vice versa, as long as you don't mind carting your gear around with you all day.

### History

Tartus seems to have been first established as a service town for the island of Arados (later called Ruad, now called Arwad) and given the name Antarados. It was taken over by Alexander the Great and then rebuilt by Constantine in 346 AD and renamed Constantina.

A chapel devoted to the Virgin Mary was built and the town became a popular pilgrimage site during the Crusader period, when it was renamed Tortosa.

In the 12th century the town became the seat of a bishop and the cathedral was constructed on the site of the ancient chapel.

## Information

There is a **tourist office** north of the cathedral but its opening hours are very erratic and it is not worth a visit.

To change **money**, the Commercial Bank of Syria has two branches: the one on the street from the clocktower takes cash only, the other just north of the cathedral takes cash and travellers' cheques.

The **immigration office** is in a small street just behind the clocktower. The office is upstairs and the street entrance is just a doorway with a black and white sign and a Syrian flag overhead.

## Cathedral & Museum

Don't be put off by the rather austere exterior of the 12th-century cathedral, the interior is all graceful curves and arches and houses a good little museum.

From the outside it looks more like a fortress and the only decoration is the five-arched windows and the reconstructed doorway. The interior consists of a nave with aisles on either side. Fragments of

| | |
|---|---|
| 1 | Post Office |
| 2 | Tourist Office |
| 3 | Commercial Bank of Syria |
| 4 | Cathedral & Museum |
| 5 | Boats to Arwad |
| 6 | Restaurant |
| 7 | Commercial Bank of Syria (cash only) |
| 8 | Hotel Tourism |
| 9 | Ambassador Hotel |
| 10 | Omaya Hotel |
| 11 | Service-taxi stop |
| 12 | Immigration Office |
| 13 | Al Baher Hotel |
| 14 | Microbus & railway station |
| 15 | Grand Hotel |
| 16 | Al Manara Restaurant |
| 17 | Karnak bus office |
| 18 | Shaati al Ahlam |

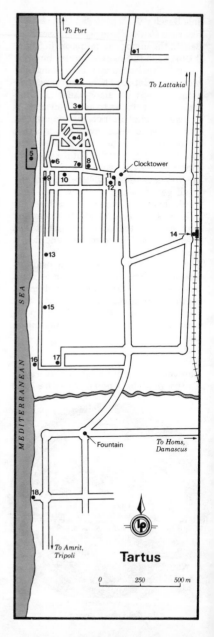

Tartus

0        250        500 m

earlier buildings have been incorporated into the construction; most obvious are the Corinthian-style capitals used in two pillars in the nave.

The second pillar on the left of the nave is built on top of a rectangular structure containing an arched passage. This is believed to have been the entrance to the original chapel where pilgrims made their devotions to the image of the Virgin Mary.

Items on display in the museum come from various sites including Ras Shamra, Arwad and Amrit. The rather crudely made sarcophagus in the central apse dates from the 2nd century AD.

The cathedral is supposedly open from 9 am to 1 pm and 3 to 6 pm daily except Tuesday but these hours are very flexible. Entry is S£1.

## Arwad

This small island, a few km south-west of Tartus, is a real gem. There are no cars or wide streets, only a maze of narrow lanes that twist and turn between the tightly packed buildings with each turn revealing something new. Small boats head out to the island every 15 minutes or so from the small fishing harbour. It costs S£2, which you pay on the island, and takes about 20 minutes. The last boat leaves the island around sunset – don't get stranded as there is no accommodation.

In Phoenician times the island was the head of a prosperous and powerful maritime state. It gradually declined in the 1st millennium BC and it was of little importance by the time it became part of the Roman Empire. During the Crusades it assumed strategic importance and even though Saladin captured Tartus in 1188, it wasn't until 1302 that the Crusaders were finally driven from their last stronghold in the East.

Today the island is a fascinating place to wander around. Right next door to the modern cafés crowded with young men watching American cowboy movies on video, you can see fishermen mending their nets and building boats with traditional methods and tools that have been used for centuries.

It's still possible to see the remains of the walls which used to protect the island from invasion, and the small fort on the highest point houses a small museum. Nothing is labelled but the attendants are eager to show off their English and guide you around.

The stalls down by the boat harbour sell the most amazing array of tacky souvenirs from shell-encrusted ashtrays to plastic toys.

## Shaati al Ahlam (Dream Beach)

Although it's certainly not my idea of a dream beach, Shaati al Ahlam is a little more relaxed than Tartus and women should have no problems swimming in bikinis. It costs S£5 per day to use the beach and there are also bungalows for rent at S£200 per day. They can accommodate up to six people and have cooking facilities.

The fancy *Shaati al Ahlam Restaurant* is very up-market and has live music in the evenings.

To get to the beach catch an orange bus heading south from the clocktower.

## Places to Stay

One of the best deals in Syria is the *Omaya (Daniel) Hotel*. The elderly owner is a great old character and is helpful and friendly. The hotel used to be called 'Daniel' (the owner's surname) but as he will tell you with a hint of sadness, he had to change it because 'it wasn't Syrian enough' and local people wouldn't stay there. It's clean and quiet and a single/double room with fan and bath costs S£30/50, S£5 less without bath.

There are a couple of other cheapies in the same street but they don't compare with the Omaya. The *Hotel Tourism* charges S£30/34/45 for single/double/triple rooms.

Some of the hotels on the waterfront by the Arwad boat dock are cheaper than they look. The *Ambassador Hotel* is enormous and has rooms with balconies overlooking the water although these front rooms are usually taken. Rooms at the back can be bargained down as they have neither the view nor the sea breeze. Singles/doubles with fan and bath cost S£40/58. The hotel next door with the large café has similar rooms and prices.

Further south are the *Al Baher Hotel* and the *Grand Hotel* but these are up-market places and the prices reflect this.

### Places to Eat

The cheap restaurants are clustered around the clocktower and the road leading south from it.

The small restaurant just behind the boat harbour sells baked fish that is heavily spiced and salted.

Along the waterfront are a few outdoor restaurants. The one next to the hotel under construction is good, although the poor monkey in the cage is a bit depressing. A meal of kebabs, hummus and salad is S£25 and cans of beer are S£15. The *Al Manara Restaurant* at the southern end of the Corniche is right on the beach.

### Getting There

**Bus** The Karnak bus station and office is a fair walk if you're staying near the boat harbour. Buses go to Homs, Damascus, Aleppo and Lattakia. As usual it's necessary to book in advance.

The chaotic microbus station is also quite a walk; a taxi from the clocktower will cost S£7. Buses leave regularly when full. To Lattakia takes 1½ to two hours and costs S£5.25; to Homs 1½ hours, S£5.

**Service-taxis** congregate around the clock-tower. Demand is not high so you may have to wait quite a while for one to fill up. Destinations include Damascus S£50, Homs S£30 and Lattakia S£30 – outrageous when you compare it with the bus fares.

**Train** The railway station is right behind the microbus station. The train to Damascus leaves at 3 pm and costs S£21 in 1st class and S£17.50 in 2nd class.

For Homs there are departures at 6.15 and 9.30 am and the 3 pm to Damascus also goes through Homs. Fares are S£11 in 1st class, S£7 in 2nd class.

## CRAC DES CHEVALIERS

The Crac des Chevaliers (Castle of the Knights) is one of Syria's prime attractions and should not be missed. It is very well preserved and can't have looked much different 800 years ago. It's open daily from 9 am to 6 pm, entry is S£1. A flash-light would be handy to explore some of the darker passages.

The fort is sited in the only significant break in the mountain range between Antakya (Turkey) and Beirut (Lebanon), a distance of some 250 km. In ancient times, anyone who controlled this gap was virtually assured of authority over inland Syria by controlling the flow of goods and people from the ports to the interior.

Even today this gap is important and carries the major road link from Homs to Tartus, as well as the oil pipeline from the fields in the far east of the country to the terminal at Tartus. Air force jets zooming low overhead – carefully ignored by the locals – are a constant, intrusive reminder that Lebanon is only a few km away.

The Crusaders began construction of the fort in 1170 and when it was completed it could house a garrison of 4000. After holding off a number of concerted attempts to take the fort, in 1271 they were finally forced to surrender to Sultan Baybars. He allowed them to march out of the castle on condition that they left the country, although it seems that they only went as far as Tartus and Tripoli. Additional towers were built by Baybars and the different Frankish and Arabic styles can be clearly seen.

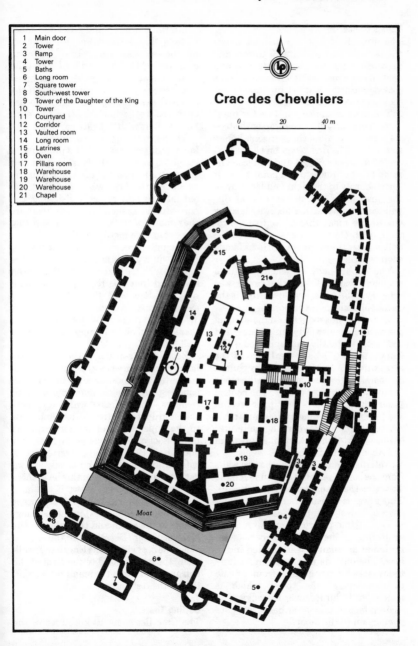

1   Main door
2   Tower
3   Ramp
4   Tower
5   Baths
6   Long room
7   Square tower
8   South-west tower
9   Tower of the Daughter of the King
10  Tower
11  Courtyard
12  Corridor
13  Vaulted room
14  Long room
15  Latrines
16  Oven
17  Pillars room
18  Warehouse
19  Warehouse
20  Warehouse
21  Chapel

## Crac des Chevaliers

0        20        40 m

Moat

## Things to See

The stronghold has two distinct parts: the outside wall with its 13 towers and main entrance; and the inside wall and central construction which are built on a rocky platform. A moat dug out of the rock separates the two walls.

The main entrance (No 1 on the plan) leads to a gently sloping ramp with steps wide enough to allow the garrison's horses to ride up. The first tower on the left (2) served as a guard room and stables. The ramp (3) continues up to a point where it turns sharply to the right and leads up to the inner fortress. The tower (4) at this point is massive with a doorway leading out to the moat through a five-metre-thick wall. On the outer wall above the doorway are the figures of two lions facing each other.

The moat here is usually full of stagnant water. When the castle was occupied this water was used to fill the baths (5) and water the horses.

The cavernous room (6) on the south of the moat measures 60 by nine metres and the roof is totally unsupported. The square tower (7) bore the brunt of the attack in 1271 and was rebuilt by Sultan Baybars. The long room leads to the tower (8) in the south-west corner. The central pillar which supports the upper level of the tower bears an inscription in Arabic recording Sultan Baybars' name in full: 'Al-Malek al-Zaher Rukh al Dunya wal din Abou al-fath Baybars'!

Walking around between the two walls from the south-west tower, you reach the Tower of the Daughter of the King (9). This tower is unusual in that it is wider than it is deep. On the facade are three rows of triple-pointed arches. A large projecting gallery, where rocks were hurled at assailants, is concealed in the face. The only danger faced by visitors today is the kitchen garbage from the café in the top of the tower which is nonchalantly hurled over the edge. The eastern face of this tower has a rear gate opening on to the moat.

Continue around and enter the inner fortress, through the tower (10) at the top of the access ramp, into an open courtyard (11). The corridor (12) on the western side of the yard is the most impressive structure in the Crac. Of the seven trusses facing the yard, two are open doorways while the other five each hold a pillar with delicate carvings.

The doors through the corridor lead to a large vaulted room (13), probably a reception room. On the far side of this is a 120-metre-long room (14) which runs the whole length of the western wall. A few old latrines (15) are still visible at the northern end. In the middle of the room are the remains of an old oven (16) measuring more than five metres in diameter.

The pillars room (17) has five rows of heavy squat pillars and the whole room is vaulted with fist-sized stones. It has been suggested that this room was used as a refectory. Rooms 18, 19 and 20 were used as warehouses. In room 19 are the remains of massive pottery oil jars and in 20 there's an old oil-mill, more oil jars and a well.

Back in the courtyard, the chapel (21) has a nave of three bays of vaults. It was converted to a mosque after the Muslim conquest and the *minbar* (pulpit) still remains. The staircase which obstructs the main door is a later addition and leads to the upper floors of the fortress. The upper floor of the Tower of the Daughter of the King (9) has been converted into a café selling tea, beer and snacks. From various vantage points on this level there are some magnificent views if the haze clears: the snow-capped peak of Kornet as-Saouda (3088 metres) in the Lebanon Range to the south and the valley of the Nahr al-Kabir (Big River) to the east.

For the best view of the Crac itself, walk along the road around to the right of the entrance and up to the small hill behind the south-west corner.

## Getting There

The Crac lies some 10 km north of the

Homs-Tartus motorway. It is roughly half-way between the two towns and can be visited in a day trip from either or en route from one to the other.

The only direct bus is a microbus from the Homs bus station at 9 am. It goes to the village of Hosn at the base of the Crac. At any other time take a bus for Tartus from Homs (or vice versa) and ask for Qalaat al-Hosn. The bus drops you at the turnoff from the motorway from where minibuses make the run up to the village of Hosn (S£2.50), 200 metres below the Crac. The whole trip takes about two hours from either town.

To return, take a minibus back to the highway and flag down a microbus.

# Orontes Valley

The Orontes River (in Arabic *Nahr al-Assi* – the rebel river) has its headwaters in the mountains of Lebanon near Baalbek. It enters Syria near Tell Nabi Mend, the Kadesh of ancient times where, around 1300 BC, the Egyptians were beaten back by the Hittites in a bloody confrontation.

Just south of the city of Homs is a dam dating back to the 2nd millennium BC. With some modern additions, it is known today as Lake Qattine and supplies Homs with drinking water and irrigates some 200 square km.

The river flows through the industrial city of Homs before reaching Hama, where the only obstruction to the flow is the ancient *norias* or waterwheels. Until quite recently the Orontes used to flow north-west from Hama and drain away in the swamps of the plain of Ghab. Now the swamps have been drained to form one of the most fertile plains in Syria and the river flows north through Antakya in Turkey before finally reaching the Mediterranean.

## HOMS

There's really nothing of interest to see in Homs but it's a busy city with a lively air. It is also one of those crossroads that most travellers have to pass through at some stage. Roads head north to Hama, east to Palmyra and the Euphrates, south to Damascus and west to Tartus and the coast.

The only building of note is the Khalid Ibn Al-Walid Mosque on the Hama road 500 metres north of the town centre. It holds the tomb of the commander of the Muslim armies who brought Islam to Syria in 636 AD.

The *souk* (market) is unusually large and busy but, as it's all modern, it's no great shakes.

## History

In ancient times, the city was known as Emesa and its people are mentioned among those who opposed the Roman conquest. The emperor Heliogabalus, proclaimed in 217 AD, was from Homs, as was Julia Domna, the wife of the emperor Septimus Serverus. It was also in Emesa that the troops of Zenobia, the ambitious queen of Palmyra, were defeated by Aurelian.

## Information

The **tourist office** is in Kouwatli St in a small booth by the footpath. There is no printed information in any language here and the woman running it seems to lock up shop and disappear most of the time.

The **post office** is on the roundabout at the western end of Kouwatli St.

For **money** exchange, the tiny branch of the Commercial Bank of Syria one block south of Kouwatli St, takes cash and travellers' cheques.

The **immigration office** is in a multi-storey building opposite the Al Hamra cinema. It's open 8.30 am to 1.30 pm Saturday to Thursday.

## Places to Stay

The cheap hotels are all along Kouwatli St between the tourist office and the souk. The best is the *Al Nasr Hotel* which only has the name written in Arabic; in English it just says Hotel. It's on the corner and the entrance is from the side street. It's clean, the manager is friendly and speaks English, and there's a large lounge room with a balcony overlooking the main street. There are a few single and double rooms for S£25/50; the rest are share-rooms for S£25 per bed. Showers are extra; S£5 for a cold one and S£10 hot, but you can bargain with the owner for a freebie.

The *Al Khayyam Hotel* next door to

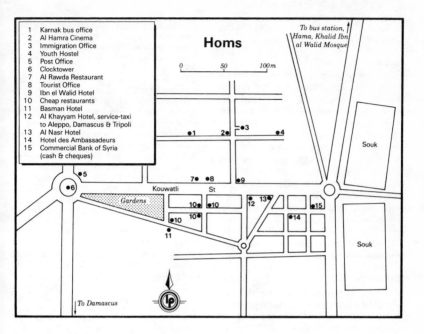

**Homs**

1 Karnak bus office
2 Al Hamra Cinema
3 Immigration Office
4 Youth Hostel
5 Post Office
6 Clocktower
7 Al Rawda Restaurant
8 Tourist Office
9 Ibn el Walid Hotel
10 Cheap restaurants
11 Basman Hotel
12 Al Khayyam Hotel, service-taxi
   to Aleppo, Damascus & Tripoli
13 Al Nasr Hotel
14 Hotel des Ambassadeurs
15 Commercial Bank of Syria
   (cash & cheques)

To bus station,
Hama, Khalid Ibn
al Walid Mosque

Souk

Kouwatli   St

Gardens

Souk

To Damascus

the Al Nasr is OK except for the slight oversight on the part of the owner to put any showers in the place! S£30 for a bed in a share room.

On the opposite corner, the *Ibn el Walid Hotel* is noisy and none too clean but is cheaper at S£20 per bed.

The *Youth Hostel* is in a very run-down building one block north of Kouwatli St and at S£15 is not worth it. It's dirty and disorganised and is only open between 6 and 8 pm.

For something a bit more up-market, the *Basman Hotel* has double rooms with bath and fan for S£100. The entrance is in the middle of a small shopping arcade.

**Places to Eat**

The *Al Rawda Restaurant* next door to the tourist office is the best available. Behind it is an enormous shady outdoor café with drinks and *nargileh*.

Other cheap restaurants are all in a group one block south of Kouwatli St and have the same old stuff – kebabs, chicken, felafel, hummus and salad.

**Getting There**

**Bus** The Karnak office and station is one block north of Kouwatli St. There are four daily buses to Damascus, the first at 6.30 am, S£12. Other buses daily to Palmyra, Hama, Aleppo, Tartus and Lattakia – book one day in advance.

The bus station for regular buses and *meecros* is about two km north of the centre – 20 minutes walk or S£8 by taxi. Buses run to Damascus every 15 minutes; S£7, two hours. A *meecro* to Hama takes 45 minutes, S£1.75. There is a direct bus to Hosn at 9 am (for the Crac des Chevaliers) but at any other time take a bus for Tartus (S£5) and ask for Qalaat al Hosn.

**Service-taxi** All the *servees* gather around the corner of the Al Khayyam Hotel on

Kouwatli St and run to Aleppo (S£50), Damascus and Tripoli (Lebanon).

## HAMA

This is one of the most attractive towns in Syria with the Orontes River flowing through the centre, its banks lined with trees and gardens and the ancient, groaning norias (waterwheels). The town's peaceful atmosphere make it a pleasant place to spend a few relaxing days.

The people here are some of the most conservative in Syria and the bizarre sight of a woman smartly dressed but with her face completely veiled in black is common. In contrast to this are the many women in local costume of full-length black dresses boldly embroidered in bright reds and yellows, their unveiled faces often tattooed with traditional markings.

### History

Although its history is not well known, Hama has been an important place for centuries. During the reigns of David and Solomon (1000 to 922 BC), the Kingdom of Hamah traded with Israel. In 853 BC it revolted against the Assyrian occupiers and defeated the troops of Samalnasar. Under Sargon II, the Assyrians got their revenge in 720 BC and deported all the citizens. In the time of the Seleucids it was known as Epiphania after Epiphanes (Antiochus IV), and was called Emath in the early Christian era.

In recent times Hama has become famous, or infamous, as the place where the true repressive nature of Assad's regime was brutally demonstrated in 1982. Amnesty International, the international human rights group, in a report presented to the Syrian Government on 26 April 1983, stated:

Shortly after dark on 2 February 1982, regular Syrian soldiers tried to raid a house in the ancient, western part of the city. Ninety soldiers led by a lieutenant surrounded a house believed to contain a large cache of arms belonging to the outlawed Muslim Brotherhood. As they started their raid, the troops were ambushed by armed *Mujahideen* (rebels). They were captured or killed and their uniforms removed. The insurgents then posted themselves on the roofs and turrets of the city.

The next morning, the citizens of Hama were apparently informed that the city had been 'liberated' and that the 'liberation' of the rest of the country would follow. The insurgents occupied government and security forces' buildings, ransacked the local armoury and began executing government officials and 'collaborators'. At least 50 people are reported to have been killed by anti-government demonstrators on this first day of protest.

The government responded by sealing off the city. Some 6000 to 8000 soldiers . . . were reportedly despatched to the city. On 11 February Syrian television showed a film of what it claimed was a cache of arms found in Hama, comprising 500 US M16 rifles, 40 shoulder-fired rocket launchers with armour-piercing rockets, and a huge arsenal of ammunition and small firearms.

According to some observers, old parts of the city were bombarded from the air and shelled in order to facilitate the entry of troops and tanks along the narrow streets. The ancient quarter of Hadra was apparently bombarded and razed to the ground by tanks during the first four days of fighting. On 15 February, after several days of heavy bombardment, the Syrian Defence Minister stated that the uprising in Hama had been suppressed. However, the city remained surrounded and cut off. Two weeks of house-to-house searches and mass arrests followed, with conflicting reports of atrocities and collective killings of unarmed, innocent inhabitants by the security forces. It is difficult to establish for certain what happened, but Amnesty International has heard that there was, among other things, a collective execution of 70 people outside the municipal hospital on 19 February; that Hadra quarter residents were executed by *Saraya al-Difa'* (Brigades for the Defence of the Revolution) troops the same day; that cyanide gas containers were alleged to have been brought into the city, connected by rubber pipes to the entrances of buildings believed to house insurgents and turned on, killing all the buildings' occupants; that people were assembled at the military airfield, at the sports stadium and at the military barracks and left out in the open for days without food or shelter.

On 22 February the Syrian authorities

Top: The 2nd-century ruins of Palmyra, Syria
Left: Bazaar stall – Aleppo, Syria
Right: Goat herders & Roman tombs – Qatura, Syria

Top: Funerary towers and oasis – Palmyra, Syria
Left: The entrance to the citadel – Aleppo, Syria
Right: Mending the fishing nets – Arwad, Syria

broadcast a telegram of support addressed to President Assad from the Hama branch of the Ba'th Party. The message referred to Muslim Brotherhood fighters killing party activists and their families and leaving their mutilated bodies in the streets. It said the security forces had taken fierce reprisals against the Brotherhood and their sympathisers 'which stopped them breathing for ever'.

When order was restored, estimates of the number of dead on all sides ranged from 10,000 to 25,000.

Heavy stuff! It is not known whether the killings were a result of the lack of supervision of troops or part of the government policy to counteract violent opposition.

Graphic evidence of the siege can still be seen in various places in the city, particularly in the area around the museum where buildings have been boarded up and the walls are pock-marked with bullet holes. Obviously this event is something that the government would rather like to pretend never happened, so it's prudent not to raise the subject.

## Information

The **tourist office** is in a small building in the gardens in the centre of town. As usual, there is no information available and the free hand-out map is inaccurate and out of date as it still has the Grand Mosque marked.

The main **post office** is on the corner of Kouwatli Avenue and the old Damascus-Aleppo highway (Sadik Avenue). The posting box is an anonymous wooden box inside on the left.

For changing **money**, the Commercial Bank of Syria is also not easy to find as there's no sign in English. The only hint is the list of exchange rates posted on the front door.

For visa extensions, the **immigration office** is hidden away upstairs in a building just opposite the footbridge in the centre of town.

## Citadel

For a good view over the city walk up to the park on top of the citadel. Nothing at all remains of the old fortress as all the stone has been carted off for use in other buildings. The area has been extensively landscaped and developed into a picnic and recreation area but seems to be about as popular as a pork chop with the locals.

## Norias (waterwheels)

Hama's main attraction is the norias, wooden waterwheels up to 20 metres in diameter, built centuries ago to provide water for the town and for irrigation. They still turn today although the water is not used. Because both the wheels and the blocks on which they are mounted are wooden, the friction produces a mournful groaning.

The norias right in the centre of town are the most interesting. In the surrounding park people come to rest and children swim in the waters by the wheels, which are also lit at night. The most impressive wheels, however, are about one km upstream from the centre at a place known as The Four Norias of Bichriyat.

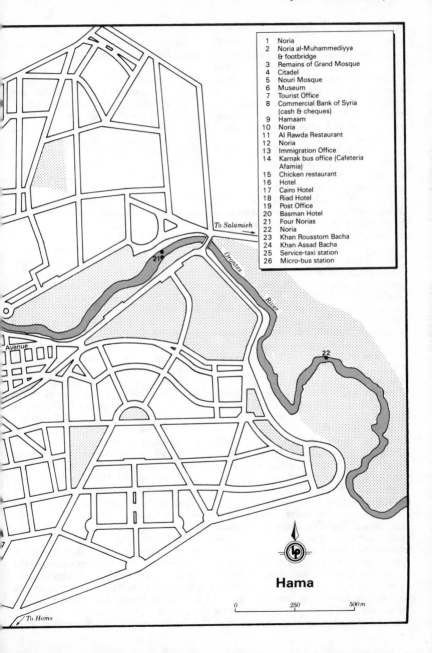

1  Noria
2  Noria al-Muhammediyya
   & footbridge
3  Remains of Grand Mosque
4  Citadel
5  Nouri Mosque
6  Museum
7  Tourist Office
8  Commercial Bank of Syria
   (cash & cheques)
9  Hamaam
10 Noria
11 Al Rawda Restaurant
12 Noria
13 Immigration Office
14 Karnak bus office (Cafeteria
   Afamia)
15 Chicken restaurant
16 Hotel
17 Cairo Hotel
18 Riad Hotel
19 Post Office
20 Basman Hotel
21 Four Norias
22 Noria
23 Khan Rousstom Bacha
24 Khan Assad Bacha
25 Service-taxi station
26 Micro-bus station

To Salamieh

Orontes River

21

22

To Homs

Hama

0    250    500 m

As the name suggests, there are four norias here – two pairs on a weir which spans the whole river. It's unfortunate that this weir also collects all the rubbish and debris which happens to be drifting down the river – everything from plastic bottles to dead sheep. On the downstream side on the left bank are two flash restaurants with terraces looking across to the wheels.

About one km from the centre in the other direction is the largest of the norias known as the Al-Muhammediyya. It dates from the 14th century and used to supply the Grand Mosque with water. At this point there is a small stone footbridge across the river which leads to an uninteresting area of parkland.

### Grand Mosque

The remains of the Grand Mosque can be seen 150 metres south of the Al-Muhammediyya noria. This once-fine building, which was a converted church on the site of a pagan temple, was completely flattened during the uprising of 1982. The site is rapidly being covered with new buildings.

### Museum

The museum is housed in the old Azem Palace, the residence of the governor, Assad Pacha al-Azem, who ruled the town from 1700 to 1742. The shady courtyard has various bits of ancient sculpture lying around, some bearing Arabic and Christian inscriptions. In the northern wall of the courtyard is an elaborate summer salon. Parts of the upstairs section were badly damaged during the uprising and are now closed. In fact you'll probably have a museum attendant tagging along while you walk around to make sure you don't pry into those areas which they'd rather were not seen. The museum is open from 8 am to 1 pm daily except Tuesday. Entry is S£1.

The area around the museum was one of the worst hit during the uprising and a wander around gives some idea of what

must have happened. Make sure there's no-one watching if you take photos of any war-damaged buildings.

### Caravanserais

The two caravanserais (khans) are notable only for their stone entrances built in alternating colours. The Khan Rousstom Bacha was at one time an orphanage but is undergoing a 'modernisation' project, so what it looks like when it's finished is anybody's guess. The big door has a feature known as an 'eyelet' which only allows one person through at a time. The Khan Assad Pacha, built in 1751, is now a technical school.

### Places to Stay

One of the best value-for-money places in Syria is the *Cairo Hotel* on Kouwatli Avenue. It's spotlessly clean and the friendly owner, Bader, speaks English and German. Doubles with fan are S£75 but bargain down to S£60. If you don't mind having no shade to retreat to in the heat of the day, a bed on the roof is S£20.

A couple of doors down is the *Riad Hotel* which has similar prices to the Cairo but is neither as clean nor as friendly.

There's a couple of cheap flophouses where S£20 gets you a bed in a noisy but otherwise satisfactory hotel. The one at the end of Kouwatli Avenue is upstairs and just has a green, black and red sign in Arabic above the door.

Hama's up-market hotel is the *Basman Hotel*, also on Kouwatli Avenue. Here you'll be paying US$8/11 for air-con singles/doubles with bath. It's a reasonable place but doesn't really offer much more than the Cairo.

### Places to Eat

In the couple of blocks along Kouwatli Avenue west of the Cairo Hotel are all the usual cheap kebab and chicken restaurants. There's about half a dozen of them here so if one doesn't have what you want, just try next door.

On the small street running from

Kouwatli Avenue to the river are a couple of chicken restaurants – the one nearer the river is good and has fans. The standard half-chicken, salad and hummus is S£18.

If you want to dine in style, the *Al Rawda Restaurant* on the banks of the river has a fine setting overlooking the norias. The food is only average; kebabs and salad will set you back S£40. Occasionally there is a band and dance performances.

For just a tea or coffee, and maybe a *nargileh* and a game of backgammon, you can't beat the outdoor café next to the Al Rawda. It's set in a garden of shady eucalypt trees and has views of the river and norias. It is a great place to escape the heat. Every so often a waiter will come around with a shiny silver coffee pot and very small cups; this is very strong Arabic coffee and is strongly flavoured with cardamom. It is drunk in tiny doses which you just knock back in one hit – a real heart-starter.

### Getting There

**Bus** If you're coming or going by Karnak bus, the station/office is right in the centre of town opposite the river. The office is actually a small loft inside the Cafeteria Afamia. There are buses to Damascus (7 am, 1 pm, S£12), Tartus (6 am, S£12) and Aleppo (5 pm, S£18).

The microbus station is on the southern outskirts of town about two km from the centre; a 20-minute walk or S£7 by taxi. *Meecros* go to Homs, Aleppo, Apamea (Suqalibiyah) and surrounding towns.

**Service-taxi** The *servees* station is right across the road from the microbus station.

**Train** The railway station is way out of town to the west. A taxi from the centre is S£10. There's not much of a station and the guy there, who will presumably sell you a ticket if you can wake him up, doesn't seem to know what times the trains run.

### QALAAT AL-MUDIQ/APAMEA

From Hama the Orontes River flows north-west and into the vast Ghab depression, some 50 km away. Once a stagnant swamp, this low-lying area of some 40 square km has, with World Bank help, been drained and irrigation ditches dug, turning it into one of the most fertile areas in Syria. Major crops are wheat, barley, sugar beet and a range of fruit trees. In olden times it is said that the Pharaoh Thutmose III came here to hunt elephants. A thousand years later Hannibal was here teaching the Syrians how to make use of elephants in war. On the eastern edge of this valley lie the ruins of the ancient city of Apamea, now known as Qalaat al-Mudiq.

Founded by Seleucus I in the 2nd century BC, the city became an important trading post and crossroad for the East. It was connected by road to Lattakia which served it as a port. In its heyday Apamea boasted a population of 120,000 and was visited by many dignitaries including Mark Antony, accompanied by Cleopatra, on his return from staging a campaign against the Armenians on the Euphrates. The city declined after the Roman era but again assumed importance during the Crusades. The fortifications around the hill-top which dominates the valley are still standing after being restored following the earthquakes of 1157 and 1170.

### Museum

In the small village at the foot of the hill is a caravanserai, dating from Ottoman times, which has been converted into a museum. The floors of the vaulted rooms surrounding the massive courtyard have been covered with the brilliant mosaics found in Apamea during excavations. Unfortunately what labelling exists is in Arabic. It's a real crime that there's nothing to stop visitors from just walking all over these priceless pieces. The museum is open from 9 am to 1 pm; entry is S£1.

## Fortifications

The fortifications on the hill are, typically, more impressive from the outside. Inside is the village of Qalaat al-Mudiq where local hustlers will try and sell you glass and coins from the ruins. Some of the pieces are obviously old and others are just as obviously made in the local workshop, so if you're interested, it's a case of buyer beware.

## Ruins

The main area of ruins is about 500 metres east of the village where the re-erected columns of the two-km-long main street (the *decumanus*) look quite incongruous standing in the middle of wheat fields and thistles. The columns themselves, originally erected in the 2nd century AD, are unusually carved with straight or twisted fluting. Along the length of the decumanus the ground is littered with great chunks of rock which were once part of structures such as the Temple of Bacchus, churches, theatre and shops. Many of these pieces are sculptured or have Greek inscriptions.

The whole site covers a large area and even in the small area where the reconstruction has taken place, excavation has been far from exhaustive. Glass fragments are everywhere and there must still be some fine pieces waiting to be unearthed.

## Places to Stay & Eat

There's nowhere to stay in Qalaat al-Madiq and unbelievably, nowhere to buy something to eat. Fortunately it's an easy day trip from Hama but bring some food and a water bottle and hat – it can be really scorching.

## Getting There

Microbuses (S£4) and service-taxis (S£6) run regularly from Hama to Suqalibiyah, 45 km from Hama, and from there minibuses go on to Qalaat al-Madiq. The whole trip takes about an hour. About halfway between Hama and Suqalibiyah at Maharde the ruins of Qalaat Sheisar rise above the escarpment on the right and a small ruined noria groans away slowly by the river on the left.

---

### The Great Kurdish Chicken Massacre

Here in Europe we tend to hear more bad news than good about the Kurds. So when I was in Syria I decided to find out for myself. I went up to the extreme north-east, which is mostly populated by Kurds.

From Qamishle I took a minibus into the wilderness. When I got off the bus in the middle of nowhere, I could make out the shape of a farm on the horizon. With only the hot sun for my companion, I set out on what seemed like an endless walk. When I reached the low loam houses I was welcomed with great friendliness, in accordance with the oriental tradition. One donkey, a few goats and a dozen chickens rested in the shadows. The owner of the farm was a young man who wore jeans and a T-shirt. He told me that he was a Kurd, like most of the people in this area, and that I should feel safe with him as my host.

'We Kurds are the strong men,' he repeated again and again, waving his pistol about. (Many young people in Syria and other Arab states have pistols.)

I laughed at his extreme self-confidence, but this obviously provoked him. He aimed his pistol at the chickens and fired. But the shot only raised dust and the chickens fluttered around nervously. Furious, the farmer fired twice more – with the same result. By this time I was afraid that I would become a victim of his rage. Suddenly the farmer turned around, threw his pistol away and ran into the house. The chickens calmed down, but then he returned . . . with a sub-machine gun. He stood near me, now tall and proud, and then fired volleys of bullets into the crowd of chickens. It was a horrible massacre. He looked at me grinning and I was forced to admire him.

After that his family treated me to the usual welcomings and tea, and later they cooked and served up the chickens, or at least those bits that weren't totally obliterated.

'Sahten,' they said, which means 'have a good appetite'!

Chris Springer, West Germany

# Aleppo

Called Halab by the locals, Aleppo, with a population of 1.8 million, is Syria's second largest city. Since Roman times it has been an important trading centre with the countries of Asia and the Mediterranean and this accounts for the European feel of its tree-lined streets, parks and up-market restaurants. After WW I it came under the French mandate and consequently it lost a lot of its importance as a commercial centre as it no longer served as a trading outlet for the south-eastern districts of Turkey.

There is a large Christian population comprised mainly of Armenian refugees from Turkey.

With its fascinating covered souks, the citadel, museum and caravanserais, it is a great place to spend a few days. There are also interesting places in the vicinity such as the Church of St Simon (Qalaat Samaan), which was the largest Christian building in the Middle East when it was built in the 4th century.

## History

Early Egyptian records show that Aleppo was established in the 8th century BC. During the reign of the Seleucids it was given the name Beroea and with the fall of Palmyra at the hands of the Romans, it became the major commercial centre between the the Mediterranean to the west and the countries of Asia to the east. The town was completely destroyed by the Persians in 611 AD and was taken during the Saracenic invasion in 638. The Byzantines overwhelmed the town in 961 although they couldn't take the citadel. In 1124 the Crusaders under Baldwin laid siege to the town.

After three disastrous earthquakes in the 10th century, both the town and fortress were rebuilt by Nureddin. After the raids by the Mongols in 1260 and 1401, the city finally fell to the Turks in 1517. It prospered greatly until another earthquake struck in 1822, killing over 60% of the inhabitants and wrecking many buildings including the citadel. During the decade of Egyptian rule, 1831 to 1840, the city once again prospered, although its importance as a trading centre declined with the discovery of the Cape route to India.

European merchants – particularly French, English and Venetian – established themselves here and set up factories, although the flood of cheap goods from Europe killed a lot of local manufacturing. Today the major local industries are silk-weaving and cotton-printing. Products from the surrounding area include wool, hides, dried fruits and, particularly, the pistachio nuts which Aleppo is famous for.

## Information

**Tourist Office** The tourist office is probably the most helpful in Syria and as well as having a good hand-out map, usually has quite a bit of printed information about what to see in Syria. It's in the gardens opposite the museum and is open every day from 8.30 am to 5 pm.

**Post Office** The main post office is the enormous building on the far side of the gardens on Kouwatli St. It's open every day from 8 am to 6 pm.

**Money** Finding the right branch of the bank to change travellers' cheques in Aleppo can be an endurance test. The branch on Baron St, with its entrance hidden away at the back of an arcade, will send you to the small exchange branch on Kouwatli St, and the guy there insists that it is the Baron St branch which changes cheques. Between the two of them they'll eventually sort it out. Either branch takes cash.

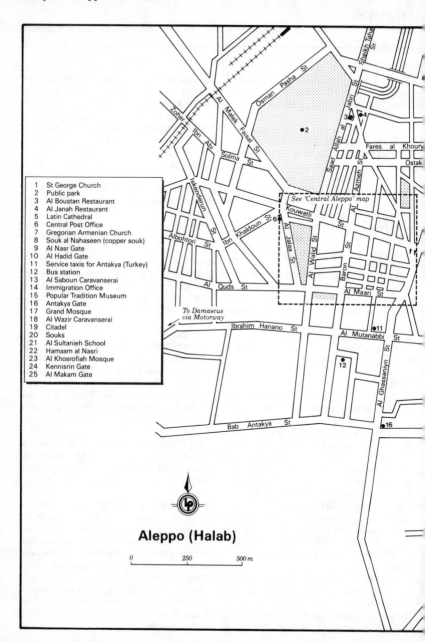

1   St George Church
2   Public park
3   Al Boustan Restaurant
4   Al Janah Restaurant
5   Latin Cathedral
6   Central Post Office
7   Gregorian Armenian Church
8   Souk al Nahaseen (copper souk)
9   Al Nasr Gate
10  Al Hadid Gate
11  Service taxis for Antakya (Turkey)
12  Bus station
13  Al Saboun Caravanserai
14  Immigration Office
15  Popular Tradition Museum
16  Antakya Gate
17  Grand Mosque
18  Al Wazir Caravanserai
19  Citadel
20  Souks
21  Al Sultanieh School
22  Hamaam al Nasri
23  Al Khosrofiah Mosque
24  Kennisrin Gate
25  Al Makam Gate

See 'Central Aleppo' map

To Damascus
via Motorway

**Aleppo (Halab)**

0        250        500 m

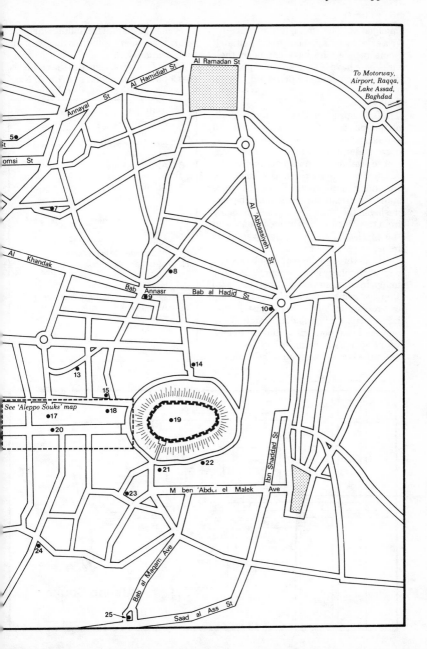

**Immigration** The immigration office for visa extensions is just north of the citadel. Some people who have extended their visas here have been asked to supply *five* passport photos, so be prepared.

## Souks

The fabulous covered souks are the main attraction of the city. This labyrinth extends over a couple of hectares and once under the vaulted stone ceiling, you're swallowed up into another world. All under one roof are the smells of cardamom and cloves from the spice stalls, the cries of the hawkers and barrow pushers, the rows of carcasses hanging from the doorways in the meat souk, and the myriad of stalls selling everything from rope to prayer mats.

A walk through the souks could take all day, particularly if you accept some of the many invitations by the merchants to stop and drink tea. There's no obligation or pressure to buy – this is just Syrian hospitality. While wandering around you may well find yourself latched onto by a young Syrian who wants to be your 'guide' and take you to the shop of his 'cousin'.

They may be helpful for finding what you want, if you don't mind paying extra for their commission.

A couple of blocks north of the citadel is the Copper Souk, not far from the Al Nasr Gate. The souks are dead on Fridays.

| | |
|---|---|
| 1 | Al-Djadid |
| 2 | Al-Dahshah |
| 3 | Al-Haradj |
| 4 | Istanbul (gold & silver jewellery) |
| 5 | Al-Wazir |
| 6 | Al-Djinfas |
| 7 | Al-Hibal (rope) |
| 8 | Al-Tarabichiah |
| 9 | Al-Ibi (textiles) |
| 10 | Al-Haur |
| 11 | Al-Itakiah (leather) |
| 12 | Al-Dra |
| 13 | Al-Bahramiah (mainly food) |
| 14 | Al-Sakatiah (mainly food) |
| 15 | Al-Batiah |
| 16 | Al-Attarin (perfumes, household goods) |
| 17 | Al-Zarb (hairdressers & textiles) |
| 18 | Al-Djumruk |
| 19 | Al-Han |
| 20 | Al-Djoukh |
| 21 | Al-Hamaam |
| 22 | Al-Makmas |

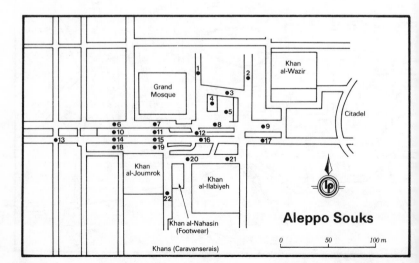

Aleppo Souks

## Caravanserais

The caravanserais (*khans*) are found in amongst the souks. Unfortunately, most are of limited interest because they are almost totally obscured by modern additions. The *Khan al-Wazir*, built in 1682, has an interesting doorway and inside is at least one low-key souvenir and carpet shop. The *Khan al-Joumrok* (Khan of the Customs) is the old headquarters of the French, Dutch and English merchants of the 16th and 17th centuries.

## Grand Mosque

On the northern edge of the souks is the Grand Mosque (Jami Zakariyeh) with its free-standing minaret dating back to 1090. The mosque itself dates back to early Islamic times but most of what remains today is from the Mameluke period. Inside the mosque is a fine, carved wooden pulpit (*minbar*) and behind the railing to the left of it is supposed to be the head of Zacharias, the father of John the Baptist, after whom the mosque is named. This is one of the only mosques where non-Muslims are admitted on Fridays, and in fact you can sit inside during the main midday mass if you don't mind participating and bowing to Mecca.

## Citadel

The citadel dominates the city and is at the eastern end of the souks. It is surrounded by a moat, 20 metres deep and 30 metres wide, which is spanned by a bridge on the northern side. Entrance to the citadel is through a 12th-century gate and behind this is the massive fortified main entrance. Although finely decorated on the outside, the inside is a succession of five right-angle turns, where three sets of solid steel-plated doors made a formidable barrier to any would-be occupiers. Some of the doors still remain and one of the lintels of the doorways has carvings of entwined dragons, and another has a pair of lions.

Once inside there are only a couple of rooms above the entrance which have been restored. The rest is a jumble of fallen stone, a result of successive invasions and the devastating earthquake of 1822. The views from the walls are terrific and you get a good idea of just how big this city is. The citadel is open from 10 am to 6 pm daily except Tuesday. Entry is S£1.

## Museums

**Aleppo Museum** The Aleppo museum has a fine collection of artefacts from Mari (Tell Hariri), Ebla (a centre of great political power in northern Syria, Anatolia and part of Mesopotamia around 1800 BC) and Ugarit (Ras Shamra). There are sculptures from Hama, and the black basalt statues at the entrance are from the temple-palace at Tell Halaf (a 9th-century BC settlement in the north-east of Syria, near present-day Ras el Ain).

It really is a fine museum and, as usual, you'll be virtually the only one there. On sale at the entrance is a guidebook to the museum for S£3. The museum is open from 9 am to 12 noon and 3 to 5.30 pm daily except Tuesday. Entry is S£1.

**Museum of Popular Art & Traditions** This is opposite the Khan al-Wazir and is housed in a palace dating back to 1354. At the time of writing it was closed for extensive restoration.

## Places to Stay – bottom end

There is a whole stack of cheap hotels on Al Maari St. The *Hotel Suez Canal* shares its entrance with the *Hotel Yarmouk*. Both are OK cheapies and charge S£25 per person in rooms with fans.

The *Claridge Hotel* is near the clocktower and has rooms for S£34 for a double. The *Syria Hotel* is similar.

Others in Al Maari St include the *Al Zahra*, *New Arab World* and the *Al Sahel* opposite the clocktower.

The figures in front of the Aleppo Museum once guarded the temple-palace at Tell Hallaf, near Ras al'Ain.

## Places to stay - middle

There's really only one place to stay – the *Baron Hotel*. If you're going to splurge once in Syria, this is the place to do it. When it was built in 1909, it was on the outskirts of town 'in gardens considered dangerous to venture into after dark'. The hotel was opened by two Armenian brothers and was called the Baron because residents of Aleppo referred to the brothers by the courtesy title 'baron'. It quickly became famous as one of the premier hotels of the Middle East, helped by the fact that Aleppo was then an important trading centre and staging post for travellers. The Orient Express used to terminate in Aleppo and the rich and famous travelling on it would often stay at the Baron. A look through the old leather-bound visitors book (kept securely stashed in the safe) turns up names such as T E Lawrence (Lawrence of Arabia), Agatha Christie, aviators Charles Lindbergh, Amy Johnston and Charles Kingsford-Smith, Theodore Roosevelt and Lady Louis Mountbatten.

The Baron today is run by Mr Mazlumian, the septuagenarian son of one of the original 'baron' brothers, who speaks with a pronounced English accent. It's still a handsome building but if it's luxury you're after, forget it! Nothing much has changed since 1909 – the beds are old and squeaky, the walls need painting, the plumbing is antediluvian and even the wrinkled old retainer working behind the bar looks like an original. But for all that the place has heaps of character and if you don't want to stay, at least stop by and have a drink in the bar. If you are staying, single/double rooms with breakfast cost a meagre US$9/14 – a bargain.

For those who want a bit of up-market luxury there's the *Ramsis Hotel* opposite the Baron, and the *Ambassador Hotel* across the street. Both are categorised by the tourist authority as two-star and charge US$8/12.

## Places to Eat

In the block bounded by Al Maari, Bab al Faraj, Kouwatli and Baron streets, are the cheapies offering all the usual stuff – the price is more variable than the food so check before you sit down.

Right on the corner of Al Maari and Bab al Faraj is a tiny restaurant which gives 'crowded' a whole new meaning – with room for 10 they pack in 20! The reason is that the food, which is vegetable and meat stews, rice and macaroni, is cheap and filling. They also serve steamed chicken if you want a change from the usual roasted variety.

There's a good *al fresco* restaurant with a fountain in a side street off Baron St,

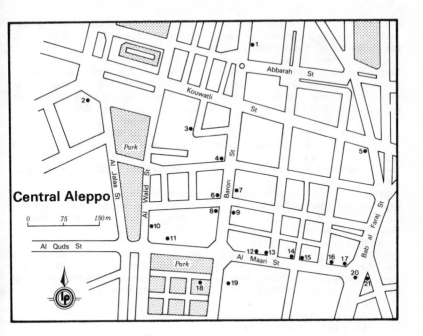

Central Aleppo

0    75    150 m

1   Commercial Bank of Syria
    (cash & cheques)
2   Central Post Office
3   Outdoor restaurant
4   Syrian Arab Airlines
5   Exchange office (cash only)
6   Ramsis Hotel
7   Baron Hotel
8   Karnak bus office
9   Ambassador Hotel
10  Karnak buses
11  Service taxis to Damascus, Beirut
12  Hotel Suez Canal & Hotel Yasmouk
13  Hotel al Zahra
14  Hotel Syria
15  Hotel New Arab World
16  Hotel Claridge
17  Restaurant
18  Tourist Office
19  Museum
20  Clocktower
21  Al Sahel Hotel & open-air cafe

just up from the Syrian Airlines office.
It's a very pleasant place to sit in the
evenings and the food is cheap – a full
meal of kebabs, salad, hummus, yoghurt
and bread is just S£16. Bottled beer is
S£12 for a 750 ml bottle.

If it's just a drink you're after, the
outside terrace at the Baron Hotel takes a
lot of beating. Your bottle of Al Chark

beer is brought to you by the shuffling old
waiter, replete with white jacket and
cloth over the arm, who then laboriously
writes out a chit (S£15 a bottle) and waits
at a discreet distance while you dig for
your money.

There are a few cafés worth trying.
Opposite the entrance to the citadel there
are two with some shady trees where you

can linger over a *shay* and watch the world go by. Back in the downtown area there's an upstairs café right on the clocktower corner. It has a view of the hectic intersection and the antics of the drivers and pedestrians are good entertainment. The entrance is in the side street, through the Al Sahel Hotel.

### Getting There

**Air** Aleppo has an international airport with regular connections to Turkey, Europe and other cities in the Middle East.

Syrian Arab Airlines have flights on weekdays to Damascus for S£92.

**Bus** The Karnak office is on Baron St diagonally opposite the Baron Hotel. The buses leave from around the back, almost opposite the tourist office. There are daily connections to Lattakia (S£20), Deir Ez-Zur (S£28), as well as Hama (S£18), Homs and Damascus (S£35).

The local bus station is a couple of blocks south of the museum. It's better organised than most Syrian bus stations and you can expect a passport check as you go in, and another as the bus is leaving. For Lattakia, buy tickets (S£10) from the window inside the building. For other places, it's just a matter of finding out which bay the bus you want leaves from. Microbuses to A'zaz (for Turkey) leave regularly from here.

Turkish buses connect Aleppo and Istanbul. Book early at the Karnak office as the buses heading north originate in Damascus and only about 10 seats are reserved for passengers getting on in Aleppo. The fare is S£270 and takes 24 hours.

**Service-taxi** *Servees* for Damascus and places south leave from opposite the tourist office.

For the Turkish border on the Antakya road, they leave from a yard one block south of the museum and cost S£10. Minibuses between the border points are

S£5, then a service-taxi or *dolmuş* takes you on to Antakya for TL 2000.

**Train** The railway station is just to the north of the big public park, about 15 minutes walk from the downtown hotel area. Local trains run daily to Damascus, Lattakia, and Deir Ez-Zur and Qamishle in the north-east.

Twice a week there's a train from Aleppo to Istanbul. It takes forever (40 hours) and costs S£117. It leaves Aleppo on Sunday and Wednesday mornings.

### Getting Around

All the things of interest are in a compact area so getting around on foot poses no problems.

Car buffs may like to ride in a taxi just for the hell of it. They are practically all enormous lumbering old American limousines from the 1940s and '50s and have the usual assortment of lights and decorations inside. Some of them light up like Christmas trees at night.

### AROUND ALEPPO

#### Qalaat Samaan (Basilica of St Simeon)

St Simeon, also known as St Simon of Stylites, was one of Syria's most unusual early Christians. In the 5th century this shepherd from northern Syria had a revelation in a dream and joined a monastery. Finding monastic life not sufficiently ascetic, he retreated to the barren hills and in 423, he sat on top of a three-metre pillar and stayed atop this and other taller pillars for the next 42 years! For his last 30 years, the pillar was some 15 metres high. Around the top was a railing and around his neck was an iron collar fastened by a chain to the pillar to stop him toppling off in the middle of the night. Rations were carried up a ladder by fellow monks and twice a week he celebrated mass on top.

Pilgrims started coming from as far away as Britain, hoping to see a miracle. St Simeon would preach to them daily from his perch, and they would shout their questions to him and he would shout his answers back. He refused to talk to women, however, and even his mother was not allowed near the column.

After his death in 459, an enormous church was built around the famous pillar. It was unique in design in that it was four basilicas arranged in the shape of a cross all opening onto a central octagonal yard covered by a dome. In the centre stood the sacred pillar. One basilica was used for worship; the other three housed the many pilgrims. It was finished in 490 and at the time was the largest church in the world. A monastery was built at the foot of the hill to house the clergy and a town with hostelries soon sprang up.

The church today is remarkably well preserved, with the arches of the octagonal yard still complete, along with much of the four basilicas. The pillar is in a sad state and is nothing more than a boulder on top of a platform. After St Simeon's death, pilgrims chipped away at it and took small fragments home as souvenirs of the holy place.

The views of the barren hills to the west are stunning and the ruins of the monastery can be seen down to the left at the foot of the hill in the village of Deir Samaan. A family has actually taken up residence in the ruins but they don't mind if you wander around.

The site is open daily and entry is S£1. The friendly caretaker speaks English, German and French and would happily talk all day given the chance.

**Getting There** Microbuses from Aleppo leave every hour or so from the bus station for the one-hour trip to the village of Daret 'Azze. From there to Qalaat Samaan is about 15 km and it's a matter of negotiating with a local for transport. There's one guy from Deir Samaan with a large red truck who often waits in Daret 'Azze to take people to Qalaat Samaan and the tombs at Qatura. Although he doesn't speak any English, he's very easygoing, will take you into his house as well as the various sites, and then leaves payment up to you. A group of five of us gave him S£40 for four hours and he seemed happy with that.

### Qatura

About five km before Deir Samaan are the old Roman tombs at Qatura. They are about one km off the road to the west. The tombs are cut into the rock and it's easy to scramble up to them. The Greek inscriptions are still clearly visible.

Right below the tombs is a natural well where young village girls bring their goats, and collect water using buckets made from old truck tyres.

# The Desert & the Euphrates

The Damascus-Aleppo highway marks roughly the division between the cultivable land to the west and the barren desert, which runs east all the way to the Euphrates.

The wide fringe of the desert gets sufficient rain to support enough vegetation to graze sheep and goats. The desert-fringe dwellers build beehive-shaped houses as protection against the extreme heat. You can see these houses on the road from Homs to Palmyra and in the area south of Lake Assad.

The desert proper extends south-east from Palmyra into Jordan and Iraq. It is not a sand desert but consists of stony treeless plains stretching to the horizon. Rainfall is extremely irregular here and it's not uncommon for two or three years to pass between falls.

Dotting this desert are the oases – the main one is Palmyra – which used to serve as way-stations for the caravans on their way between the Mediterranean and Mesopotamia.

## PALMYRA

Known to the locals as Tadmor, Palmyra is Syria's prime attraction and is one of the world's great historical sites. If you're only going to see one thing in Syria, make it Palmyra. Even if you have seen enough ruins to last you a lifetime and the thought of one more is enough to make you groan, make the effort to see this one as it really is something special. Rare is the chance when you can see a site as important and impressive as this without bus loads of rubbernecks to contend with. Apart from a few Bedouin and the occasional traveller or tourist, the ruins of Palmyra are deserted.

The oasis is really in the middle of nowhere – 150 km from the Orontes River to the west and 200 km from the Euphrates to the east. This is the very end of the Anti Lebanon Mountains and the final fold of the range forms a basin, and on the edge of this a spring rises. Known as Efca ('source' in Aramaen), it is slightly sulphurous and is said to have medicinal qualities.

The ruins of the 2nd-century AD city have been extensively excavated and restored and cover some 50 hectares. The new town, with a population of about 4000, has been built about 500 metres from the ruins and is a very easygoing place.

### History

Tadmor is mentioned in tablets as early as the 19th century BC. It became an important staging post for caravans travelling from the Mediterranean to the countries of the Gulf. It was also an important link on the old Silk Route from China and India to Europe. The city prospered greatly by levying heavy tolls on the caravans and with the invasion of the Romans in the 1st century AD, it became something of a buffer between the Persians and the Romans. The name was changed from Tadmor (the City of Dates) to Palmyra (the City of Palms).

The emperor Hadrian visited the city in 130 AD and declared it a 'free city'. In 217, under the emperor Caracella, the city became a Roman colony. This gave its citizens equal rights with Rome and freed them from paying Roman taxes. During this period the great colonnaded street was enlarged, temples were built and the citizens grew extremely wealthy on the caravan trade – some even owned ships sailing in the Arabian Gulf. In 137 AD an enormous stone tablet bore the inscription of the 'Tariff of Palmyra' (now in a museum in Leningrad). It set out the taxes payable on each commodity which passed through the city, as well as the charges for the supply of water.

The colony gradually evolved into a

Top: The 12th-century castle Crac Des Chevaliers – Hosn, Syria
Left: An ancient *noria* (water wheel) – Hama, Syria
Right: Two women in traditional dress – Hama, Syria

Top: Shopping for vegetables – Maalula, Syria
Left: The Roman theatre at Bosra, Syria
Right: Western gate of the Temple of Jupiter – Damascus, Syria

kingdom ruled by Odenathus, a brilliant military leader who had earned the gratitude of Rome by freeing the emperor Valerian from capture by the Persians. For this Valerian bestowed upon him the title of 'Corrector of the East'.

The city's downfall began when Odenathus was assassinated in 266 in suspicious circumstances. His second wife, the famous half-Greek/half-Arab Zenobia, took over in the name of their son, who was still a minor. It was suspected that Zenobia was involved in her husband's death but it was never proved. Claiming to be descended from Cleopatra, she was a woman of exceptional ability and ambition. Fluent in Greek, Latin, Aramaic and Egyptian, she continued to rule over the empire and under her leadership its boundaries were extended as far as Persia and Egypt. The 18th-century traveller, Edward Gibbon, in his book titled *The Decline & Fall of the Roman Empire* said of her:

She equalled in beauty her ancestor Cleopatra and far surpassed that princess in chastity and valour. Zenobia was esteemed the most lovely as well as the most heroic of her sex. She was of dark complexion. Her teeth were of a pearly whiteness and her large black eyes sparkled with an uncommon fire, tempered by the most attractive sweetness. Her voice was strong and harmonious. Her manly understanding was strengthened and adorned by study.

She was also a ruler with a sense of humour. A merchant was to be punished for overcharging and was summoned to the theatre to appear in front of the queen and the public audience. The merchant stood alone in the arena and shook with fear, thinking that a wild beast was to be set upon him. When the beast was released the crowd roared with laughter – the merchant turned around to be confronted by a chicken.

With her sights set on Rome, she declared complete independence and had coins minted in Alexandria which bore her image and that of her son.

The emperor Aurelian couldn't stomach such a show of open defiance and after defeating her forces at Antioch and Homs in 271, he besieged Palmyra itself. Zenobia was defiant to the last and instead of accepting the generous surrender terms offered by Aurelian, she made a dash on a camel through the encircling Roman forces. She headed for Persia to appeal for military aid, only to be captured by the Roman cavalry at the Euphrates. The city then surrendered, but escaped with only a fine for its insurrection. Zenobia was carted off to Rome as Aurelian's trophy and was paraded in the streets, bound in gold chains. She spent the rest of her days in Rome, some say in a villa provided by the emperor, others say that she chose to fast to death rather than remain captive.

Whatever became of her, it was the end of Palmyra's prosperity and its most colourful figure. The emperor Aurelian wrote of her in a letter:

Those who say I have only conquered a woman do not know what that woman was, nor how lightning were her decisions, how persevering she was in her plans, how resolute with her soldiers.

Zenobia's coin

The city itself was destroyed by Aurelian in 273 following another rebellion when the inhabitants massacred the 600 archers stationed there. Aurelian's troops were particularly brutal. The residents were slaughtered and the city was set to the torch. It was never able to recover its former glory and became a Roman outpost. The emperor Diocletian fortified it as one in the line of fortresses that marked the boundary of the Roman Empire. Justinian rebuilt the city's defences in the 6th century but by this stage it had lost all its wealth and declined steadily with the drop in caravan traffic.

It fell to the Muslims in 634 and was finally and completely destroyed by a devastating earthquake in 1089. It seems that a Jewish colony existed there in the 12th century but the city had passed into legend by then.

In 1678 it was rediscovered by two English merchants living in Aleppo and the tales of Odenathus and Zenobia fascinated Europe, mainly because nobody had any idea that this once-important city had even existed.

Excavations started in 1924 and until then, the Arab villagers used to live in the courtyard of the Temple of Bel before being moved to the new town. Restoration has seen the number of standing columns go from 150 in the 1950s to over 300 now. Some of the earlier restoration work, particularly noticeable on the tetrapylon, was crudely executed.

Today it's easy to spend a couple of days wandering around the site, the funerary towers, and the 17th-century Arab castle on the hill.

### The Ruins

**Temple of Bel** The best place to start is the Temple of Bel at the eastern edge of the site. The temple itself is in a massive courtyard some 200 metres square. Originally this courtyard was surrounded by a 15-metre-high wall but only the northern side is original, the rest is of Arab construction. The western wall, which contains the entrance and a small souvenir shop, was built out of fragments of the temple when it was fortified. A double colonnade used to run around three sides of the interior while the fourth side (the western side) had a single row of columns much taller than the others. Some of these can be seen to the right and left of the entrance.

Just to the left of the entrance inside the courtyard is a passage which enters the Temple from outside the wall and gradually slopes up to the level of the courtyard. This is where the sacrificial animals were brought into the precincts. In front of the shrine are the ruins of a banquet hall. The podium of the sacrificial altar is on the left, and the remains of another platform on the right, possibly used for religious purification ceremonies.

The shrine itself is unusual in design in that the entrance is in one of the sides rather than the ends, and is offset from the centre. Inside, the shrine has porticoes at either end, with ceilings cut from single blocks of stone. The northern one is highly decorated and the ceiling has a rosette and the centre is a cupola featuring a bust of Jupiter and signs of the zodiac. In the corner by this portico is a staircase to the roof where it is thought that sacrifices took place. The view from here is great but be careful where you put your feet as there are gaping holes into the portico below. The stepped ramp leading to the southern portico suggests that it may have contained a portable idol used in processions.

Around the back of the shrine is a pile of old railway tracks which were used to remove trolleys of rubble during the original excavations. The temple enclosure is open daily from 8 am to 1 pm and 4 to 6pm. Entry is S£1.

**The Great Colonnade** This column-lined street formed the main artery of the town and ran from the main temple entrance to the monumental arch, and then on for 700

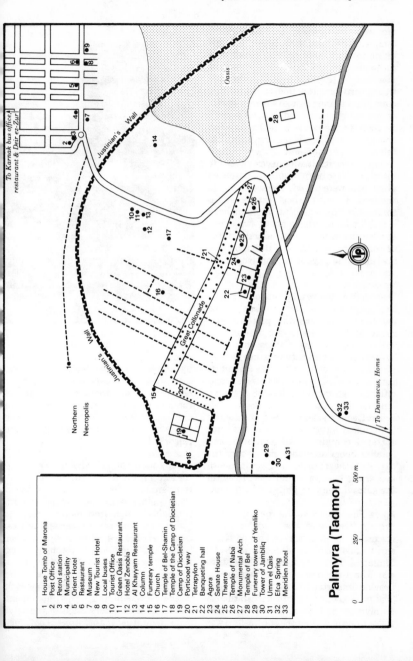

1    House Tomb of Marona
2    Post Office
3    Petrol station
4    Municipality
5    Orient Hotel
6    Restaurant
7    Museum
8    New Tourist Hotel
9    Local buses
10   Tourist Office
11   Green Oasis Restaurant
12   Hotel Zenobia
13   Al Khayyam Restaurant
14   Column
15   Funerary temple
16   Church
17   Temple of Bel-Shamin
18   Temple of the Camp of Diocletian
19   Camp of Diocletian
20   Porticoed way
21   Tetrapylon
22   Banqueting hall
23   Agora
24   Senate House
25   Theatre
26   Temple of Naba
27   Monumental Arch
28   Temple of Bel
29   Funerary towers of Yemliko
30   Tower of Jambliq
31   Umm el Qais
32   Efca Spring
33   Meridien hotel

**Palmyra (Tadmor)**

0        250        500 m

To Karnak bus office,
restaurant & Deir ez-Zur

Justinian's Wall

Oasis

Northern
Necropolis

Justinian's Wall

Great Collonade

To Damascus, Homs

metres or so, ending at the funerary temple. The section between the Bel temple and the arch no longer exists and the main road from Palmyra to Damascus now winds through here. Overloaded trucks, carrying cotton from the Euphrates, come thundering through within a couple of metres of the arch and this traffic can't be good for the ruins. In fact it looks as though the keystone of the arch is ready to fall out at any moment.

The street itself was never paved, to allow camels to use it, but the porticoes on either side were paved. The section up to the tetrapylon is the best restored and is impressive in its scale. Each column has a small jutting platform about two-thirds of the way up, designed to hold the statue of some rich or famous Palmyrene who had helped to pay for the construction of the street.

**Theatre** The theatre is on the south side of the street between two arches in the colonnade. Beneath the platforms on many of the columns are inscriptions with names for the statues that once stood there. It seems the statues were of prominent people such as emperors, princes of Palmyra, magistrates and officials, high-ranking priests and caravan chiefs.

The free-standing facade of the theatre is designed along the lines of a palace entrance complete with royal door and smaller doors on either side. From the rear of the theatre a pillared way led south past the senate house and agora to one of the gates in the wall built by Justinian.

**Agora** The agora was the equivalent of a Roman forum and was used for public discussion, and as a market. Four porticoes surrounded a courtyard measuring 84 by 71 metres. The dedications of the statues which once stood on the pillars and walls, provide important clues for historians. The portico on the north had statues of Palmyrene and Roman officials, the eastern one had senators, the western was

Theatre, Palmyra

for military officers while on the south side, merchants and caravan leaders were honoured. Today there is nothing left of the statues and most of the pillars are only a metre or so high. Adjoining the Agora is the banqueting hall used by the rulers of Palmyra.

**Tetrapylon** About a third of the way along the street is the reconstructed tetrapylon (four groups of four pillars). Only one of these pillars is of the original granite (probably brought from Aswan in Egypt). The rest are just coloured concrete and look pretty terrible – a result of some rather hasty and amateurish reconstruction. Each of the four groups of pillars supports 150,000 kg of solid cornice and a statue used to stand between the pillars on each of the four pedestals. This monument marks a major intersection of the city; from here the main street continues north-west, and another smaller pillared street leads south-west to the Agora.

**Funerary Temple** The main street continues for another 500 metres and ends in the impressive, reconstructed portico of the funerary temple, dating back to the 3rd century. This was the main residential section of town and streets can be seen leading off to both sides.

**Camp of Diocletian** This lies to the south of the funerary temple along the porticoed way. The area here is littered with fallen stones and the intricacy of the carvings can be seen at close quarters. It is believed that Diocletian built this camp on the original site of the Palace of Zenobia, but excavation so far has not been able to prove this.

**Temple of Bel-Shamin** This small shrine is near the Zenobia Hotel and is dedicated to the god of storms and fertilising rains. Although it is permanently closed, the six columns of the vestibule have platforms for statues and bear inscriptions. The one on the far left has an inscription in Greek and Palmyrene praising the secretary of the city for his generosity during the visit of 'the divine Hadrian' and for footing the bill for the construction of the temple. The text is dated at 131 AD.

**Funerary Towers of Yemliko & Jambliq** These lie to the south of the city wall at the foot of the hill of Uum el Qais. They are worth visiting, but the best of them are kept locked. The only way to see them is to hire a three-wheeled motorised cart and get the museum attendant to bring the keys along. Although it's in walking distance, they don't allow you to take the keys and the attendant is not prepared to walk. The cart shouldn't cost more than S£10 per person and you need to buy a ticket from the museum before setting off.

The square towers were built as tombs and contained coffins in niches on up to five levels. The interior was often decorated with cornices and friezes. The

Monumental Arch, Palmyra

towers closest to the town are not locked and can be easily explored. The views from the top in late afternoon are great.

## Qalaat Ibn Maan

To the west the dominating feature is the Arab castle, Qalaat Ibn Maan, built in the 17th century by Fakr ed-Din the Maanite. You can't miss it, just jump the wall and head uphill. It is surrounded by a moat and a footbridge across it still stands. The castle is not open but the views of Palmyra and the surrounding desert make the 45-minute scramble up the rubble slope well worthwhile. It's best to go up in the late afternoon when the sun is behind you and the shadows are long.

## Museum

The museum is between the ruins and the new town and is open daily, except Tuesday, from 9 am to 1 pm and 4 to 6 pm; entry is S£1. The descriptions are in English which is unusual for Syrian museums. It has an excellent array of statuary from Palmyra, most in surprisingly good condition considering they have been buried in the sand for a thousand years. Upstairs, they don't seem to bother with the lights, so you'll probably have to switch them on yourself. The attendants are helpful though.

## Places to Stay

Right by the ruins is the *Hotel Zenobia* which dates back to the French Mandate and has a certain faded elegance. The rooms have fans and are reasonably clean. Prices seem to depend on how much the manager thinks he can get out of you; S£60 is about right.

If you don't mind being a bit further away, the *Orient Hotel* is in the new town and is good value. The friendly Algerian manager speaks French, German and some English and cooks a mean chicken if you want to share the cost of buying one. The rooms are a bit dingy and have up to six beds. Bargain down to S£50 for a double with bath.

The only other hotel in town is the *New Tourist Hotel* but as it's right by the mosque you'll get the early-morning call if you stay here.

By the Efca Spring, some 3 km from town on the other side of the ruins, is the new *Meridien Hotel* with five-star facilities and prices.

## Places to Eat

There isn't a lot of choice in Palmyra. Out by the Zenobia Hotel on the road to the ruins are two outdoor restaurants next to the tourist office. The *Green Oasis Cafe* is the better of the two but the owner is none too friendly. A kebab sandweech is S£10 and a full meal is S£25 per person. The *Al Khayyam Restaurant* next door is much the same.

Back in town there's a couple of small restaurants. The one with the red and yellow sunshade over the footpath does a good half chicken, salad, hummus and bread for S£19.

At the Karnak bus office there's quite a reasonable restaurant where you can get sandwiches, kebabs and drinks. It's only open until 6 pm.

Next door to the mosque is the local tea shop where you can sit and watch the world go by.

## Getting There

**Bus** The Karnak bus station/office is about 200 metres north along the main street. Getting buses to Damascus and Homs can be a problem as they come from the towns of the north-east and are often full. The most reliable bus for Damascus (S£28, three hours) goes at 3 pm – get to the office at 1 pm if you want to be sure of a seat. For Deir Ez-Zur (S£18, two hours), the bus arrives from Damascus at 12 noon but get there at 10 am for a seat. There are other departures to Homs and Damascus but it's just a matter of waiting at the office. At least there is quite a decent restaurant to wait in.

The local buses leave for Damascus and Homs every hour or so when full, from a station one block east of the New Tourist Hotel. The fare to Damascus is S£11 and the trip takes four hours.

# Euphrates River & the North-east

The Euphrates River (*al-Furat* in Arabic) starts out high in the mountains of eastern Anatolia in Turkey and winds through the north-east of Syria into Iraq, finally emptying into the Shatt al-Arab waterway and the Persian Gulf – a total distance of over 2400 km. The Euphrates is a cool green and it makes a change to see some water and fertile land after all the desert of the interior.

One of the few tributaries of the Euphrates, the Kabur, flows down through north-eastern Syria to join it below Deir Ez-Zur. These two rivers make it possible to irrigate and work the land and in recent years the cotton produced in this area has become an important source of income for the country.

The oilfields at Qaratchok in the far north-eastern corner of the country have been producing oil for over a decade. Petroleum products account for something over 60% of all exports and reserves are estimated at 300 million tonnes. A major new find has been made near Deir Ez-Zur which, when it is developed, may have major economic and even political implications for Syria.

## LAKE ASSAD

By the time the Euphrates enters Syria at Jarablos (once the capital of the Hittite empire) it is already a mighty river. A dam was constructed to harness the Euphrates for irrigation water and hydroelectricity production.

Work on the dam began at Tabaqah in 1963 and the reservoir started to fill in 1973. Now that it's full, it stretches for some 60 km. It's Syria's pride and joy and the electricity produced was supposed to make the country self-sufficient. Recently however, the flow of the Euphrates has been reduced by the construction in Turkey of another large dam and Syria (and Iraq) are concerned that the Turks may at any time decide to regulate the flow for political reasons.

The lack of water in the river has meant that the hoped-for surfeit of electricity just hasn't materialised and in fact, as you are probably well aware by now, there are power cuts every day for at least four hours.

The dormitory town of Al-Thaura ('The Revolution') was built at Tabaqah to accommodate dam workers and peasants who had to be relocated because of the rising water levels. Not only were villages inundated but also some sites of historical and archaeological importance. With aid from UNESCO and other foreign missions, these were investigated, documented and, where possible, moved to higher ground. The 27-metre-high minaret of the Maskana mosque and the 18-metre-high minaret from Abu Harayra were both segmented and transported, the latter to the centre of Al-Thaura.

### Getting There

**Bus** There are regular microbuses between Al-Thaura and Raqqa.

**Train** Al-Thaura is on a branch line of the Aleppo/Deir Ez-Zur main line and there are twice-daily connections to Aleppo.

### RAQQA

There's really nothing to do or see in Raqqa but it can be a good base from which to visit Lake Assad and the walled city of Rasafah, 30 km to the south.

### Places to Stay

There are a few hotels around the souk, about 200 metres north of the bus station.

## Getting There

**Bus** From the bus station there are regular microbuses west to Al-Thaura and Aleppo, and east along the Euphrates to Deir Ez-Zur.

**Train** Raqqa has similar train connections – to Aleppo and Deir Ez-Zur.

## RASAFAH

This old walled city is in the middle of absolutely nowhere and as you approach it is quite a sight to see it rise out of the featureless desert. The walls, enclosing a quadrangle measuring 500 by 300 metres, are virtually all still complete. Rasafah is a bit of hassle to get to, but it can be done in a day-trip from Raqqa and is worth the effort.

Inside the walls are the remains of a Byzantine basilica built to honour Saint Sergius. The city was taken over by the Omayyed caliph Hisham, who built a palatial summer residence here. This was completely destroyed by the Abbasids in 743 and the city fell into ruin.

There is nobody at the site selling water, or anything else for that matter, so bring food and water with you – it gets stinking hot in summer.

## Getting There

It requires a little patience to get to Rasafah as transport is infrequent. Catch a bus from Raqqa for Al-Thaura or Aleppo and get off at the turn-off at As Saddayn – that's the easy bit. Now it's just a matter of waiting for a pick-up to take you out to the ruins for S£5. Wait a while – one will turn up eventually.

## DEIR EZ-ZUR

This is a very pleasant desert town on the Euphrates and is a crossroads for travellers visiting the north-east of Syria. Roads fan out to the north-east to Qamishle and Turkey, south-east to Mari, Abu Kamal and Iraq, south-west to Damascus and north-west to Raqqa and Aleppo.

There's not much to see in the town but a stroll along the river bank, particularly at sunset, is a popular activity. The suspension bridge is only for pedestrians and bicycles, and on the other side is a small recreation ground where you can swim with the locals.

If you're taking the train along the river towards Aleppo, keep an eye out for the ruins of the castle of Halabiye, about 60 km upstream on the south bank. This was called Zenobia in Palmyrene times and was founded by the famous queen of the same name. There used to be a ford across the river at this point and the walls of the keep come right down to the river bank. Of the castle itself, nothing remains except the outer walls.

## Places to Stay

The best place is the *Raghdan Hotel* right behind the Karnak bus station. It's on an arm of the Euphrates, so it gets some breeze and the rooms have shutters, fans and a washbasin. There's a TV lounge on each floor. The only drawback with this place is that the toilets are inexcusably filthy at times. Single/double rooms are S£47/63.

Along the main street one block from the Karnak station are a number of cheaper hotels. The *Hotel Al Arabi Al Khabir* has beds for S£20. The *Hotel Ghassan* is right next door and is much the same. Both these places are noisy as they're right on the street – try to get a room at the back.

Right by the souk on the corner of the main street is the *Hotel Amal* which is even noisier than the other two and costs S£25 for a bed.

## Places to Eat

Around the hotels on the main street you'll find the same roast chickens, kebabs, hummus and salad that you get everywhere.

For the same food but in different surroundings, the *Restaurant Cairo*, also on the main street, is a big cavernous place. The front part is for eating in only, while in the enormous room at the back, beer and *araq* are also served – don't be surprised if a tipsy Syrian sits down and starts to babble away to you! S£40 buys you a meal of kebabs, hummus and salad.

Down at the river by the footbridge are a couple of outdoor restaurants right on the river banks. They are great places to sit in the evening and sip a beer. Food here costs about the same as in the Cairo.

### Getting There
**Bus** The Karnak station is right in the thick of things in the centre of town. It's part of a new shopping complex one block back from the river arm, but has no identifying signs. Buses head north-east to Hassake, Qamishle and Ras al'Ain daily but as these come from Damascus, they may be full. The same applies to the bus to Abu Kamal, which comes through at 3 pm. There are three buses for Damascus, at 7 and 11 am and 2.30 pm; S£47, five hours.

The local bus station is a couple of km south of town. A taxi is the easiest way to find it. Buses run from here to Abu Kamal along the Euphrates, to Hassake in the north-east and west to Raqqa.

**Train** The railway station is across the river to the north of town, about three km from the centre. If you feel like a half-hour walk to get there, cross the footbridge, get to the T-junction and turn right. The alternative is to catch one of the yellow minibuses which run from the railway booking office (next to the Karnak office) to the station for S£3. These only run when a train is due to leave. The booking office itself is open from 7 am to 10 pm.

Trains to Aleppo leave at 9.04 am, 5.40 and 9.35 pm; S£33 in 1st class, S£23 in 2nd and it takes five hours. There are two trains daily to Qamishle (S£22) through the desert, but the bus trip is much more interesting as it follows the heavily cultivated Kabur River region and goes through many small villages.

## QAMISHLE
This is a frontier town right on the Turkish border in the north-east. The place is full of Kurds and Turks and the cheaper hotels will quote prices in Turkish lire rather than Syrian pounds.

There is nothing to see but the mix of people makes the place interesting. Because of its proximity to the border, you can expect passport checks at the hotels during the night, and when getting on or off buses or trains.

### Places to Stay & Eat
None of the cheapies amount to much. The *Chahba Hotel* is about the best of a bad lot. The old manager is quite happy to put clean sheets on the bed, which is just as well because it looks like they haven't been changed since Adam was a lad. There's plenty of rooms so it's no trouble getting one to yourself; S£20 per person. The entrance is in an arcade behind the Semiramis Hotel.

The *Hotel Omaya* is the local Turkish hangout. It's noisy, gloomy and none too clean but the manager is amiable enough. A double room costs S£35 with fan; dirt and flies are provided at no extra cost.

The *Hotel Hadaya* is the cheapest of the up-market hotels at US$8/12 for a single/double. The *Semiramis Hotel* is Qamishle's premier establishment and charges US$9/13 for singles/doubles. Expatriate workers, mostly from Eastern Europe, sometimes stay here as it's the closest town to the oilfields and there are also a couple of foreign-sponsored agricultural programmes nearby.

Just opposite the Semiramis is a reasonable restaurant with an outdoor terrace upstairs. Just for a change you can have kebabs, hummus and salad, or even roast chicken.

### Getting There
**To/from Turkey** The Turkish border is only about one km from the centre of Qamishle – a 15-minute walk.

**Bus** The Karnak bus station is right in the centre. Buses leave daily at 8 am and 1 pm for the nine-hour trip to Damascus; S£72.

The local bus station is out of town to the south.

**Train** The railway station is, typically, a long way from the centre. A share-taxi there should cost S£4, or S£10 if you take one alone.

There is a booking office in the centre, 50 metres up from the Karnak station and almost opposite the Chahba Hotel. It's open until 7 pm and the friendly official speaks English and is helpful, and not just with train info.

The train to Damascus leaves at 6.30 pm and takes 15 hours going via Deir Ez-Zur and Aleppo. It costs S£53 in 2nd class, S£75 in 1st and a sleeper will set you back S£193. There's also a train at 7 am which goes only to Aleppo.

## ABU KAMAL, MARI & DOURA EUROPOS
Abu Kamal is another frontier town, this time 140 km south-east of Deir Ez-Zur close to the Iraqi border. This border has been closed for some years because of Syria's support for Iran in the Gulf war.

The spectacular ruins of Mari, an important Mesopotamian city dating back some 5000 years, are about 10 km north of Abu Kamal. The only way to get out to them is by taxi. The Royal Palace here was enormous, measuring 200 by 120 metres with over 300 rooms. There are quite large chunks of pottery lying around all over the place. Most of the good stuff found here is on display in the museums in Aleppo and Damascus.

Also of interest near Abu Kamal are the ruins of Doura Europos at Salhiye, 40 km back towards Deir Ez-Zur. This fortified town, built by the Macedonians and

named after the village where Alexander the Great was born, sits on a cliff overlooking the Euphrates some 90 metres below. It also served as an important defensive town for the Palmyrenes against the Persians. Buses running between Deir Ez-Zur and Abu Kamal drop you a couple of km away on the main road, and from there it's an easy walk through the crumbling walls.

The god Itur-Shamagan, from Mari

### Places to Stay & Eat
There are a few cheap hotels and restaurants in Abu Kamal.

### Getting There
Karnak buses run daily from Abu Kamal to Damascus at 7 am, S£72, seven hours. Local microbuses run alongside the river to Deir Ez-Zur.

# South of Damascus

The area from Damascus south to the Jordanian border, 100 km away, is fertile agricultural land and is intensively farmed, particularly with watermelons. In the late summer you'll probably see more melons for sale by the side of the road than you've ever seen in your life. Often, however, it looks as though the farmers are trying to grow polythene bags – the fields are littered with them.

The Golan Heights in the south-west were originally Syrian territory but were occupied by the Israelis during the Arab-Israeli war of 1967. Following a peace agreement which ended the 1973 war, the Israelis partially withdrew.

The area known as the Hauran is a black basalt plain which straddles the Jordan/Syria border and is also known as Jebel Druze. The black rocks used for construction give the villages of the area a strange brooding quality.

## GOLAN HEIGHTS

The Golan is a name that most people would have heard of in various news reports on the Middle East, but probably have only a vague idea where it is, or what its significance is.

It is the only area where Israel and Syria have a common border and so it has been the scene of bitter conflict over the years. The 1967 war saw the Israelis clear the Golan of Syrian troops and Damascus itself was threatened. During the war of 1973, a delicate truce was negotiated between Israel and Syria by US Secretary of State, Henry Kissinger, who spent almost a month shuttling back and forth between Damascus and Israel. The truce saw Syria regain some 450 square km of territory lost to the Israelis during the war as well as some small, symbolically important pieces lost in the 1967 war. A complicated demilitarised buffer zone supervised by United Nations forces was also established. It varies in width from a few hundred metres to a couple of km.

Before the Israelis withdrew from Quneitra however, they evacuated the 37,000 Arab population and set about systematically destroying the town, removing anything that could be un-screwed, unbolted or wrenched from its position. Everything from windows to light fittings were sold to Israeli contractors. Once the buildings had been stripped, they were pulled apart with tractors and bulldozers. It is reported that some graves were even broken open and ransacked.

All this makes Quneitra look more like a bombed-out city than anything else. It has become something of a national propaganda showpiece demonstrating the hard-nosed approach of the Israelis. It is in the area controlled by UN forces and is an eerie place to visit. As the demilitarised zone is only a few hundred metres wide at this point, the Israeli flag can be seen flying not far away.

In 1981 the Israeli government decided to annex the Golan Heights, a move that attracted worldwide criticism. It seems the Israelis are never likely to yield what they have now, as the Golan Heights under Syria would pose an unacceptable threat to the Israeli settlements close to the Heights. The Syrians on the other hand see the occupation of the Golan as outwardly hostile and illegal.

The stalemate continues but Syria is not prepared to accept it as a *fait accompli*. It was reported recently that the country was spending US$3 billion over the next three years to build up to an effort to retake the Golan.

You need a special permit to get through the UN checkpoint just before Quneitra. These are easily obtained in Damascus from the UN office in Avenue Adnan el Malky, at the top end near the Libyan Peoples' Bureau.

## Getting There

Catch a *meecro* to the UN checkpoint at Khan Ureinibah from the station next to the Karnak station in Damascus, and from there walk or hitch the few km into Quneitra.

It's possible that the friendly Syrian soldiers at Checkpoint Alpha, the sole crossing between Syria and Israel and open only to UN personnel, will find you a lift back to Damascus in a UN vehicle.

## DER'A

There's nothing of interest in this southern town, 100 km from Damascus, although it can make a good base for visiting the ruins at Bosra, and you'll probably end up staying here if you want to tackle the Jordan border by public transport.

There's a tourist office on the Damascus road, just north of the railway line.

## Places to Stay & Eat

There are a couple of nondescript hotels not far from the *meecro* and Karnak stations. The *Hotel Al Salam* is not bad and charges S£20 for beds in noisy rooms.

At the minibus station there are a number of the standard restaurants and cafés.

## Getting There

**To/from Jordan** This border is straightforward enough. Hitch or walk the three or four km from Der'a to the Syrian checkpoint. Once through formalities here, it's another three or four km to the Jordanian checkpoint. The soldiers here won't allow you to walk the last km or so to the immigration post but are friendly and will flag down a car or bus for you. From the Jordanian side, at Ramtha, minibuses go on to Irbid, and from there to Amman.

The number of trucks lining the road on this border is staggering – at times they are queued up for kilometres waiting to cross. The drivers are well prepared for the wait. Each truck has a well-stocked food-box on the side complete with teapot and gas stove and you'll see the drivers sitting next to their trucks making a brew and having a chat while they sit it out.

**Bus** The Karnak office is right opposite the *meecro* station. There's a couple of departures daily for Damascus; S£10, 1½ hours. It's not possible to pick up the Karnak bus to Amman which runs through here.

The microbus station is typically chaotic. Buses for Bosra depart when full every half hour or so and take one hour; S£2.50. There are both big buses and microbuses doing the run to Damascus. The bigger ones are faster and stop less frequently. Demand for seats is high in the afternoon and getting on a bus can be a real shitfight. It's a comical performance because all the men will fight and push to get a seat while the women wait resignedly until the door is clear. They then walk on and the men give up the seats that they've just fought so hard for! The trip takes about 1½ hours and costs S£5.

## BOSRA

The town of Bosra lies between two wadis, both of which run into the Yarmouk River. It is 40 km east of Der'a across fertile plains littered with black basalt rocks.

It is a weird and wonderful place. Apart from having possibly the best preserved Roman theatre in existence, the rest of the town is built in, around and over old sections of Roman buildings. It is built almost entirely out of black basalt blocks and the blocks in the new houses have mostly been filched from ancient Roman buildings.

Altogether it's a strange mixture of architectural styles and, as the *Cook's Travellers' Handbook* of 1934 says, 'a zealous antiquary might find weeks of profitable enjoyment among the ruins'. That is probably quite true, but for most people one day is enough to see everything at a leisurely pace. It is possible to visit Bosra in a day-trip from Damascus using public transport but it's less hectic if you use Der'a as a base.

## History

Bosra is mentioned in Egyptian records as early as 1300 BC and during the 1st century AD it became the northern capital of the Nabataean kingdom; Petra was the capital in the south.

In 106 AD the area was annexed by the Romans and Bosra became the capital of the Province of Arabia and was named Nova Trajana Bosra. This was the seat of a praetorian legate, administrator of the region and in command of the 3rd Legion which was garrisoned mainly at Bosra. It was this and the fact that Bosra was still on the caravan routes that allowed it to prosper and flourish. When Phillip of Bostra became the emperor of Rome he raised the town to the status of metropolis and coins were minted here.

During the Christian era it was also important as the seat of a Primate with 33 priests subject to him. It fell to the Muslims and according to tradition, it is here that Mohammed encountered the Nestorian monk Boheira who told him of his future vocation as a Prophet.

The Crusaders twice tried unsuccessfully to take the fortress in the 12th century and the Mongols seriously damaged it during their invasion in 1261.

The city still managed to prosper as it was on the pilgrimage route to Mecca, and because of the tradition of Mohammed and the monk, pilgrims would often stop here for up to a week. This route became unsafe about the end of the 17th century and the pilgrims started using a route further to the west – Bosra was on the way down.

## Citadel & Theatre

The citadel is a curious construction as it is largely a fortified Roman theatre. The two structures are in fact one – the fort was built around the theatre to make it an impregnable stronghold.

The first walls were built during the

Omayyed and Abbasid periods, with further additions being made in the 11th century by the Fatimids.

After the Crusader attacks of 1140 and 1183, it was realised that there was not enough room to house all the Ayyubid troops stationed there, so during the period 1202 to 1251, nine towers were constructed. These towers were encircled by a deep moat and a five-span bridge was erected.

The big surprise on entering the citadel is to find the magnificent 15,000-seat theatre. The theatre was almost completely obscured by later buildings and only this century have these been cleared away to reveal its fine lines. It is a rarity amongst theatres of the time in that it is completely free-standing and is not built into the side of a hill.

The stage is backed by rows of Corinthian columns and the whole facade was originally faced with white marble. The stage had a wooden roof and the rest of the theatre was covered by silk awnings to give protection from the elements. As if this wasn't refinement enough, perfumed water was also sprayed in the air and the fine mist fell on the heads of the spectators.

In one of the towers of the citadel is a fairly flash café which has good tea and the only toilets in the place. There's also quite a good popular tradition museum in one of the other towers depicting local costumes and culture. The citadel is open daily from 8 am to 6 pm daily and entrance is S£1; in the rest of the town you can wander around at any time.

## Other Sights

North of the citadel is the **main street** of the old city running roughly east-west. At the western end is the large *Bab al-Haoua* (Gate of the Wind). Along the cobbled main street are the remains of columns found on the site during excavations.

The *Bab al-Qandil* (Gate of the Lantern), on the main street near the citadel, dates to the 3rd century. An

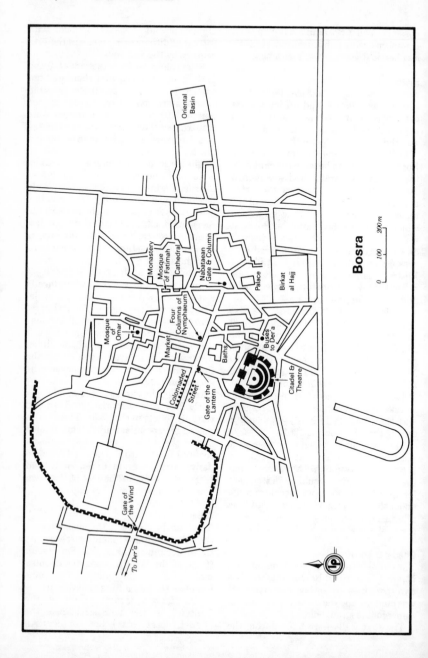

Bosra

0    100    200 m

Oriental Basin

Monastery
Mosque of Fatimah
Cathedral
Nabataean Gate & Column
Palace
Birkat al Hajj

Four Columns of Nymphaeum

Mosque of Omar

Market

Baths

Buses to Der'a

Colonnaded Street

Gate of the Lantern

Citadel & Theatre

Gate of the Wind

To Der'a

inscription on the right-hand pillar states that it was erected in memory of the Third Legion which was garrisoned here.

Next up are the four enormous Corinthian **columns**, looking somewhat out of place. This is what is left of the *nymphaeum* which supplied water to the people and gardens.

Just past these is another column and lintel that has been incorporated into a modern house. The thought of a few tonnes of basalt plummeting through the ceiling one night would surely be cause for instant insomnia. It is believed that this is what remains of a pagan sanctuary built by one of the kings of Bosra to protect his daughter from death. A dismal failure it seems as the daughter was brought a bunch of grapes in which a scorpion was hiding. It promptly stung and killed her.

Right opposite this are the **Roman baths** which are at present being excavated by French archaeologists. It was a complicated series of rooms where the bather moved from one pool-room to the next, finally arriving at the steam bath.

The **Mosque of Omar** lies about 50 metres north of the main street. Built in about 720 AD, it is one of the three oldest mosques in the world (the others are at Medina and Cairo). The basalt roof tiles replaced the original wooden ones in the 11th century.

The **monastery** is the oldest church in Bosra and is thought to have been built in the 4th century. This is supposedly where Mohammed met the monk Boheira. The facade has been totally rebuilt but the side walls and apse are original.

Between the monastery and the main street lies the **cathedral** in a sorry state of decay. It was the first building to have a circular dome above a square base, but it was poorly constructed in the first place (*circa* 512 AD) and before its final demise, had been rebuilt a number of times. The emperor Justinian used the church as the model for cathedrals he wanted built at Constantinople and Ravenna and it seems the architects managed to do a better job of it and the two still stand.

At the eastern end of the street is the **Nabataean gate and column**. The gate is the main entrance to the palace in which the Nabataean king Rabbel II lived. The column is the only one of its kind in Syria and bears the typical simple Nabataean capital.

Further out of town are two **cisterns** which used to supply the town with water.

### Places to Stay & Eat
There are no hotels in Bosra, although there is a *Youth Hostel* inside the citadel. It costs S£10 and there are basic cooking facilities. You also get locked inside the citadel at 6 pm. Damascus or Der'a offer better alternatives.

Around the entrance to the citadel are a couple of shops selling felafels and drinks.

### Getting There
Microbuses run from Der'a to Bosra regularly, take half an hour and cost S£2.50.

# Jordan

Lithograph of Petra by David Roberts, 1839

# Facts about the Country

## HISTORY SINCE WW I

The Arabs joined the British drive to oust the Turks in June 1916 after British assurances that they would be helped in their fight to establish an independent Arab state. This was one month after the British and French had concluded the secret Sykes-Picot agreement, whereby Syria and Lebanon were to be placed under French mandate and Jordan and Palestine would go to the British.

This betrayal was further heightened by the famous Balfour Declaration in 1917. It was actually a letter written by the British Foreign Secretary, Arthur Balfour, to a prominent British Jew, Lord Rothschild. It stated that:

His Majesty's Government view with favour the establishment in Palestine of a National Home for the Jewish people, and will use their best endeavours to facilitate the achievement of this object, it being clearly understood that nothing shall be done which may prejudice the civil and religious rights of existing non-Jewish communities in Palestine, or the rights and political status enjoyed by Jews in any other country.

It was destined for trouble from the start. Palestine was not a country with defined borders; historically it was the region that lay to the west of the Jordan River. The Arabs were also outraged by the implication that they were the intruders and the minority group, when in fact it is estimated that at the end of WW II they accounted for some 90% of the population. They felt, however, that the Zionists were no real threat and that the only implication was that they would have to recognise the rights of the established minority of Jews.

During the 1920s Jewish immigration proceeded at a rate which didn't cause any alarm, and in fact in 1927 there was a net emigration due to limited economic prospects in Palestine. The calm was shattered in 1929 by a riot at the Western Wall in Jerusalem over religious practices. This led to the first major attacks against Jews by Arabs.

The 1930s saw an increase in both the immigration of Jews and the level of antagonism between the two communities. Hitler's rise to power and the persecution of the Jews accelerated the numbers arriving. The Arabs became increasingly alarmed at Zionist intentions to create a Jewish state and Palestine became the focus for Arab nationalism.

Feeling more and more threatened, the various Arab groups, now united in the Arab Higher Committee, called for a general strike and boycott of British goods. The Jews for their part protested and rioted.

It finally became clear to the British that the mandate was unworkable and the Peel Commission reported that cooperation between Arabs and Jews in a Palestinian state was just not on. It recommended a partition of Palestine - rejected by both Arabs and Jews - and this was also rejected a year later by another commission which favoured a different partition, also rejected by both communities. Arab rebellion became increasingly violent and was met with escalating aggression from the Zionists.

As a way out of the stalemate, the British Government, by now desperate for a solution, proposed in the White Paper of 1939 that a new bi-national state of Palestine be created in the next decade. Until that occurred, Arabs and Jews would participate in the administration of the existing territory. The immigration of Jews would be limited to 75,000 over five years and any further immigration would have to have Arab approval.

The White Paper was categorically rejected by the Zionists and although generally welcomed by the Arabs, they officially rejected it. It did, however, serve to quieten the area down for the duration of the war and the two communities on the whole cooperated with the British.

## Partition

After WW II the situation became even messier. Up until the war, any plans for a separate Jewish state really lacked a lot of credibility because of the small Jewish minority, but with the flood of refugees from persecution in Europe, it is estimated that Jews made up about 30% of the population.

In 1945 the Zionists urged the British to withdraw the White Paper and allow the immediate entry of 100,000 Jews into Palestine. With Zionism gaining influence in the USA, this was endorsed by President Truman. The British, seeing no other alternative, set up yet another commission, the Anglo-American Commission of Inquiry, which in essence recommended the immediate admission of 100,000 refugees and the continuance of the mandate. After refusing to accede to that demand, the British, having run out of options, referred the question to the United Nations.

On 29 November 1947 the UN voted in favour of the partition of Palestine. Not surprisingly it was approved by the Jews, not only because it supported their claim for a separate state of Israel in Palestine, but it also gave them a proportionately much larger territory than the Arabs. The Arab leaders, shocked and enraged that the Jews had been given over half the area including the valuable coastal strip, not only boycotted the decision but made it known that they intended to oppose it by force. The war was on.

Highly trained and organised Israeli forces proved much too strong for the poorly led and ill-equipped volunteers from other Arab countries who had flocked to Palestine to support the Arab cause. Israel was soon well in control of its allotted area as well as entrenching itself in some strategic areas allotted to the Arabs. After a massacre of an entire village of Arabs by Israeli forces, a mass exodus of nearly one million Arabs followed, giving the Jews their much-needed majority and at the same time placing strain on Jordan.

The State of Israel was proclaimed on 14 May 1948 and the next day the British mandate finished. Fighting continued but by mid-1949 Israel had concluded separate armistice agreements with Egypt, Syria, Transjordan and Lebanon. The Jews were left with all of Galilee, most of the Mediterranean coast, the Negev desert, a large strip giving it access to the Red Sea and all of Jerusalem except for the north-east section. This, along with the remaining Arab share of Palestine, was annexed by Transjordan in April 1950 and became the Hashemite Kingdom of Jordan under King Abdullah, the brother of Faisal.

One of the effects of the mass migration of Palestinians was that Jordan's population effectively doubled and refugee camps were set up in the Jordan Valley, and near Amman.

King Abdullah was assassinated outside the Al Aqsa Mosque in Jerusalem in July 1951, and after his son Talal ruled for a year and was declared mentally unbalanced, his grandson Hussein came to power at the age of 17. With great skill and a good deal of luck he has managed to stay there ever since. In 1956 he sacked Glubb Pasha (who had headed the Arab Legion and was Chief of Staff of the Jordanian Army) because of his taunts that Hussein was only a British puppet. After elections held that year, the newly formed pro-Nasser government broke ties with England and the last British troops left Jordanian soil by mid-1957. With US support Hussein staged a coup against his own pro-Nasser government, partly because it had tried to open a dialogue with the Soviet Union.

With the union of Egypt and Syria in

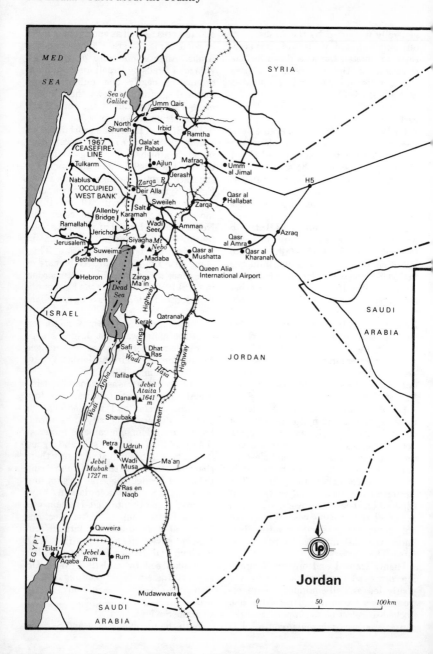

Jordan

To Baghdad

IRAQ

JORDAN

SAUDI
ARABIA

1958, Jordan feared for its own position and tried a federation with their Hashemite cousins in Iraq. This lasted less than a year as the Iraqi monarchy was overthrown and British troops were sent in to Jordan to protect Hussein from a Nasserist takeover led by discontented Palestinian refugees.

## The PLO

At an Arab summit meeting in 1964, the Palestine Liberation Organisation, with its own army, was formed to represent the Palestinian people. The Palestine National Council (PNC) was established within the PLO as its executive body – the closest thing to a Palestinian government. It included representatives from many Arab countries, various guerila organisations, student bodies and trade unions.

At about the same time, an organisation called the Palestine National Liberation Movement was set up. It was known as al-Fatah which is the reversal of its Arabic initials. One of the stated aims of both the PLO and al-Fatah was to train guerillas for raids on Israel.

A power struggle for control of the guerilla organisations saw al-Fatah become the dominant force within the PLO and its leader, Yasir Arafat, became chairman of the executive committee of the PLO in 1969.

In 1974 the PLO made a major gain in its bid for international recognition. At the UN General Assembly it was invited to take part in a debate on the 'Palestine question' and the vote favoured the PLO as the legitimate representative of the Palestinians. The Arab summit in Morocco the next month also decided in favour of the PLO representing the Palestinians in any peace negotiations.

After the disaster of the Black September hostilities in Jordan in 1973, the PLO concentrated its activities in Lebanon.

## The Six-Day War

The early 1960s saw Jordan's position improve dramatically with aid from the United States and a boom in tourism, mainly in Jerusalem's old city, but it lost out badly in the Six-Day War of 1967.

The build-up to the war had seen severe Israeli warnings against increasingly provocative Palestinian guerila raids into Israel from Syria. With President Nasser of Egypt promising to support Syria in the event of an Israeli attack, the Syrians stepped up the raids and in May '67 announced that Israel was amassing troops in preparation for an assault. Egypt responded by asking the UN to withdraw its Emergency Force from the Egypt-Israel border, which it did. Nasser then closed the Straits of Tiran (the entrance to the Red Sea), effectively nullifying the Israeli port of Eilat, and within five days of Jordan and Egypt signing a mutual defence pact, the Israelis knew they were alone and surrounded.

On 5 June 1967 the Israelis despatched a pre-dawn raid that wiped out the Arabs' only real fighting force. They completely destroyed the Egyptian Air Force on the ground and in the following days they clobbered Egyptian troops in the Sinai, Jordanian troops on the West Bank and stormed up the Golan Heights in Syria.

The outcome for Jordan was disastrous. Not only did it lose the whole of the West Bank and its part of Jerusalem, which together supplied Jordan with its two principal sources of income – agriculture and tourism – but it saw the influx of another wave of Palestinian refugees.

On 22 September 1967 the United Nations passed the now-famous Resolution 242 which called for the Israeli withdrawal from the areas it had taken in the recent war, and for all countries in the Middle East to respect the rights of others 'to live in peace within secure and recognised boundaries'. Jordan was among the Arab countries to accept it although it was rejected by Syria and Iraq as it implied recognition of Israel.

After the defeat of 1967, the Palestinians became more militant and although there was tacit agreement with the Jordanian Government that they would operate freely out of their bases in the Jordan Valley, they also expected immunity from Jordan's laws. The country became increasingly unsettled and by 1970 the Government had virtually become just one of many other factions vying for power.

Clearly this couldn't last and the showdown came in September of that year in an incident that came to be known as the 'Black September' hostilities. The Palestinians, in their most daring deed to date, hijacked four commercial aircraft and flew three of them to the north of Jordan and held passengers and crew hostage. Acting on orders from King Hussein, the army moved in and in a brief civil war wiped out all resistance here and throughout the country and deported many of the leaders. A Syrian force sent in to support the guerillas was also beaten off. An agreement signed in Cairo between Arafat and Hussein saw the guerillas recognise Hussein's authority and the Palestinians had to choose between exile or submission.

Jordan was not directly involved in the October War of 1973 but did send a small number of troops to assist Syria. The Camp David accords of 1978 were a result of a peace initiative by Egypt's President Sadat and saw a peace agreement reached between Egypt and Israel. King Hussein, along with most Arab leaders, rejected the results outright and isolated Egypt because the agreement neither required the Israelis to withdraw from occupied territories nor asserted Arab sovereignty over them.

In the '80s Jordan's position remains delicate as the struggle for power and the search for a peace settlement continues. Relations with Syria are cool because Jordan supports Syria's arch rival Iraq in the Gulf War. Hussein is also fearful that attempts within Israel to resolve the Palestinian issue could result in Jordan becoming the new independent Palestinian state in which there is hardly likely to be room for a Jordanian monarch. To avert this he has made many attempts over the years to foster support from Palestinians, particularly those on the West Bank. His latest effort towards this was a proposal in 1986 to spend US$500 million on development in the badly depressed West Bank. The West Bank Palestinians are strongly pro-PLO and are wary of the latest move saying that King Hussein is now cooperating with the Israelis.

A peace settlement still seems to be as far away as ever, especially now that King Hussein has dumped Yasir Arafat as an 'unreliable partner' and closed all Arafat's al-Fatah faction offices after accusing the PLO of meddling in Jordan's internal affairs.

## GOVERNMENT

The constitution of 1952 states that Jordan is a constitutional monarchy with representative government.

The king is vested with wide-ranging powers – he appoints and can dismiss judges, approves constitutional amendments, declares war and is the armed forces commander. He approves and signs all laws, although his power of veto can be over-ridden by a two-thirds majority of both the houses of the National Assembly.

The Council of Ministers is appointed by the king, is led by the prime minister and can dismiss Cabinet members. The prime minister chooses his cabinet which is responsible for general policy and co-ordination of the work of various departments.

The bicameral National Assembly is vested with legislative power and consists of the 30-member Senate, appointed by the King, and the 60-member House of Deputies elected by all citizens over the age of 18 years. Traditionally 30 members are elected from the East Bank and 30 from the West Bank and of the 60 seats, 50 must go to Muslims and 10 to Christians.

The Parliament was reconvened in 1984 after having been suspended in 1974 because elections could not be be held on the West Bank and because King Hussein had agreed that only the PLO could speak for the Palestinians. During that time the constitution was amended and the House of Deputies was replaced by the National Consultative Council, which elects West Bank members.

For administrative purposes the country is divided into eight *muhafazat* (governates) – three on the West Bank and five on the East.

## ECONOMY

Considering that Jordan is definitely not one of the oil-rich Middle Eastern countries and has little in the way of natural resources, its economy is in remarkably good health.

Dealt a severe blow by the loss of the prime agricultural land of the West Bank and the tourist attraction of Jerusalem in 1967, the economy has been showing a consistent growth rate of between 4% and 6% – quite an achievement. It is even more remarkable in light of the fact that in recent years, aid from the oil-rich Gulf

countries, set at US$1250 million by the 1978 Baghdad agreement, has been falling far short of the mark with only Saudi Arabia fulfilling its pledges.

Agriculture is concentrated in the Jordan Valley where ambitious irrigation schemes now make cultivation possible on thousands of hectares. Important crops are fruits, vegetables and cereals. On the highlands which form the eastern edge of the Jordan Valley, crops such as tobacco, wheat, barley and beans are grown. Agriculture can only be practised on about 10% of the land area but provides employment for more than 20% of the workforce.

The various industries account for about 20% of the gross domestic product. Phosphate mining is carried out from vast reserves at Hasa and is a major export. Copper from the Wadi Araba, south of the Dead Sea, is also exported. Manufacturing ranges from cement and batteries to toys, beer and matches.

Oil is yet to be found in commercially viable quantity but the Government is hopeful and exploration continues. Crude oil, imported via the Tapline from Saudi Arabia, is refined by the Jordanian Refining Company.

Tourism in Jordan took a long time to recover after the loss of Jerusalem and only in the last few years has it reached the levels of the pre-1967 years. Remittances from some 300,000 Jordanians working in the Gulf states, usually in white collar jobs, also make up an important portion of foreign earnings.

## GEOGRAPHY, WEATHER & CLIMATE

Jordan can easily be divided up into four major regions: the Jordan Valley, the West Bank plateau, the East Bank Plateau, and the Jordan desert.

### Jordan Valley

The dominant physical feature of the country is the fertile valley of the Jordan River. Forming part of the Great Rift Valley of Africa, it runs the full length of the country from the Syrian border in the north, down to the salty depression of the Dead Sea, and south to Aqaba and the Red Sea. The river itself is fed from the Sea of Galilee, the Yarmuk River and the valley streams of the high plateaus to the east and west.

The Dead Sea, at 394 metres below sea level, is the lowest point on earth, and the soils of this central area of the Jordan Valley are highly saline and support no vegetation. To the south of the Dead Sea, the Wadi Araba is a desolate region with absolutely no attraction. Potash is mined at Safi and it is hoped the area contains other minerals as it is useless for anything else. On the western side of the Dead Sea are Israeli *kibbutzim* on the occupied West Bank which are fertile havens in the desert.

The only town of any size in the valley is Jericho on the western side.

The weather in the valley is oppressive in summer – it feels like you're trapped in an airless oven. Daily temperatures are well in excess of 36°C. Rainfall is low at only 200 mm annually.

### West Bank Plateau

West of the Jordan Valley, the desolate hills of the Judaean and Samarian Mountains (famous in Biblical times) rise to about 1000 metres above sea level.

The plateau is broken by long shallow valleys running west to the Mediterranean and short steep ones draining into the Dead Sea. This is the Holy Land and has the famous cities of Jerusalem and Bethlehem.

The weather is a lot milder on the plateau than in the valley but expect temperatures of 30 to 35°C daily in summer. The winters are short but things get mighty unpleasant with rain, cold winds and temperatures around 7°C. Average annual rainfall is about 400 mm.

### East Bank Plateau

The East Bank plateau is broken only by the gorges cut by the perennial streams of the Wadi Zarqa, Wadi Mujib and Wadi el Hasa which flow into the Jordan River.

This area contains the main centres of population: Amman, Irbid, Zarqa and Kerak. It's also the region with the sites of most interest: Jerash, Kerak, Madaba and Petra.

The climate is similar to that of the West Bank plateau. Snow in Amman is not unheard of and even Petra gets the occasional fall.

### The Desert

All the rest of the East Bank, or about 80% of it, is desert stretching into Syria, Iraq and Saudi Arabia. In the north it's volcanic basalt while the south is sandstone and granite which sometimes produces some amazing sights – the area of Wadi Rum is one of the most fantastic desert-scapes in the world.

Climate is extreme – summertime temperatures to bake your brains, and days in winter when cold winds howl down from central Asia. Rainfall is minimal; less than 50 mm annually.

### Distances

Jordan is really a tiny country with a very curious shape. Its total area, including the West Bank, is about 98,000 square km or about the same size as Portugal. The strange kink in the Jordan-Saudi Arabia border is known as 'Winston's hiccup' because the story goes that the British Secretary of State, Winston Churchill, drew the boundary after having had a more than satisfactory lunch in Jerusalem one day back in 1920.

Distances are short – it's only about 430 km from Ramtha in the north to Aqaba in the south.

### When to Visit

The best time to visit Jordan is in spring or autumn when the daytime temperatures aren't going to knock you flat and the winds aren't too cold.

If you find Amman too cool in winter, head down to Aqaba on the Red Sea which enjoys fine weather and is something of a winter resort.

## FLORA & FAUNA

The pine forests of the north give way to the cultivated slopes of the Jordan Valley where cedar, olives and eucalypts are dominant. South towards the Dead Sea the vegetation gives way to mud and salt flats.

Animals found in the desert regions include the camel (of course), desert fox, gazelle, sand rat, hare and jerboa (a small rodent). The hills to the north-east of the Dead Sea are home to boars, badgers and goats. For parts of the year, the Azraq Oasis is home to hundreds of species of birds migrating from Europe and the near East. Despite the apparent diversity of the wildlife, in practice you'll be lucky to see anything more exotic than camels and goats.

In the Red Sea in the Gulf of Aqaba, there's a huge variety of tropical fish and coral which makes for some of the best scuba-diving in the world.

## PEOPLE

The population of Jordan is about 3.3 million, of which about 40% were refugees from the wars of 1948 and 1967.

### Ethnic & Religious Groups

The majority of Jordanians are Arabic-speaking Arabs descended from various tribes that have migrated to the area over the years from all directions.

More than 92% are Sunni Muslims; 6% are followers of Christianity and are mainly found in Amman, Madaba, Kerak and Salt.

The majority of Christians follow the Eastern Orthodox Church which is headed by the Patriarch of Jerusalem. The languages of the liturgy are Greek and Arabic.

Other minor Christian groups include the Eastern Catholics, who recognise the supremacy of the pope and are headed by the Patriarch of Antioch, Jerusalem and

Alexandria; the Roman Catholic, headed by a patriarch appointed by the pope; the Assyrian Church, whose members number about 1,000 and live in Jerusalem; and the Syrian Orthodox Church, where Syriac is the liturgical language.

There are small communities of non-Christian minority groups which include: the Druze, who are members of a sect which is an off-shoot of Shia Islam; the Samaritans, who number about 200 and live near Nablus on the West Bank and only believe that the first five books in the Bible are authentic; the Bahais, another off-shoot from Shia Islam and also numbering about 200; the Circassians, a group of about 25,000 who first settled in Jordan in Wadi Seer and Na'ur in about 1878 and trace their heritage back to Indo-European Moslem tribes in the 12th century; and the small community of Chechens who are related to the Circassians and are Shia.

### Palestinians

As mentioned earlier, about 40% of the population are Palestinian refugees who fled from the West Bank during the wars of 1948 and 1967. The exact number of refugees is unknown as they came flooding over during the fighting.

Their welfare is taken care of by the UNRWA (United Nations Relief & Works Agency) which provides basic services such as health, welfare and education. Some of the refugees are still housed in the refugee camps on the East Bank but are still determined to ultimately settle in their own homeland, Palestine.

On arrival in the East Bank, all refugees were immediately granted Jordanian citizenship and today they play an important part in the political and economic life of the country as they occupy high positions in government and business.

### The Bedouin

These desert dwellers number about 40,000 in Jordan and although many have given up the nomadic lifestyle, there are still large numbers who wander the deserts in the traditional manner.

They camp for a few months at a time in one spot and graze their herds of goats, sheep or camels. When the sparse fodder runs out, it is time to move on again. All over the east and south of the country you'll see the black goat-hair tents set up; sometimes just one, often three or four together.

The Bedouin family is a close-knit unit. The women, as usual, do most of the domestic work, the men are the providers and the children are put to work tending the herds from an early age.

Often the only concession these people make to the modern world is the acquisition of a Land Rover or pick-up truck, and occasionally a kerosene stove.

The Bedouin are renowned for their hospitality and it is part of their creed that no traveller is turned away.

The Jordanian government provides services such as education and housing, both of which are often passed up by the *bedu* ('desert dwellers' in Arabic) in favour of the lifestyle which has served them so well over the centuries.

## HOLIDAYS

As is the case in most countries, holidays are either religious (Islamic or Christian) or celebrations of important days in the country's history. For Islamic holidays see that section in the Facts About the Region chapter.

### Christian Holidays

For the celebration of Christian days in Jordan the Eastern calendar is used; this can be as much as one month behind the Gregorian. Easter is the main festival in the Eastern Church, bigger even than Christmas, so it's a good time to be in Jerusalem.

### Other Holidays

The following holidays all relate to the Gregorian calendar and are fixed.

15 January
   Tree Day (Arbor Day)
22 March
   Arab League Day
1 May
   Labour Day
25 May
   Independence Day
11 August
   King Hussein's Accession
14 November
   King Hussein's Birthday

# Facts for the Visitor

## VISAS

Visas are required by all foreigners entering Jordan. These are issued at the border or airport on arrival, or can be obtained from Jordanian consulates outside the country.

Tourist visas are valid for one month and cost anything from nothing for Australians (heaven knows why) to US$20 for many European nationalities. If you're coming from Syria, a visa obtained in Damascus will be cheaper than in Europe. Multiple-entry visas are also available for a nominated number of visits. Visas can be extended for a further two months without any hassle, but only in Amman.

Getting a visa issued at the border is quite straightforward but it may take longer to get the formalities over and done with.

Any evidence of a visit to Israel will immediately disqualify you from entering Jordan, despite the contradictions in the regulations for crossing the King Hussein Bridge to the West Bank and Israel.

If you plan on travelling to the West Bank and further on into Israel, it's possible to return to Jordan within one month of crossing into the West Bank, as long as your visa is still valid. See the Getting There chapter for details of this crazy crossing.

## MONEY

| | | | |
|---|---|---|---|
| USA | US$1 | = | JD0.300 |
| Australia | A$1 | = | JD0.200 |
| France | F10 | = | JD0.450 |
| W Germany | DM1 | = | JD0.150 |
| Canada | C$1 | = | JD0.200 |
| Japan | Y100 | = | JD0.180 |
| UK | £1 | = | JD0.460 |
| | | | |
| USA | JD1 | = | US$3.40 |
| Australia | JD1 | = | A$5.00 |
| France | JD1 | = | F22 |
| W Germany | JD1 | = | DM6.60 |
| Canada | JD1 | = | C$5.00 |
| Japan | JD1 | = | Y555 |
| UK | JD1 | = | £2.20 |

The currency in Jordan is the dinar (JD), known as the *geedee* among hip young locals, which is made up of 1000 fils. You will also often hear *piastre* or *girsh* used, which are both 10 fils, so 10 girsh equals 100 fils. Often when a price is quoted to you the ending will be omitted, so if you're told that something is 25, it's a matter of working out whether it's 25 fils, 25 girsh or 25 dinar!

The coins in circulation are 5, 10, 25, 50, 100 and 250 fils. The values of the coins are written in English; the numerals are only in Arabic.

Notes come in JD0.500, 1, 5, 10 and 20 denominations. For everyday travelling, the JD5 note is about as large as you want to carry. Changing 10s and 20s can be a real nuisance.

There are no currency restrictions or declaration forms in Jordan and therefore there's no blackmarket.

### Changing Money

Changing money in Amman is simplicity itself. There are moneychangers (and banks) all over the downtown area but as rates vary from one to another it pays to shop around. You'll also find that many will only take cash but there are plenty that will take both cash and cheques. Banks give the same rate but may take commission on travellers' cheques.

The only other towns with money-changers are Aqaba and Irbid; anywhere else you'll have to deal through one of the many banks which is no problem except they are open much shorter hours than the changers.

## COSTS

Jordan is, unfortunately, not a cheap country to travel in. Even the most basic accommodation will cost at least US$3.40, and often much more. Food and transport are also costly, particularly if you've just come from Syria or Egypt.

With careful budgeting US$12 per day is possible as long as you don't mind eating felafel and shawarma every day. Having your own tent will bring down the cost to some extent but the camping sites are limited.

## INFORMATION

Tourist information is sparse in Jordan although the Ministry of Tourism & Antiquities does put out a few glossy brochures and posters. There are tourist offices in Amman, Petra and Jerash although these seem to exist just to keep a few people employed rather than to actually serve any useful purpose.

At Jerash there are Tourist Police but these guys keep a very low profile and don't like to venture out of the air-conditioned comfort of the Rest House.

## ACCOMMODATION

There are no Youth Hostels so it's a matter of shelling out for a room. A bed in a share room in a cheap hotel costs about JD1.250 or possibly JD1 but you'll be pushing to find anything cheaper than that. It's sometimes possible to sleep on the roof, which in summer is a good place to be, but this will still cost at least JD1.

Especially in Amman, the cheap places

can be incredibly noisy from the traffic so try to get a room towards the back of the building.

The most surprising thing about accommodation in Jordan is that there are towns, some of them quite large like Jerash and Madaba, that have no hotel at all. Other towns, like Ajlun and Azraq, only have flash hotels where you're looking at JD7 or more.

The cheap hotels may insist on hanging on to your passport to put in the 'safe', which is usually the drawer in the desk at the front. If you want to keep it with you (where else is there to have it?), a little friendly persuasion usually works.

For those with the money and the inclination, there are five-star hotels in Amman, Petra and Aqaba. Tariffs at these places start at about JD20 and head for the sky.

## SAFETY

Jordan is a very safe and friendly country to travel in. The military keep a low profile and you would be unlikely to experience anything but friendliness, honesty and hospitality here. The closest you'll come to being kidnapped is someone dragging you into their house to drink tea or stay the night! If this happens don't hesitate to accept – Arabs pride themselves on their hospitality.

It is safe to walk around anywhere day or night both in Amman and other towns.

### Theft

As is the case in Syria, theft is not a problem for people who take reasonable care with their gear. Leaving your bag in the office of a bus station or hotel for a few hours should be no cause for concern. Share rooms in hotels are also quite OK as a rule.

### Women Alone

Women travelling alone in Jordan will find that Jordanian men are a little less hung-up about western women and sex than a lot of men in other Middle Eastern countries, but it still pays to dress and behave modestly. Walking the streets of Amman in shorts and a singlet would be as embarrassing for them as it would be for you.

There are some activities, such as sitting in the tea shops, which are usually men-only activities and although it's quite OK for western women to enter, in some places the stares may make you feel a little uncomfortable.

## BUSINESS HOURS

Government departments are open from 8 am to 2 pm daily except Friday. Businesses keep to much the same hours. Banks are open from 9.30 am to 1.30 pm Saturday to Thursday.

Small shops and moneychangers are open long hours, from about 9 am to 8 or 9 pm. Some close for a couple of hours in mid-afternoon. Fridays are pretty dead – there are always a few shops open but no moneychangers except at the airport.

The *souks* (markets) and street stalls are open every day and in fact Friday is often their busiest day.

During Ramadan, the Muslim month of fasting, business hours are shorter and because of the restriction on eating or drinking during the day, it can be difficult to find a place that's open in daylight hours, particularly in out-of-the-way places.

## ELECTRICITY

Jordan's electricity supply is 240 volts. Most of it is generated by the two large oil-fired generating plants in Zarqa and Amman. Supply is reliable and uninterrupted.

## MEDIA

The press in Jordan is given a surprisingly free reign and censorship is rare.

The daily English-language newspaper, the *Jordan Times*, has a reasonably impartial outlook and gives good coverage of events in Jordan, elsewhere in the

Middle East, and worldwide. It also has a What's On listing which includes films, exhibitions, flight information, emergency telephone numbers and even the latest market prices of fruit and vegetables.

The *Jerusalem Star* is a weekly newspaper which has more feature articles, reviews of all the Middle Eastern Arabic newspaper editorials and some great cartoons (The Far Side by Gary Larson).

Jordan Television broadcasts on two channels; one in Arabic and the other a combination of English, French, Hebrew and Arabic. Jordanians are avid TV watchers and you can see them in the tea shops glued to the sets following the latest developments in American soaps; wrestling also draws big audiences.

Radio Jordan also transmits in Arabic and English. The English station is on 855 kHz AM and 99 kHz FM in Amman and Aqaba. It's mostly a music station but has some news coverage.

The Hebrew transmissions on both the radio and TV are aimed at Israelis living on the West Bank in the hope that they might see the Arab point of view.

## POST & TELECOMMUNICATIONS
### Post
The postal service is generally efficient and letters arriving from Europe can take as little as three or four days. On the other hand, letters posted from Jordan take up to two weeks to Australia and the US. Letters to the USA and Australia cost 240 fils; postcards 160 fils.

There is no postal service between Jordan and Israel, which in this case includes the West Bank. If you tell any Jordanians that you are going to the West Bank they may well ask you to take letters to post to relatives living there.

**Parcel Post** Sending a parcel is quite an involved and expensive process. There's a parcel office behind the main post office in Amman. A 5-kg to 7-kg parcel to Australia or the US costs JD5.250 by sea mail and can take up to six months to arrive.

## Telephone

The local telephone system has a terrible reputation for unreliability but thankfully this is changing. Calls cost 50 fils and most shopkeepers and hotels will let you use their phone which is better than trying to use the few noisy public phones.

Overseas calls can be made easily from offices in Amman and Aqaba but these cost the earth; JD1.750 per minute with a three-minute minimum and it may take up to 30 minutes or so to get the connection.

As with the postal service, there are no connections between Jordan and Israel.

## Telex & Telegram

The telephone offices in Amman and Aqaba can be used for sending telexes and telegrams but these too are expensive. Five-star hotels will send them for guests – for a fee.

## TIME

Jordan is two hours ahead of GMT in winter (October to April) and three hours ahead in summer (May to September).

Time is something that Arabs always seem to have plenty of. A bit of patience goes a long way when dealing with them.

## WHAT TO BRING

With the high temperatures in summer, a hat, sunglasses and water bottle are all essential items. Other things that are handy and take up only a little space are: a Swiss army knife, a torch (flashlight), a few metres of nylon cord for a washing line, and a tennis ball cut in half makes a handy fits-all sink plug.

If you're going to be in the area in winter, make sure you have some warm clothes and a windproof and waterproof jacket.

## THINGS TO BUY

Jordan doesn't have a lot to offer the souvenir hunter. Most things are horrendously over-priced and many, such as the inlaid backgammon boards and boxes, come from Syria anyway.

Bedouin rugs, and tapestries done by Palestinian women are popular but you need to look carefully to make sure they are actually hand made.

Brass and copper coffee pots are one of the better buys but are difficult to transport and usually come from Syria where you can pick them up for about 75% less. Small bottles of coloured sand from Petra, skillfully poured into the bottle to form intricate patterns, are sold for anything from 500 fils upwards. Naturally-occurring coloured sand was originally used; these days the sand is artificially coloured (what else is new?).

In Amman and Aqaba there are a few low-key souvenir shops which have all this stuff but fleecing the tourist has not been developed into the fine art that it is in many countries and it is still possible to pick up the occasional bargain.

## FILM & PHOTOGRAPHY

Kodak and other brands of film are widely available at the tourist sites in Jordan and in Amman itself, but don't expect to pay less than you would at home.

Always ask permission before photographing anyone, particularly women, and be careful when taking pictures in and around Aqaba as Israel is only just 'over there' and the Saudi border is only 12 km away. Photography in military areas is forbidden.

## BOOKS

For a detailed look at the main archaeological sites, there are a number of books available.

A couple of excellent guides by Rami Khouri, former editor of the Jordan Times, are titled *Petra – A guide to the capital of the Nabataeans* and *Jerash – A frontier city of the Roman East* (Longmans UK, 1986, available from the Jordan Distribution Agency, Amman). They give full details of the two sites and have excellent maps and plans.

Written in 1959, *The Antiquities of Jordan* (G Lankester Harding, Jordan Distribution Agency, 1984, JD3.750) is a bit dated but is still the most comprehensive guide to archaeological sites in Jordan and includes those on the West Bank. The author was Director of the Department of Antiquities in Jordan for 20 years.

The book published by the Middle East Economic Digest (MEED), titled *Jordan – A MEED Practical Guide* and published in 1983, is aimed more at the businessman and resident expatriate, and so as well as general information, has chapters on business and trade matters.

The Fodor's book, *Jordan & the Holy Land* (Kay Showker, 1984, JD3), is mainly for the group tourist or those with a vehicle and lists only up-market establishments.

For rock-climbing and walking, *Treks & Climbs in the Mountains of Rum & Petra* by Tony Howard (Jordan Distribution Agency, 1987) is an excellent handbook full of walks, climbs, four-wheel drive and camel treks.

Top: The oval forum at the Roman city of Jerash, Jordan
Left: Abu Darwish Mosque on Jebel Al Ashrafiyeh – Amman, Jordan
Right: The 'Bedouin Supermarket' – Petra, Jordan

Top: The monastery at Petra, Jordan
Left: First glimpse through the gorge of the Treasury – Petra, Jordan
Right: Desert Patrolman on sentry duty – Wadi Rum, Jordan

# Getting There

Jordan can be reached by air, overland from Israel, Syria, Iraq or Saudi Arabia and by sea from Egypt.

## AIR
The Queen Alia International Airport in Amman is a modern facility and there are regular connections to Europe, the Middle East and Asia.

Royal Jordanian, the country's flag carrier, is a cheap airline and flies to places such as Europe, the US, Thailand and Singapore.

There is a JD3 departure tax on all international flights.

Alia: The Royal Jordanian Airline

## From Australia
There are no direct connections between Australia and Jordan but Student Travel offers a fare of A$1430 return and A$880 one-way from the east coast with British Airways.

The full economy fare quoted by Royal Jordanian is A$3740 return and A$1870 one-way.

## From Europe
Discount fares are big business in London and you can get some of the best deals to just about anywhere. Bucket shops dealing in these tickets abound and a hunt around a few of them will give you an idea of what's available. Two of the more reliable ones are *STA*, 74 Old Brompton Rd, London SW7; and *Trailfinders* at 46 Earls Court Rd, London W8.

Typical fares to Amman are £580 return and £215 one-way with Aeroflot.

Athens is another good discount centre and Royal Jordanian fly direct four times a week.

## From the USA
The cheapest way from the US to the Middle East is a return flight to London and a bucket-shop deal from there.

Royal Jordanian fly direct from both Los Angeles and New York. The full economy fare from the west coast is US$1492 one-way and US$2984 return.

## From Asia
Singapore, Penang, Bangkok and Hong Kong are all good places to look for cheap fares but as Jordan is a bit off the beaten track, there is not much discounting on these routes.

Aeroflot offers a fare of S$850 one-way and S$1700 return from Singapore to Amman via Moscow.

Royal Jordanian fly to Singapore, Bangkok and New Delhi. The economy fare from New Delhi to Amman is Rs 5222 one-way and Rs 10,444 return.

From Pakistan there are flights with PIA and the fare is Rs 6545 one-way and Rs 13,090 return.

## From North Africa
There are regular flights with Royal Jordanian between Amman and Cairo and Tunis.

Unless you are really pushed for time, the route through the Sinai and then ferry to Aqaba is a more interesting (and cheaper) alternative than flying from Cairo.

## OVERLAND
### To/From Syria
**Bus** The only border crossing between Syria and Jordan is at Ramtha/Der'a and as the traffic is heavy it gets extremely crowded during the day.

Twice a day air-conditioned JETT

buses (Jordan Express Tourism Transport), the government-owned bus company, run between Amman and Damascus. The afternoon bus is actually the Syrian Karnak bus returning to Damascus. The trip takes about seven hours depending on the border crossing and is the easiest way to make the crossing. It costs JD3 from Amman, S£75 from Damascus and you need to book 48 hours in advance as demand often exceeds supply.

It is also possible to cross this border with a combination of local bus, walking and hitching. See the Irbid (Jordan) and Der'a (Syria) sections for details of this crossing.

**Service-taxi** The *servees* are slightly faster than the buses and run at all hours. However, they usually get a far more thorough search at the border so you often save no time at all. They leave from around the Abdali bus station in Amman, or from next to the Karnak station in Damascus; JD4 or S£100. They also operate between Damascus and Irbid in northern Jordan for the same price.

**Car & Motorbike** It's no problem bringing your own vehicle to Jordan. Fuel is readily available everywhere and the quality is good although some stations may not stock super.

### To/From Iraq

**Bus** The border between Jordan and Iraq is open but it is almost impossible to get a tourist visa for Iraq. Unless you're going there to work, they'll give you the knock back.

If you do have a visa however, there are daily direct JETT buses between Amman and Baghdad. They cost JD10, depart at 6 pm and take 16 hours.

**Service-taxi** The *servees* are faster but over a long distance the bus is probably more comfortable. Book at the offices either side of the Abdali bus station in Amman.

### To/From Saudi Arabia

There are no direct connections to Saudi Arabia – it's a matter of doing it in stages on local transport, that is of course if you can get a visa. These are notoriously difficult to get and the only visas dished out to tourists are transit visas which allow you to travel along the Tapline (Trans Arabia Pipeline) in three days. The entry to Saudi for this route is from Azraq, 90 km south-east of Amman.

### To/From Israel & the West Bank

**West Bank Permit** This is one of the crazier results of international conflict. The Jordanians insist (quite rightly) that in going to the West Bank you are not leaving Jordan so they don't stamp you out of the country but give you a permit. The Israelis on the other hand reckon that by entering the West Bank you are entering Israeli territory and will stamp you in (on a loose sheet if you ask for it), so theoretically you are in two countries at once!

So, first of all, if you are travelling from Jordan to the West Bank, you need a permit from the Ministry of Interior in Amman. They take about three days to issue so get things moving as soon as you get to Amman if you don't want to be held up. As you don't have to leave your passport, you can travel around for a while and come back to collect the permit.

Go to the Ministry of Interior armed with a pen, a passport photograph and a 50 fils revenue stamp, available from the post office or outside the Ministry. *Don't* ask for a permit to visit Israel or tell them that you intend going further into the West Bank. You then fill in a couple of forms, hand them in and get told when to collect your permit. This is usually only a couple of days but it may take longer. Collecting the permit is a little more complicated as you have to go to room A for this then room B for a signature then room C for another signature and so on. The whole process takes an hour or so.

The permit allows you a one-month stay on the West Bank. Of course, once you are across the King Hussein Bridge, as far as the Israelis are concerned you are in Israel and are free to travel anywhere around the country. You can return to Jordan within the month as long as your Jordanian visa is still valid and your passport hasn't got an Israeli stamp in it. Even if you don't intend returning to Jordan, make sure you ask for the stamp on a separate sheet of paper when you cross the bridge as Israeli stamps are bad news when travelling in the Arab world.

Despite the fact that entry into Jordan is prohibited if there's any evidence of a visit to Israel in your passport, it is possible to cross from Israel. To do this you must have a Jordanian visa before you get to Israel because for obvious reasons they are not available there. Once across the bridge you cannot go back to Israel and must leave Jordan by another route.

**King Hussein (Allenby) Bridge** The King Hussein Bridge is the only place where people can cross the Jordan River and is only open until 1 pm Sunday to Thursday, until 11 am on Fridays and is closed altogether on Saturday (the Jewish *shabbat* – Sabbath). JETT buses are the only vehicles allowed to take passengers across the bridge and there's a terminal on either side. It's not possible to walk, hitch or take a private vehicle across.

If you're coming from Amman on a JETT bus, you get taken to the foreigners' terminal where your permit is stamped and then the minibus continues to the bridge for another permit check. The bridge itself is small and narrow and only about 30 metres long, which is a bit of a disappointment if you're expecting something large and imposing. Once across the bridge there are two Israeli passport checks before you arrive at the immigration terminal on the West Bank. Here everything is super-efficient and the Israeli officials are very polite and very thorough. There are moneychanging facilities and you have to pay a tax of JD2.500 to enter Israel. From the West

Bank terminal, share taxis (*sheruts*) run to Jericho, Jerusalem and other places on the West Bank.

If you leave Amman by service-taxi, it works out costing exactly the same but takes longer and is more of a hassle. The taxis stop at the service-taxi terminal on the East Bank where everyone is unloaded, permits checked and then everyone is loaded back on to JETT buses. It's fairly well organised but takes time, so if you choose to go this way, leave Amman early – the last bus leaves from the terminal at 11 am.

**Note** It is important to note that with the sometimes unstable political climate, the slightest disturbance on either side can see the bridge close without notice for days on end. When this happens, no-one seems to know when it is likely to re-open so you just have to sit it out.

**Bus** From Amman, there is one JETT bus daily except Saturday at 6.30 am which costs JD2.500. This takes you right to the terminal on the other side of the bridge. On a good day you can be in Jerusalem by 10 am.

**Service-taxi** Going by *servees* is not going to save you a cracker but if you want to be with the locals it's the way to go. Taxis leave Abdali station in Amman up until about 9.30 am and cost JD1. When they drop you at the terminal, a further charge of JD1.500 is made for the ride across the bridge.

## SEA
### To/From Egypt
There are car ferries from Aqaba to Nuweiba in Sinai and to Suez. The ferry terminal is a few km south of Aqaba; JD1 for a taxi.

To Suez they run every second day at 11 am and take 15 hours. The fare is JD17 in a dormitory, JD20 for a Pullman seat, JD22 tourist class and JD27 1st class. It's also possible to take a JETT bus from

Aqaba to Cairo. This service uses the Nuweiba ferry and takes 15 hours; the cost is JD15 which includes the price of the ferry.

The Nuweiba service started up in April '85 and has proved very popular. There are two sailings daily from Aqaba, at 12 noon and 4 pm. The trip takes three hours and costs JD7.500. One of the boats is Egyptian, the other Jordanian and both are staffed by Filipinos. From Nuweiba tickets cost E£25. The port at Nuweiba is totally unprotected from southerly winds which is no problem for about 350 days of the year when the winds come from the north. On days when a southerly is blowing it's possible that the ferry will have to wait offshore until the wind subsides. This can take several hours and occasionally even overnight.

Tickets for both ferry services can be bought on the day of departure from any of the travel agents along the waterfront in Aqaba. There is also an Egyptian Consulate in Aqaba and visas are issued on the spot. It's a lot easier than doing battle at the crowded consulate in Amman.

# Getting Around

## AIR

Being such a small country there is hardly any need for an internal air network. The only available route is between Amman and Aqaba.

Royal Jordanian, the country's flag carrier, flies nine times a week between the two cities. The fare is JD13 one-way and JD18 return; the flight takes only 45 minutes.

## ROAD
### JETT Bus

The enormous blue and white buses belonging to the JETT bus company run on limited routes within the country and run charter tours.

Between Amman and Aqaba there are five services daily. The trip takes five hours and costs JD3.

The only other destinations are the King Hussein Bridge (6.30 am, JD2.500) for the West Bank, and Petra. The trip to Petra is mainly for those who want to see it in a day-trip from Amman, which is far too short a time to appreciate it. The round-trip costs JD13 – a real tourist rip-off. This price includes lunch at the Government Rest House in Petra and admission to the site. To take the bus just one-way is still JD6.

### Bus/Minibus

Large private buses, usually air-conditioned, run north from Amman to Irbid (700 fils) and south to Aqaba (JD2.500).

All smaller towns are connected by 20-seater minibuses. These operate infrequently and leave when full. Trying to establish the correct fare can be difficult – ask the other passengers what they are paying. If you pick up a bus in between two towns, you have to pay the full fare from one to the other even though it may be over half-way when you pick it up.

Always establish the fare before taking the ride or you may be taken for a ride.

### Service-taxi

By far the most popular mode of transport is the *servees*. These are usually Peugeot 504 station wagons with seven seats or Mercedes sedans with five seats.

They operate on all routes and because of the limited number of seats, it usually doesn't take long for one to fill up. They cost about 50% more than the minibuses but are much faster as they rarely stop along the way to pick up or set down passengers.

### Hire Car

Most things in Jordan are expensive and hire cars are no exception. If there are four or more of you to split the cost, it can be a good way of seeing a bit of the country, especially the desert castles in the east which are not serviced by public transport.

There are a dozen or more rental agencies in Amman and a couple in Aqaba. The smaller concerns are a lot cheaper than the international crowds like Budget and Avis. See the Amman and Aqaba sections for details.

A small car with unlimited km can be found for JD11 per day with a minimum rental period of three days. Limited-km deals work out much more expensive if you're going to be doing more than 75 km per day. They cost from JD6 per day plus 36 fils for every km over 75.

### Hitching

Hitching is definitely feasible in Jordan. The traffic varies a lot from place to place but you generally don't have to wait long for a lift.

A lot of drivers will pick someone up as a way of subsidising their own trip. If you want to avoid a possibly unpleasant

133

situation when you get out, ask beforehand if payment is expected and if so, establish how much they want. If you're not prepared to pay at all, it's still possible to get around but you may have to knock back three or four lifts before you find a freebie.

Make sure you have a hat and some water to fight the heat if you have to wait a while for a lift. Hassles when hitching are rare but lone women should definitely not hitch and even one single male traveller wrote in to warn about the truck drivers who may have 'designs on your body'.

## TRAIN

There is a railway line from the Syrian border in the north to the Saudi border in the south. This is the Hejaz railway line built early this century to take the pilgrims from Damascus to Mecca but at present there are no scheduled passenger services along it.

Goods trains use the Hejaz line and the new line built to take the phosphate from Hasa to Aqaba and it may be possible to hitch a ride on one of these.

## LOCAL TRANSPORT
### Bus

Amman has an efficient and cheap public bus network but none of the buses have either the destination or the number in English so unless you can read Arabic or know which one to catch, their usefulness is limited.

### Service-taxi

Amman is also well served by *servees* and these are by far the best way of getting around. They too have nothing in English but are a lot easier to track down than the buses.

Irbid also has a couple of service-taxi routes.

### Taxi

In all other places you'll have to walk, which poses no problems, or take one of the many regular taxis. These are metered and the drivers usually speak a fair amount of English, especially in Amman. Late at night they will probably charge more than is shown on the meter.

## TOURS

The only scheduled tour is operated by JETT to Petra. This tour is really only for those who have limited time in Amman and want to see something of Petra. The drive takes three hours each way which doesn't leave much time for sight-seeing.

It costs JD13 for the round-trip including lunch and entry to the site and leaves Amman daily at 6.30 am.

Any travel agent in Amman should be able to organise longer trips if you want to do it that way.

# Amman

Amman is certainly never going to win any prizes for being the most interesting city in the world and in fact has very few attractions. The downtown area is a busy, noisy, chaotic jumble of traffic – both human and motorised – and just crossing the street on foot successfully is a major achievement. Nevertheless, Amman is the hub of all roads in Jordan so it's highly unlikely that a visitor to Jordan will not pass through it.

Amman has grown incredibly in recent years and now sprawls over a large area. Standing on top of one of the 13 or so *jebels* (hills) that the city is built on and surveying the scene, it's easy to get the impression that the sprawl is nothing more than thousands of concrete blocks with very little greenery to break up the glaring monotony.

Unfortunately modern Middle-Eastern, low-budget architecture is extremely boring and Amman is no exception. Most houses and buildings are built with the same materials from about half a dozen different designs, so most buildings look remarkably alike.

Having condemned Amman in that respect, it must also be said that it's one of the friendliest cities you're likely to visit. Most of the residents are Palestinians who fled from west of the Jordan during the wars of 1948 and 1967 and settled in Amman. They are generally well educated, friendly, speak a fair amount of English and are eager to chat with a foreigner. In almost every encounter a Jordanian will say to you 'Welcome in Jordan', and you get the feeling that they really mean it.

The shops in downtown Amman are full of Western goods – from cameras to cuddly toys – and if it wasn't for the chaotic traffic and the wailing of the *muezzin* from the mosques, you could almost be somewhere in Europe.

## History

Excavations in and around Amman have turned up finds from as early as 3500 BC. Occupation of the town, called Rabbath Ammon in the Old Testament, has been continuous and objects found in a tomb dating back to the Bronze Age show that the town was actively involved in trade with Greece, Syria, Cyprus and Mesopotamia.

Biblical references are many and reveal that by 1200 BC Rabbath Ammon was the capital of the Ammonites. During David's reign, he sent Joab at the head of the Israelite armies to besiege Rabbath, after having been insulted by the Ammonite king Nahash.

It seems David was not the most benevolent of rulers. After taking Rabbath he burnt the inhabitants alive in the brick kiln (II Samuel 12), and before the town had been taken he sent Uriah the Hittite 'in the forefront of the hottest battle' (II Samuel 11) where he was bound to be killed, simply because David had taken a liking to Uriah's wife Bethsheba.

The town continued to flourish and supplied David with weapons in his ongoing wars and his successor, Solomon, erected a shrine in Jerusalem to the Ammonite god Molech. From here on, the only Biblical references to Rabbath are prophecies of its destruction at the hands of the Babylonians, who did in fact take over but did not destroy the town.

The history of Amman between then (*circa* 585 BC) and the time of the Ptolemies of Egypt is unclear. Ptolemy Philadelphus (283-246 BC) rebuilt the city during his reign and it was named Philadelphia after him. After brief occupation by the Nabataeans, it was taken by the Romans under Herod around 30 BC. The city was totally replanned and rebuilt in typically grand Roman style.

At the time of the Arab invasion in the

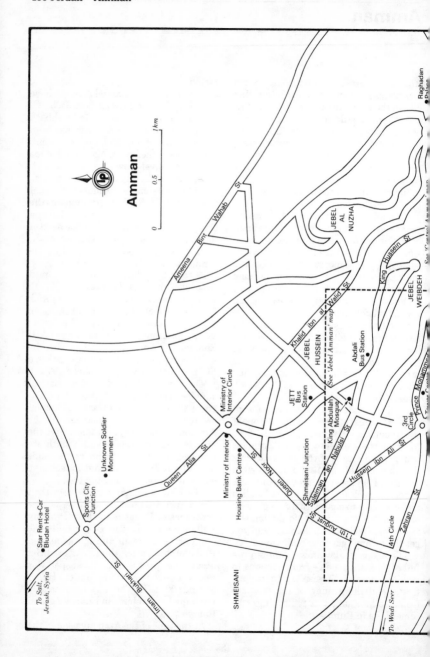

Amman

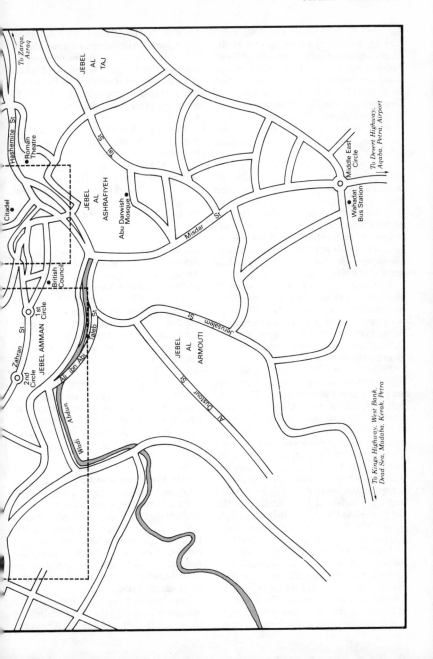

7th century, the town was still alive and kicking, and living on the caravan trade. Its fortunes gradually declined and it was nothing more than a sad little village when a colony of Circassians was resettled here in 1878. It became the centre of Transjordan when Emir Abdullah made it his headquarters in the early 1920s.

Since then it has gone ahead in leaps and bounds to become a modern bustling city.

### Orientation

Amman is built on seven major *jebels* and it can be mighty confusing to begin with. The downtown area is at the bottom of four of these hills, which means that wherever you want to go from there is up, and these hills are steep! The centre of downtown is the area immediately around the King Hussein Mosque.

The only way to make any sense of Amman in a short time is to pick out the major landmarks on the *jebels*. There are no street signs and each street seems to have about three different names anyway. Asking someone for directions to a street is generally useless.

From the citadel on top of Jebel al Qalaa you can get a view of the surrounds and try and get your bearings. The main hill is Jebel Amman, where you'll find most of the embassies and flash hotels. The traffic roundabouts on Jebel Amman are numbered as you leave the downtown area, so you go from 1st circle up to 7th circle and beyond. Just to confuse matters, 4th circle is not a circle at all but a regular junction with traffic lights. The main landmark on Jebel Amman is the Jordan Tower Centre just below 3rd circle – it's the high, circular white tower topped by a 'crown'.

Jebel Hussein is the next one to identify as there are two major bus stations here and also the Ministry of Interior for West Bank permits. It's north-west of the citadel and the Housing Bank Centre sticks out a mile – it's the tall, terraced building with the creepers hanging down

the sides and the illuminated Alia sign on top. Closer to the downtown area, also on Jebel Hussein, is the big blue dome of the spanking new King Abdullah Mosque. It's also easy to identify as it's the only building that is not grey or white! Close to the mosque are the Abdali and JETT bus stations.

To the south of citadel hill is Jebel Al Ashrafiyeh. It's the tallest and steepest of the *jebels* and has the curious Abu Darwish Mosque on the top, built in alternating layers of black and white stone. To get to the top for an excellent view, take a No 26 service-taxi from behind the Church of the Saviour.

### Information

**Tourist Office** There's no tourist office in Amman but you can go to the Ministry of Antiquities & Tourism (tel 642311) just up from 3rd circle. They have a few glossy brochures, a good map of Jordan and another of Amman. Unless you want a few free wall posters, it's not really worth the effort. To get there, catch a No 3 service-taxi and get out just after 3rd circle; the ministry is one block over to the left.

*Your Guide to Amman* is a free monthly booklet which lists embassies, airlines, travel agents, rent-a-car companies and has other useful and not-so-useful information. Pick up a copy at the tourist office or any of the airlines or travel agents.

**Post & Telecommunications** The main post office in Amman is very handily located right in the downtown area on Prince Mohammed St. The poste restante mail is kept in a box on the counter and you can look through the lot. Bulky mail and large envelopes are kept on the other side of the counter so ask to look through those as well. The office is open from 8 am to 6 pm daily except Friday.

The main office for international telephone calls is in the street up behind the post office, opposite the Al Khayyam

Cinema. It's open from 7 am to 11 pm and the staff are helpful. International connections can take up to half an hour and the costs are high: JD1.750 per minute to the US and Australia, JD1.250 to Europe, and there's a minimum of three minutes. For directory assistance for local calls, ring 640444.

The parcel post office is in the same street as the telephone office, down near the corner of Prince Mohammed St. It looks more like a shop-front than a post office. It is right opposite a rear entrance to the main post office. Posting a parcel is time consuming but simple enough. Take the parcel *unwrapped* to the customs office on the 1st floor of the main post office, after a perfunctory search they clear it and direct you to the parcel office where it gets weighed and you pack it. Parcels will not be sent unless they're wrapped in cotton, which you can buy for a few hundred fils in any fabric shop. The office is open from 8 am to 1 pm.

**Money** There are moneychangers all over the downtown area as well as numerous foreign and local banks. The rates vary so check them out before changing. If you want to get money on a Visa card, the Petra Bank is the agent. Banks are open from 9.30 am to 12.30 pm; moneychangers open from 10 am to 2 pm and 4 to 8 pm. There's a branch of the Arab Bank at the airport which is open from 8 am to 8 pm.

The American Express agent is International Traders (tel 661014) but the office is out in the swish suburb of Shmeisani and is not on any public transport route – you'll have to take a taxi. The office is open from 8 am to 12 noon and 3 to 6 pm daily except Friday.

**Immigration** For a visa extension you need to go to the Department of Foreigners (*sho-orn ajaneb*) in Suleiman al Nabulsi St. It's right on the No 7 service-taxi route up near the blue King Abdullah Mosque. Extensions are for two months, take two minutes to issue and are free.

**Permits & Visas** If you want to stay in Petra overnight, officially you need a permit issued by the Department of Antiquities. In practice it's quite easy to stay overnight without the permit, or you can get it in Petra itself. To get one in Amman, contact the Antiquities office on Zahran St above 3rd circle, almost opposite Zahran Palace, the home of King Hussein's mother.

The Ministry of Interior for West Bank permits is at the roundabout known as Ministry of Interior circle, although this circle is in the process of being 'upgraded' so all the roads to it may be closed. Take a service-taxi No 6 from Cinema Al Hussein St and get off near the Housing Bank Centre.

The Syrian embassy is past 3rd circle in a side street off to the right. Take a *servees* No 3 and get out at the Ministry of Foreign Affairs. Visas are issued the same day and a one-month tourist visa costs JD1.750. You need two passport photos, and a letter of introduction from your embassy, preferably stating your profession. Any mention of being a journalist or writer is a guarantee of hassles in Syria. Applications are accepted from 8.30 am to 11 am and you pick up the visa at 1 pm the same day.

The Egyptian consulate is just off Zahran St above 1st circle. It can be a real shitfight here. Try and catch the attention of one of the officials who will then lead you through the hordes and take care of your application. Unless you really need to get it here, the consulate in Aqaba is much quieter and easier to deal with.

**Embassies** Addresses of some of the embassies in Amman include:

Australia
    4th circle, Jebel Amman, tel 673246
Canada
    Shmeisani, tel 666124
France
    Jebel Amman, tel 641273
Germany
    Jebel Amman, tel 641351

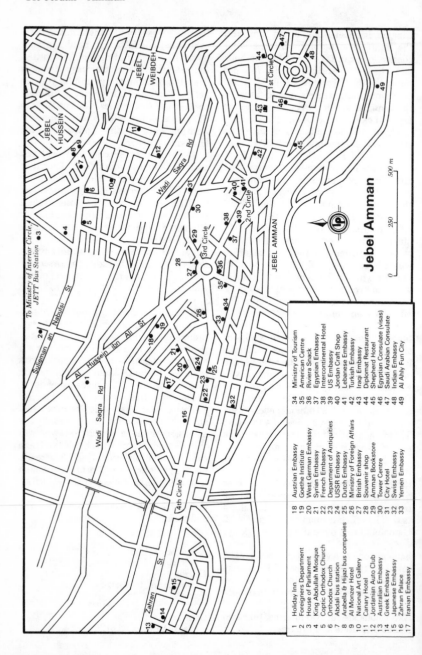

Jebel Amman

0    250    500 m

1 Holiday Inn
2 Foreigners Department
3 House of Parliament
4 King Abdullah Mosque
5 Coptic Orthodox Church
6 Orthodox Church
7 Abdali bus station
8 Arabella & Hijazi bus companies
9 Al Monzer Hotel
10 National Art Gallery
11 Canary Hotel
12 Jordanian Auto Club
13 Australian Embassy
14 Greek Embassy
15 Japanese Embassy
16 Zahran Palace
17 Iranian Embassy

18 Austrian Embassy
19 Goethe Institute
20 West German Embassy
21 Syrian Embassy
22 French Embassy
23 Coptic Orthodox Church
24 USSR Embassy
25 Dutch Embassy
26 Ministry of Foreign Affairs
27 British Embassy
28 Souvenir shop
29 Amman Bookstore
30 Tower Centre
31 City Hotel
32 Swiss Embassy
33 Yemen Embassy

34 Ministry of Tourism
35 American Centre
36 Riviera Snack
37 Egyptian Embassy
38 Intercontinental Hotel
39 US Embassy
40 Jordan Craft Shop
41 Lebanese Embassy
42 Turkish Embassy
43 Iraqi Embassy
44 Diplomat Restaurant
45 Shepherd Hotel
46 Egyptian Consulate (visas)
47 Saudi Arabian Consulate
48 Indian Embassy
49 Al Ahly Fun City

Iraq
    Zahran St, 1st circle, Jebel Amman, tel 639331
Japan
    4th circle, Jebel Amman, tel 642486
Saudi Arabia
    1st circle, Jebel Amman, tel 814154
Syria
    3rd circle, Jebel Amman, tel 641076
United Kingdom
    3rd circle, Jebel Amman, tel 641261
USA
    Zahran St, Jebel Amman, tel 644371

**Bookshops & Libraries** There are three bookshops in Amman worth mentioning. The Jordan Distribution Agency is the best and is closest to downtown. They have a wide range of books on the Middle East as well as a fair stock of international magazines and newspapers. It's on the main street from the post office up to 1st circle. The University Bookshop, at the small roundabout on Jebel Weibdeh, and the Amman Bookshop, in the tower centre just below 3rd circle, have a similar but smaller range.

The British Council (tel 636147) on Zahran St, Jebel Amman east of 1st circle, has a good library, current newspapers and on Monday nights they show free feature films. The library is open from 8.30 am to 1.30 pm and 4 to 6 pm Saturday to Thursday.

The American Cultural Centre (tel 641520) also has a library and newspapers and is a good place to escape the heat for an hour or so. It's just across the far side of 3rd circle and is open Sunday to Thursday from 8 am to 5 pm. On Monday and Tuesday it stays open to 7 pm.

The French Cultural Centre (tel 637009) is by the roundabout at the top of Jebel Weibdeh, the hill directly behind the post office. It is open 9 am to 1 pm and 3 to 6.30 pm daily, except Friday and Sunday.

**Hash House Harriers** If you want to meet a few of the local expatriates, the Hash House Harriers is a social jogging club where the emphasis is on the social side of things rather than the jogging. They meet every Monday night at 6 pm and after a short run there's a barbecue and drinks. Men pay JD2.500 and women JD2, which pays for the barbecue and copious quantities of Amstel beer. To find out where it's on, ask someone at the British embassy or British Council.

**Airlines** Addresses of the airlines that fly to and from Jordan include:

Royal Jordanian
    King Hussein St, tel 639351
Aeroflot
    Intercontinental Hotel, Jebel Amman, tel 641510
British Airways
    Intercontinental Hotel, Jebel Amman, tel 641430
Egypt Air
    Zaatarah & Co, King Hussein St, tel 630011
KLM
    King Hussein St, tel 622175
Middle East Airlines
    King Hussein St, tel 636104
Saudia
    King Hussein St, tel 639333
Syrian Arab Airlines
    tel 622147

**Shopping** Right by 2nd circle is the Jordan Craft Shop (tel 644555). It looks like a normal house but has some excellent hand made articles for sale. Prices are high but this is quality stuff, a lot of it made by Palestinian refugees. There's another good souvenir shop right next door to the British embassy.

**Roman Theatre**
The restored Roman theatre, five minutes walk east of downtown, is really the only surviving remnant of the Roman city of Philadelphia. It was cut into the side of the hill and can seat 6000 people. In recent years it has once again become a place of entertainment, and productions are put on at irregular intervals. Just in front of the theatre are the remains of a

colonnaded square and various other buildings, but these are of little interest. Entrance is free but you will probably be accosted by a guide trying to rope you into shelling out a dinar to have him show you around.

## Citadel

Nothing much remains of the citadel on top of the hill; it's just a bare rectangular area with the ruins of a few buildings, notably a Byzantine church and a castle built by the Omayyeds. The Romans actually fortified an ancient fortress already on the site and surrounded it with a protective wall. There was also a temple dedicated to Hercules dating from the time of the Emperor Marcus Aurelius (161-180 AD). On the northern slope of the citadel is an enormous water cistern cut into the rock.

## Museums

**Folklore Museum** This is one of two small museums housed in the wings of the Roman theatre. The Folklore Museum is in the right wing of the theatre and houses a collection of items showing the traditional life of the local people – a Bedouin tent complete with all the tools and utensils, musical instruments, woven rugs and a camel saddle. It's open from Sunday to Thursday from 9 am to 5 pm, closed Tuesday and Friday. Entry is 250 fils.

**Museum of Popular Traditions** This is in the left wing of the Roman theatre and has well-presented displays of traditional costumes, jewellery and utensils, and a section of mosaics from Madaba. It is open the same hours as the Folklore Museum but entry is 150 fils.

**Archaeological Museum** On the southern edge of Jebel Qalaat is the Archaeological Museum, from where you get a great view of the Roman theatre and backyards full of washing and assorted debris. The museum itself is small but has quite a

good collection of ancient bric-a-brac ranging from 6000-year-old skulls from Jericho to artwork from the Omayyed period. It's open from 9 am to 4 pm daily except Tuesday and Friday; entry is 250 fils.

## Places to Stay – bottom end

The downtown area is thick with cheap hotels. Along King Faisal St practically every building is a hotel. Most of these places have shops on the ground floor, a tea shop on the 2nd and then rooms on the 3rd and 4th. They are nearly all noisy as hell, the din from the street is penetrating and seems to be worse on the upper floors. Try to get a room at the back.

The *Bader Hotel* (tel 637602) is one of the better ones and is only 50 metres from the post office. It's set back slightly from the street and the entrance is along an alleyway with a small restaurant that spills onto the footpath. The rooms are generally clean, have a fan, bath and hot water. The charges are set at JD2.200/3.500/4.500 for singles/doubles/triples but they may try for more. It has a fridge where you can store any food you have. Nabir, the young son of the owner, is helpful and speaks a little English. You can store small amounts of luggage here for free. A good place.

Opposite the Bader is the *Cliff Hotel* (tel 623795) which is also clean and friendly. The entrance is through the side alley. Small rooms on the roof are JD1 per person, but you'll need to bargain. These rooms are stifling in summer but you can put the beds out in the open air. For a bed in a triple room you pay JD1.250, which is standard charge for beds in a lot of the downtown cheapies. There is a good TV lounge in the reception area. Next door is the *Vinici Hotel* which has similar prices but is not as friendly.

Another in this category of cheapies is the *Baghdad Grand Hotel* which is only about 30 metres down from the Cliff Hotel. It's far from grand but is quite OK. Beds in a share-room cost JD1.250,

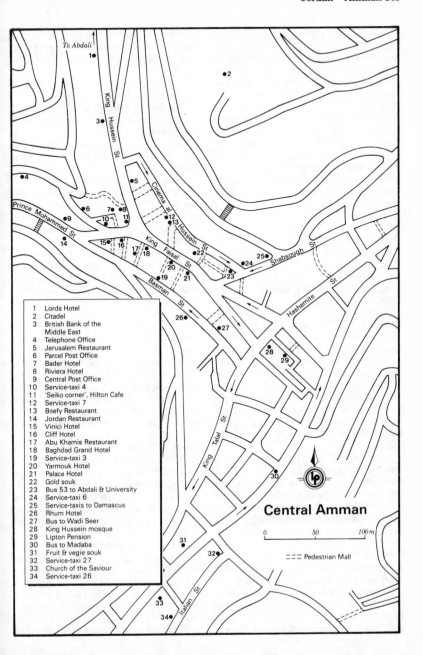

1 Lords Hotel
2 Citadel
3 British Bank of the
   Middle East
4 Telephone Office
5 Jerusalem Restaurant
6 Parcel Post Office
7 Bader Hotel
8 Riviera Hotel
9 Central Post Office
10 Service-taxi 4
11 'Seiko corner', Hilton Cafe
12 Service-taxi 7
13 Beefy Restaurant
14 Jordan Restaurant
15 Vinici Hotel
16 Cliff Hotel
17 Abu Khamis Restaurant
18 Baghdad Grand Hotel
19 Service-taxi 3
20 Yarmouk Hotel
21 Palace Hotel
22 Gold souk
23 Bus 53 to Abdali & University
24 Service-taxi 6
25 Service-taxis to Damascus
26 Rhum Hotel
27 Bus to Wadi Seer
28 King Hussein mosque
29 Lipton Pension
30 Bus to Madaba
31 Fruit & vegie souk
32 Service-taxi 27
33 Church of the Saviour
34 Service-taxi 26

**Central Amman**

0          50          100 m

= = = Pedestrian Mall

doubles/triples with fan cost JD2.500/3.500. The tea shop on the 1st floor is a very friendly place. The manager is always smiling and the regular clients are mostly Palestinians from Hebron. You can sit on small balconies overlooking the street.

The *Lords Hotel* on King Hussein St is big and cavernous and a bit gloomy but this does help to keep it cool in summer. Quiet rooms at the back cost JD2/3.500 for singles/doubles with fan and hot water. It is centrally heated in winter and even has room service. This is a good place to head for if you're after a bit of privacy.

### Places to Stay - middle

For something a bit better, the *Rhum Hotel* (tel 623162) on Basman St has decent rooms with bath and fan. The rates are surprisingly cheap at JD2.500/3.500 for singles/doubles.

The *Lipton Pension* is right behind the King Hussein Mosque and is the only tall building there. The windows of the rooms are only a stone's throw from the minaret so unless you want an early-morning call, forget this place. It's overpriced anyway at JD4/6.500 for singles/doubles.

For a bit of three-star comfort, try the *City Hotel* on the road up to 3rd circle from downtown. The rooms have fan and bath and cost JD6.600/8.800 for singles/doubles.

Another good one in this category is the *Canary Hotel* (tel 638353) on Jebel Weibdeh opposite the Terra Sancta College. This is about the cheapest of the air-conditioned places and rooms cost JD4.950/JD7.700 for singles/doubles with bath.

### Places to Stay - top end

Amman also has its share of five-star international hotels. The closest to downtown is the *Jordan Intercontinental* (tel 641361) on Zahran St mid-way between 2nd and 3rd circles, right opposite the American Embassy. Others include the *Amra* (tel 815071) at 6th circle, the *Regency Palace* (tel 660000) in Shmeisani and the *Holiday Inn* (tel 663185).

### Places to Eat

**Cheap Eats** If you're on a fairly tight budget, all you'll be eating in Amman is felafel and shawarma as the restaurant prices are over the top and you are paying more for where you eat rather than what you eat.

Breakfast is easy. Right by the Cliff Hotel is a couple of alleys with small shops that sell yoghurt, milk, fruit, butter, bread and all sorts of cheeses. Stock up with goodies and put your own breakfast together.

In the alley that leads to the Bader Hotel is a good cheap restaurant for felafel, hummus and fuul. A filling meal with bread and tea is only about 300 fils. Just around the corner in King Hussein St are three shawarma stalls next to each other. The price of a shawarma is set by the government at 170 fils and a couple of these make a reasonable lunch.

In the same lane as the Baghdad Grand Hotel is a good place called the *Abu Khamis & Abu Saleh Restaurant*. There is no sign in English but it's a big place with a chicken-roasting oven out the front. They have a good range including chicken (600 fils for half), stuffed green peppers (320 fils), excellent potato chips (140 fils), a variety of meat and vegetable stews (300 fils), rice (120 fils) as well as salads, hummus and bread.

The *Jerusalem Restaurant* on King Hussein St is another good place, again with no sign in English. The front window is full of sweets and pastries. The best dish here is the traditional *mensaf* – boiled lamb on a bed of rice with pine nuts and a delicious cooked yoghurt sauce. It's not cheap at JD1.100 but it is excellent. For dessert try *mahalabiya wa festa* – a milk pudding with crushed pistachio nuts for 250 fils.

Just off Cinema Al Hussein St is the

*Beefy* café, a fast-food-type place with decent hamburgers and chips. There's nowhere to sit so you stand up at the counter or take away. A burger with cheese and egg is 400 fils. Another burger place is *Riviera Snack* up at 3rd circle. The food isn't as good but you can sit outside and watch the traffic roar by; 330 fils for a burger and they also have good draught beer.

**Other Restaurants** For a meal with a view, try the restaurant on the 23rd floor of the *Jordan Towers* building, just below 3rd circle. It's worth the trip just for the view. Soups are JD1 to JD2; main courses JD2 to JD4 or you can just sit in the bar where a can of Amstel will set you back a cool JD1.100.

On the ground level of the towers building is the *Chicken Tikka Inn* with good curries for around JD1.500, soups 500 fils. It's open from 12 noon to 4 pm and 6.30 to 11 pm.

Right on 1st circle, the *Diplomat Restaurant* has a good range of dishes for JD1 to JD3. It's open until quite late and they have tables on the footpath where you can sip on a beer.

Some of the tea shops downtown make good places to sit and write letters, meet the locals or read. The *Hilton Cafe* is right on 'Seiko Corner', above the Seiko sign at the corner of King Hussein St and King Faisal St. You get a good view from here and they serve hot and cold drinks. The entrance is just up King Hussein St. The café on the 1st floor of the Baghdad Grand Hotel is another good one.

**Getting There**

**Air** The only internal route is from Aqaba; nine flights per week with Royal Jordanian, JD13 one-way, JD18 return.

There's a departure tax of JD3 for international flights.

**JETT Bus** The JETT bus office/terminal is on King Hussein St, about 500 metres past the Abdali station. If you arrive from

Syria on a Karnak bus, this is where you'll end up. To get downtown take a No 6 service-taxi (70 fils) heading downhill and ride it to the end. It drops you in Cinema Al Hussein St right in the centre. If you want to walk it takes about 30 minutes, or a normal yellow taxi costs about 400 fils. Tickets for the buses should be booked two days in advance.

There's one bus daily to the King Hussein Bridge for the West Bank at 6 am; JD2.500. See the Jordan Getting There section for more details.

Buses for Damascus leave at 7 am and 3 pm (JD3), and there's a daily bus to Petra at 6.30 am for JD6!

The No 6 service-taxis start running at about 5.30 am so you can catch one from downtown for any of these early-morning departures.

**Bus/minibus** There are two bus stations in Amman; Abdali for transport north and west, and Wahadat for buses south.

Abdali station is on King Hussein St, about 20 minutes walk (uphill) from downtown. A service-taxi No 6 or 7 from Cinema Al Hussein St goes right by it. Minibuses run to Jerash, Salt and South Shuneh in the Jordan Valley. There's no timetable and they just leave when full. There are also air-conditioned Hijazi and Arabella buses which run to a timetable for the two-hour trip to Irbid (700 fils). Buy tickets from their offices on the northern side of the station.

Wahadat station is way out to the south of town by the traffic roundabout called Middle East Circle. A service-taxi No 27 from downtown near the fruit and vegie *souk* goes to Middle East Circle. This is where all buses heading south leave from. Nothing runs to a schedule so it's just a matter of getting a seat and waiting. Irregular minibus departures for Kerak (750 fils) and Wadi Musa/Petra (JD2). There are also large air-conditioned buses for Aqaba for JD2. Bargain to get the correct fare on these buses as they tend to ask for whatever they think you'll pay.

Local red and white town buses run to Madaba (200 fils) every 20 minutes or so from downtown near the fruit and vegie souk.

**Service-taxi** The *servees* are faster and more convenient than the buses but are more expensive. Because they only carry five or seven people, they fill up a lot faster than the buses and don't stop along the way. They use the same stations as the buses (Abdali and Wahadat).

From Abdali they run to Jerash, Salt, Wadi Seer and the King Hussein Bridge.

From Wahadat there are departures for Kerak (JD1, two hours), Madaba (300 fils, 30 minutes), Wadi Musa (JD2.500, three hours) and Aqaba (JD3, five hours).

With both the buses and *servees* there are many more departures in the morning.

**Hitching** To hitch you need to start out of town. For the King's Highway it's easiest to catch a town bus to Madaba and hitch from there. For the Desert Highway take an airport bus (500 fils) and get off where it turns off the highway.

If you're heading north take a *servees* No 49 from Abdali station to Sweileh which will put you right on the highway.

### Getting Around

**Airport Transport** The Queen Alia International Airport is about 35 km south of the city. Buses make the 45-minute run every half hour from 5.30 am to 8 pm from the Abdali bus station for 500 fils.

**Service-taxi** The local bus system is hard to figure out as nothing is in English so the *servees* are the way to go. They are all white Mercedes of varying vintages with writing on the front doors giving the number and destination, but only in Arabic, so if you're going to use them you'll have to be able to read the numbers. They start from a given point and run along a set route. There's a standard charge of 50 to 70 fils depending on the

route and you pay the full amount regardless of where you get off. Some of the more useful routes are:

No 2 – from Basman St near the Hussein Mosque to 1st and 2nd circle; 60 fils.
No 3 – from Basman St to 3rd and 4th circles; 70 fils.
No 4 – from the side street right near the post office up to Jebel Weibdeh; 60 fils.
No 6 – from Cinema Al Hussein St to Ministry of Interior Circle going past the Abdali and JETT stations; 70 fils.
No 7 – from Cinema Al Hussein St, up King Hussein St past Abdali station and King Abdullah Mosque, and along Suleiman an Nabulsi St.
No 26 – from behind the Church of the Saviour downtown up to the top of Jebel Al Ashrafiyeh at the Abu Darwish Mosque, for a good view; 60 fils.
No 27 – from near the fruit and vegie souk out to Middle East Circle for Wahadat bus station; 70 fils.

**Taxi** Regular taxis are yellow with a green panel on the driver's door. These guys are keen and if you do any walking in Amman you'll get sick and tired of getting honked at as they prowl for fares.

Before getting in, insist that they use the meter and don't stand for any bullshit about having to pay extra for baggage or other extras they may feel inclined to tack on.

Late at night they will often only take you for a negotiated price and nothing will change their minds. When this is the case you just have to know what is a good price and bargain.

**Hire Car** One of the cheapest rent-a-car agencies is Star Rent-a-Car (tel 604904) out by Sports City Junction. The guy there is helpful and willing to do a deal. For unlimited km he charges JD11 per day with a three day minimum. This includes insurance above the first JD50 and he'll deliver the car to you downtown. If you're going to be doing less than 75 km per day, the cheapest agency is Al Jabal (tel 606669) where a brand new car costs JD6 per day plus 36 fils per km after 75 km which includes insurance after the first JD50. Another cheapie is Satellite Rent-a-Car (tel 625767) near the Abdali bus station. They charge JD10 per day plus 36 fils per km.

## AROUND AMMAN
### Salt

The village of Salt, 30 km north-east of Amman, used to be the administrative centre for the area during the time of Ottoman rule. It was passed over as the new capital of Transjordan in favour of the small village of Amman. The result is that Amman has been transformed from small village to modern city while Salt has retained its charm.

There's not really anything special here but if you wander around the town you will see some fine examples of Ottoman architecture. It's a curious sight to see a Turkish house which has had a typically modern, concrete-block upper floor added. The town is the only one in Jordan where you don't get the feeling that it has been thrown together in the last 10 or 15 years. Salt is worth a visit if you have half a day to kill.

**Getting There** A minibus from Abdali costs 150 fils for the 45-minute trip. *Servees* will cost you 270 fils.

From Salt there are also minibuses heading down into the Jordan Valley to South Shuneh.

### Wadi Seer & Araq al-Amir

The narrow fertile valley of Wadi Seer is a real contrast to the bare, treeless plateau of Amman to the east. The ruins of the building of Qasr al-Abid (Castle of the Slave) and the caves, known as Araq al-Amir (Cave of the Prince), are another 10 km down the valley from the village of Wadi Seer.

The caves are up to the right of the road and are in two tiers, the upper one forms a long gallery along the cliff face. The caves were apparently used as stables and that is still their function – the local villagers use them to house their goats and store chaff.

The castle is about 500 metres down the valley and can be seen from the caves. There is still some mystery as to when and why it was built but it is believed that it was built in the 2nd century BC by Hyrcanus of the powerful Jewish Tobiad family. The 1st-century historian, Josephus, in his book *Antiquities of the Jews*, talks of a castle of white stone which was decorated with carvings of 'animals of a prodigious magnitude'.

Today reconstruction of the palace is complete. A lone French archaeologist spent three years making detailed drawings of the fallen stones. He then made cardboard cut-outs of each stone and tried to piece it all together. He has spent a further seven years on the actual reconstruction. The result is a fine monument which, up until now, has been completely ignored by tourists.

The finest part is the north entrance with one of the original carved beasts, an enormous lion, in place over the doorway. The whole place is unique in that it was built out of the largest blocks of any building in the Middle East. The largest measures seven by three metres but as they were only 20 cm or so thick, the whole construction was quite flimsy and the earthquake of 362 AD completely flattened it.

Another unusual sight in this valley are the refugees from Afghanistan who walk around with large sacks on their backs, buying and selling second-hand clothing.

**Getting There** A No 42 bus from Basman St in downtown Amman runs to Wadi Seer regularly. This is one of the few town buses which displays a number, although it is in Arabic. The trip takes an hour and costs 100 fils. Service-taxis from Abdali also run this route.

From Wadi Seer you catch a minibus for 100 fils which will take you right to the end of the road at Araq al-Amir.

Carved lion, Araq al-Amir

It may also be possible to get to Wadi Seer by the old road from Salt.

### Qasr al Mushatta

Qasr al Mushatta is 35 km south of Amman near the airport. It was the biggest and most lavish of all the Omayyed castles but for some unknown reason it was never finished. Today it looks far from grand, especially as the elaborate carving on the facade was stripped and shipped off to a museum in Berlin after the palace was given to Kaiser Wilhelm, just before WW 1, by Sultan Abd al Hamid of Turkey. Some pieces of this are still lying around the site and they give some idea of how it must have once looked.

One unusual feature of the building is that the vaults are made from burnt bricks – an uncommon material in buildings of this style.

This site is kept locked at night, but is opened each day by the soldiers who are part of the airport security and live in a tent close by.

**Getting There** The Qasr al Mushatta is right at the airport and can be visited by public transport. Take an airport bus from Abdali station in Amman. At the airport terminal walk on about 600 metres to the checkpoint and you can see the castle off to the left. If you go by car, turn right at the roundabout by the Alia Gateway Hotel and the road will take you right around the perimeter of the airport to the castle.

# North of Amman

The area to the north of Amman is the most densely populated in Jordan, with the major centres of Irbid and Jerash as well as dozens of small towns dotted in amongst the rugged and relatively fertile hills. In this area lie the ruins of the ancient Decapolis cities of Jerash and Umm Qais (Gadara), and the 12th-century castle of al-Rabad.

North of Irbid, the country flattens out to the plains of Hauran which stretch away to the Syrian border, while to the west lies the Jordan Valley – one of the most fertile patches of land in the Middle East.

## JERASH

Situated some 50 km north of Amman, Jerash is one of Jordan's major attractions, second only to Petra. Lying in the Gilead Hills right on the road that leads to Ramtha and on to Syria, it is the best example in the Middle East of a Roman provincial city and is remarkably well preserved.

The modern town of Jerash, which lies on the east bank of a small tributary of the Zarqa River, has a sizeable population of Circassians who were settled here by the Turkish authorities late last century.

The main ruins of Jerash are on the west of the same stream and were rediscovered in 1806 by a German traveller, Seetzen. Excavations were started in the early 1920s. Prior to that most of the city was buried under sand which accounts for the good condition of many of the buildings.

In its heyday it is estimated that Jerash had a population of around 15,000 and although it wasn't on any of the trade routes, its citizens prospered from the good corn-growing land which surrounds it.

Today the excavations have revealed two theatres, an unusual oval-shaped forum, temples, churches and baths.

Despite its importance as a historical site, with the slump in tourism in the Middle East in the last few years, there's rarely more than a handful of people there at any one time. It's open daily, except Friday, from 9 am to 7 pm and entry is 500 fils.

There's a Visitors Centre with a souvenir shop and post office and a Government Rest House which sells refreshments.

### History

Although there have been finds to indicate that the site was inhabited in Neolithic times, it was from the time of Alexander the Great (332 BC) that the city really rose to prominence.

In 63 BC the Roman emperor Pompey conquered the region and Jerash became part of the Roman province of Syria and soon after became one of the cities of the Decapolis. Over the next two centuries trade was established with the Nabataeans and the city became extremely wealthy. A completely new plan was drawn up in the 1st century AD and it centred on the typical feature of a colonnaded main street intersected by two side streets.

With the emperor Trajan's exploits around 106 BC, which saw the annexation of the Nabataean kingdom and even more wealth finding its way to Jerash, many of these new buildings were torn down to be replaced by even more imposing structures.

In 129 AD, when the emperor Hadrian visited and stayed for some time, the town administration went into top gear again and to mark a visit of such importance, the Triumphal Arch at the southern end of the city was constructed.

Jerash reached its peak in the beginning of the 3rd century when it was bestowed with the rank of Colony, but from then on it went into a slow decline. With the trade caravans now defunct because of the sea trade, the decline continued steadily. The only respite was during the reign of Diocletian (*circa* 300 AD) which saw a minor building boom.

By the middle of the 5th century, Christianity had become the major religion of the region and the construction of churches proceeded at a startling rate. During the reign of Justinian (527-565 AD) no less than seven churches were built, mostly out of stones filched from the earlier pagan temples and shrines.

With the Persian invasion of 614 and the Muslim conquest of 636, followed by a series of earthquakes in 747, Jerash was really on the skids and its population shrunk to about 25% of its former size.

Apart from a brief occupation by a Crusader garrison in the 12th century, the city was completely deserted up until the arrival of the Circassians in 1878.

### The Ruins

When approaching from Amman, the **Triumphal Arch** is first to come into view. Although its present height is daunting, it was twice as high when it was first built. One unusual feature of the construction is the wreaths of carved acanthus leaves above the bases of the pillars which look like they'd be more at home on the top. Behind the arch is the **hippodrome**, the old sports field which used to be surrounded by seats, some of which are now in the process of being restored. The entrance to the site is from behind the new Government Rest House, built just outside the south gate. Once inside the gate, the **Temple of Zeus** is the ruined building on the left. It is presently being restored to its former glory, when a flight of stairs supported by vaults led up to it. The temple itself was built in the latter part of the 2nd century on a holy site from earlier times.

The **Forum** is unusual because of its oval shape, presumably because some natural feature or existing building prevented it from being round. The reconstructed Ionic columns surrounding it are an impressive sight. The centre is paved with limestone and other softer blocks and the podium in the centre was the base for a statue.

The **South Theatre** behind the Temple of Zeus was built in the 1st century and could once hold 5000 spectators. The back of the stage was originally two-storeys high and has now been rebuilt to the first level. From the top of the seats you can get an excellent view of the ruins with the modern town of Jerash in the background.

On the far side of the Forum, the **Colonnaded Street** stretches for over 600 metres to the North Gate. The street is still paved with the original stones and the ruts worn by thousands of chariots over the years can be clearly seen. The columns on the west side are of uneven height, and were built that way to complement the facades of the buildings that once stood behind them.

At the two main intersections ornamental *tetrapyla* were built. The **Southern Tetrapylon** consisted of four bases each supporting four pillars topped by a statue. Only the south-eastern base has been rebuilt. The intersection was made into a circular plaza at the end of the 3rd century. The cross street runs east, downhill to a bridge spanning the small river and on to the **eastern baths** just behind the present bus station, and west to a gate in the city wall.

The steps of the **Cathedral** are on the left about 100 metres after the intersection. The gate and steps actually cover the remains of an earlier temple. Next to the steps is the **Nymphaeum**, the main ornamental fountain of the city and a temple to the Nymphs. The two-storey construction was elaborately decorated and faced with marble slabs on the lower level and plastered and painted on the upper. Water used to cascade over the facade into a large pool at the front and the overflow from this went out through carved lion's heads to drains in the street below.

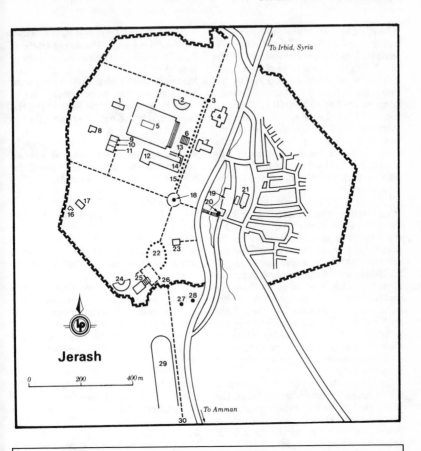

**Jerash**

0        200        400 m

| | | |
|---|---|---|
| 1 | Synagogue Church | |
| 2 | North Theatre | |
| 3 | North Tetrapylon | |
| 4 | West Baths | |
| 5 | Artemis Temple | |
| 6 | Artemis Temple Stairway | |
| 7 | Viaduct Church | |
| 8 | Church of Bishop Genesius | |
| 9 | Church of St Cosmos & St Damianus | |
| 10 | Church of St John | |
| 11 | Church of St George | |
| 12 | Church of St Theodore | |
| 13 | Nymphaeum | |
| 14 | Cathedral | |
| 15 | Colonnaded street | |
| 16 | Mortuary Church | |
| 17 | Church of St Peter & St Paul | |
| 18 | South Tetrapylon | |
| 19 | Bus & Service-taxi station | |
| 20 | Mosque | |
| 21 | East Baths | |
| 22 | Forum | |
| 23 | Museum | |
| 24 | South Theatre | |
| 25 | Temple of Zeus | |
| 26 | South Gate | |
| 27 | Government Rest House | |
| 28 | Visitors Centre | |
| 29 | Hippodrome | |
| 30 | Triumphal Arch | |

Next on the left is the most imposing building on the site, the **Temple of Artemis**, dedicated to the patron goddess of the city. Inside the Great Gate of the temple is a flight of stairs leading up to the courtyard where the temple stands. Large vaults had to be built to the north and south of the temple to make the courtyard level. Originally the temple was surrounded by pillars but only the double rows at the front remain. The temple was fortified by the Arabs in the 12th century but was destroyed by the Crusaders.

Back on the main street opposite the Great Gate is the **Viaduct Church** built over what was once the road leading up to the Temple of Artemis. Further up the main street is the second major intersection and the **Northern Tetrapylon**, dedicated to the Syrian wife of the Emperor Septimus Serverus. This was different from the southern one in that it was four arches surmounted by a dome. The **West Baths** are just downhill from the north tetrapylon. Dating back to the 2nd century, it is one of the earliest examples of a dome being put on a square room, although it's all a bit of a jumble today.

The **North Theatre** just to the north of the tetrapylon is much smaller than the south theatre and is in the process of being restored. From the north tetrapylon it is about 200 metres to the **North Gate**, across the stones and weeds.

Just to the south of the Temple of Artemis lie the ruins of a number of **churches**. In all, 13 have been uncovered and it is widely believed that there are more to be found. To the west of the Cathedral is the Church of St Theodore built in 496 AD, and to the west of this, the churches of St Cosmos, St Damianus, St John and St George. They were all built around 530 AD and opened on to one another. The floors of all three were finely decorated with mosaics, some of which can now be seen in the Museum of Popular Tradition in Amman. Little remains of the other churches.

In the tiny **museum** just to the east of the Forum is a good selection of artefacts from the site, ranging from pottery theatre tickets to jewellery, glass and Mameluke coins such as the *tetradrachma*. The staff are very helpful and eager to explain anything and although the museum is brand new, there are plans to expand it.

The whole site takes a good few hours to wander around and absorb and one can only imagine what it would be like if the other 90% of it was excavated!

### Places to Stay & Eat

Surprisingly perhaps, there is no hotel in Jerash but its proximity to Amman makes it an easy day trip or you could go on to stay at Ajlun, but be warned that the only hotel there costs JD7.700 for a single room.

The *Government Rest House* by the entrance has an expensive restaurant but it costs nothing to sit in the air-conditioned cool and have a glass of cold water.

By the bus station is the usual collection of cafés selling the usual felafel and shawarma.

For something a bit better, try the *Lebanon Restaurant* just west of the traffic roundabout on the road to Ajlun at the southern end of town.

### Getting There

The minibus and service-taxi station is right by the east baths. From Amman, take a service-taxi (500 fils, 45 minutes) or minibus (300 fils) from Abdali station, or hitch from the Sweileh roundabout.

From Jerash, there are minibuses to Irbid, Mafraq and Ajlun (200 fils), 25 km to the west.

If you're staying at Jerash after about 5 pm, be prepared to hitch back to Amman as all transport stops running soon after that. The Tourist Police, who for the most part hide in the air-conditioned Visitors Centre, may help by flagging down a car for you.

## AJLUN

The trip to Ajlun, 25 km to the west of Jerash, goes through some beautiful small pine forests and olive groves.

The attraction of the town is the Qalaat al-Rabad, a castle built by the Arabs as protection against the Crusaders. It stands on a hill two km to the west of the town and from the top you get fantastic views of the Jordan Valley to the west. It's a tough uphill walk but the minibuses heading that way will give you a lift until they turn off about 500 metres before the castle. A taxi to the top will cost about JD1 for the round trip.

It was built by one of Saladin's generals in 1184 and enlarged in 1214. After the fall of the Crusaders, it was used as an administrative outpost for Damascus. Destroyed by the Mongols in 1260, it was rebuilt later the same century by the Mamelukes.

It is a fine example of Islamic military architecture and with its hill-top position, was one in a chain of beacons and pigeon posts that allowed messages to be transmitted from the Euphrates to Cairo in the space of a day.

It's quite well preserved and there is no entry fee.

In the town of Ajlun itself, the only thing of interest is the mosque in the centre. Its minaret is said to date back some 600 years.

### Places to Stay & Eat

The only formal accommodation in Ajlun is the *Alrabad Castle Hotel* perched on the side of the hill about 500 metres before the castle. It has commanding views of the valley and town but the prices are just as stunning – JD7.000/9.800 for singles/doubles with fan, bath and balcony.

It may be possible to stay at the Christian college two km back towards Jerash but don't count on this.

If you have your own tent, it is possible to camp in the small patch of forest just to the west of the castle. Take the track to the right 50 metres before the castle and after the second concrete shed, there's a small track off to the right. Watch out for the old gaping cisterns and the ant nests.

By the traffic roundabout in the centre is the *Green Mountain Restaurant* which has – surprise, surprise – roast chicken, hummus, salad and bread for 600 fils.

The *Ajlun Tourist Park* is on the left-hand side of the road about one km on the Jerash side of Ajlun. It has a beautiful view of the castle across the valley. A beer will set you back 600 fils and a meal of kebabs is JD1.250.

### Getting There

There are regular minibuses from Jerash which leave from the roundabout in the centre of the town; 200 fils for the 25-km, half-hour trip.

At a push it would be possible to go from Amman to Jerash and Ajlun and on to Irbid in one day.

To get to Irbid, there are large air-conditioned buses running throughout the day for 200 fils. Competition for seats is keen in the mornings with all the students heading off for the Yarmuk University in Irbid.

## IRBID

Irbid really has nothing to offer the visitor, but it is a handy base for making the trip out to Umm Qais and Al Hemma, right up on the Syrian border with views of the Golan Heights and the Sea of Galilee.

The university on the south of town was the scene of some unrest in early 1986 when students demonstrated against the lack of student participation in the running of the university. In the ensuing clash with police, three of the demonstrators were trampled to death. The riot was seen as part of a growing resentment within the country at the lack of participation within the present governmental structure.

There are a few moneychangers open for long hours in the main street as well as the usual banks.

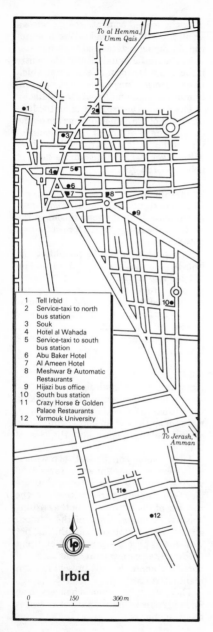

To al Hemma,
Umm Qais

1 Tell Irbid
2 Service-taxi to north
   bus station
3 Souk
4 Hotel al Wahada
5 Service-taxi to south
   bus station
6 Abu Baker Hotel
7 Al Ameen Hotel
8 Meshwar & Automatic
   Restaurants
9 Hijazi bus office
10 South bus station
11 Crazy Horse & Golden
   Palace Restaurants
12 Yarmouk University

To Jerash,
Amman

Irbid

0      150      300 m

## Places to Stay

There are a few sleazy hotels in the busy downtown area. The best is the *Hotel al Wahada* but the sign in English only says Hotel. It's friendly and clean and only has triple rooms; JD1.500 for a bed. The *Al Ameen Hotel* is not as good and the rooms don't have fans.

The entrance to the *Abu Baker Hotel* is up a stairway with a Bank of Jordan sign on it. The walls are painted a sickly shade of pink and the owner is none too friendly. It is the cheapest in town, however, at JD1 for a bed.

## Places to Eat

The *Meshwar Restaurant* near the roundabout by the post office has shawarma, felafel and various cooked animal organs as well as fresh juices. A couple of doors down is the *Automatic Restaurant* where kebabs cost JD1, or a half chicken and salad is 600 fils. A can of beer is also 600 fils.

Out by the university are a couple of student hangouts. The *Crazy Horse Restaurant & Coffee Bar* has good sandwiches with all sorts of fillings for 200 fils. The place is always full of chatty students. Next door is the *Golden Palace Restaurant* which is a little more formal and has meals and drinks.

## Getting There

Irbid has two bus stations. The northern one is about a 20-minute walk from the centre, or a service-taxi runs past it for 50 fils. There are minibuses from this station to Umm Qais (150 fils) and Al Hemma, and to Ramtha for the Syrian border.

The south bus station is a similar distance from the centre. Service-taxis for 55 fils leave all the time from the main street. From here there are Arabella buses to Amman about five times daily. They run to a set schedule, are air-conditioned and the two-hour trip costs 700 fils. There are also minibuses to Ajlun, Mafraq, Jerash and North Shuneh in the Jordan Valley.

*Servees* to Amman cost 750 fils and take two hours.

**To Syria** If you want to go direct to Damascus there are Syrian service-taxis operating out of the south bus station. The trip takes about three hours and costs JD3.

To cross on your own, take a minibus from the north bus station to Ramtha, the Jordanian border post. After the formalities the soldiers will flag down a vehicle to take you to the Syrian side. Once you're through there, it's a three or four km walk or hitch to Der'a, the first town, from where there are buses to Damascus and Bosra.

## AROUND IRBID
### Umm Qais

Thirty km north-west of Irbid right in the corner of Jordan is Umm Qais with views over the Golan Heights and the Sea of Galilee to the north and the Jordan Valley to the south.

This is the ancient Graeco-Roman town of Gadara, one of the cities of the Decapolis and, according to the Bible, the place where Jesus cast out the devil from two men into a herd of pigs (Matthew 8: 28-34).

The city was captured from the Ptolemies by the Seleucids in 218 BC, and the Jews under Hyrcanus captured it from them in 100 BC. When the Romans led by Pompey conquered the East and the Decapolis was formed, the fortunes of Gadara increased rapidly and building was undertaken on a typically large scale.

The Nabataeans controlled the trade routes as far north as Damascus. This interference with Rome's interests led Mark Antony to send Herod the Great to conquer them. The Nabataean king was finally overcome in 31 BC. Herod was given Gadara following a naval victory, and he ruled over it until his death in 4 BC when the city became independent once again.

With the downfall of the Nabataean kingdom at the hands of Trajan in 106 AD,

Western Theatre, Umm Qais

Gadara continued to flourish up until the 7th century, but by the time of the Arab conquest it was little more than a small village.

### Things to See

The best ruins are on a hill at the western end of the town of Umm Qais. Here the western theatre, in a sorry state of repair, has incredible views from the seats, out over the Sea of Galilee. Right in the middle of the front row is the headless statue of a goddess made of white marble, which is in stark contrast to the black basalt of the theatre. It is quite bizarre to see this figure sitting there as though the performance had not yet finished. The houses of the modern village are built mostly out of black basalt blocks taken from the ruins of other buildings.

### Al Hemma

The baths of Al Hemma are a further 10 km from Umm Qais, down the hill towards the Golan. They were famous in Roman times for their health-giving properties and are still used today, but you have to be keen to want to jump into the smelly water.

**Getting There** There are regular minibuses to Umm Qais from Irbid for 150 fils. Transport beyond to Al Hemma is very infrequent – just wait by the side of the road for a vehicle and hitch. You need your passport for the trip down as there's a military control point on the edge of Umm Qais.

# The Jordan Valley

Forming part of the Great Rift Valley of Africa, the fertile valley of the Jordan River was of great significance in Biblical times and is now the food bowl of Jordan.

The river rises in the mountains of Lebanon and flows down into Lake Tiberias (the Sea of Galilee), 212 metres below sea level, before draining into the Dead Sea which, at 392 metres below sea level, is the lowest point on earth. The actual length of the river is 360 km but as the crow flies the distance between its source and the Dead Sea is only 200 km.

It was in this valley some 10,000 years ago that humankind first started to plant crops and abandon the nomadic lifestyle for permanent settlements. Villages were built, primitive water-harnessing schemes were undertaken and by 3000 BC, produce from the valley was being exported to neighbouring regions. The river itself is highly revered by Christians because Christ was baptised by John the Baptist in its waters.

Since 1948 the Jordan River has marked the boundary between Israel and Jordan from the Sea of Galilee to the Yarbis River, and from there to the Dead Sea it marks the 1967 cease-fire line between the two countries.

In the 1967 war with Israel, Jordan lost all its land west of the river – the area known as the West Bank. The population on the east bank of the valley dwindled from 60,000 before the war to 5000 by 1971. During the '70s new roads and fully-serviced villages were built and the population has now soared to over 100,000. There are no cities along the river course although the Roman city of Pella (Tabaqat Fahil) used to occupy a commanding position on the eastern bank.

Ambitious irrigation projects such as the East Ghor Canal have brought substantial areas under irrigation. The hot dry summers and short mild winters make for ideal growing conditions and two and even three crops a year are grown. Thousands of tonnes of fruit and vegetables are produced annually with the main crops being tomatoes, cucumbers, melons and citrus fruits. The introduction of portable plastic greenhouses saw a seven-fold increase in productivity and this has meant that Jordan can now afford to export large amounts of produce to surrounding countries.

Apart from the Dead Sea, there is little of interest in the valley for the visitor today, though Deir Alla and Pella may be of interest to budding archaeologists.

## Deir Alla

The site of Deir Alla (the House of God) is to the right of the main road, 35 km north of South Shuneh. Although there is little to see today, the site is of historical importance. Jacob is said to have rested here after wrestling with an angel and named the place Succoth, mentioned in the Old Testament book of Joshua.

On the small *tell* (hill) an impressive sanctuary was built around 1500 BC and was in use up until 1200 BC when it was abandoned after being destroyed by a massive earthquake. Dutch archaeologists excavating the site have found figurines and incense burners on the site.

Deir Alla was a Persian settlement in the 3rd century BC, but it was later abandoned until the Arab era when it served as a cemetery for nearby villages.

## Pella

Another 30 km north near the village of Mashari are the ruins of the ancient city of Pella (Tabaqat Fahil) two km east of the road. Although the site was inhabited from as early as 5000 BC, it was during the Graeco-Roman period that Pella flourished. The city takes its name from the birthplace of Alexander the Great and was one of the cities of the Decapolis, the commercial league of ten cities formed by Pompey after his conquest of Syria and Palestine in 64 BC. It was to Pella that Christians fled persecution from the Roman army in Jerusalem in the 2nd century AD.

The city reached its peak during the Byzantine era and by 451 AD there was a Bishop of Pella. The defeat of the Byzantines by the invading Arab armies at the Battle of Yarmouk in 635 spelled the end for Pella. Apart from brief occupation by the Mamelukes in the 13th and 14th centuries, the town remained uninhabited until the 19th century.

In 1979 joint Australian-American excavations began and are still in progress. When fully uncovered, it is thought that the site may be as extensive as Jerash. Today Roman pillars, ancient tombs and a Byzantine theatre can be seen in the rugged green hills.

## Getting There

The Jordan Valley can be reached by minibus from Irbid to North Shuneh in the north or by service-taxi to South Shuneh from Amman. The road from Salt to Deir Alla doesn't carry a lot of traffic but hitching is possible.

There are regular connections by both minibus and service-taxi between North and South Shuneh.

## DEAD SEA

The Dead Sea (in Arabic *Bahr Lut* – the Sea of Lot) is 75 km long and from six to 16 km wide and has no outlet. The name becomes obvious when you realise that the high salt content (33%) makes any plant and animal life impossible. The concentration of salt has nothing to do with it being below sea level but comes about because of the high evaporation rate which has, over the years, led to the build up of salts. Despite the fact that the Jordan River flows into the sea, the actual level of the sea is falling as more and more water is diverted from the river each year for irrigation.

Whatever the reason for the salt build up, it certainly makes for an unusual swimming experience. The higher density of the water makes your body more buoyant so drowning or sinking is virtually impossible. Swimming is also just about impossible as you're too high in the water to be able to stroke properly, but of course you can always float on your back while reading the newspaper and get your picture taken. While swimming you will probably discover cuts that you never knew you had as the water gets into them and stings like crazy, and if any water gets into your eyes, be prepared for a few minutes of agony. After a dip in the Dead Sea you are left with a mighty uncomfortable, itchy coating of salt on your skin which you can't get off quick enough – don't swim where there are no showers or freshwater springs.

At the southern end of the sea the Jordanians have started to exploit the high potash content of the mineral-rich water. Vast evaporation ponds covering some 100 square km were built and each day over one million tonnes of water are pumped into them. The concentrated potash salts are then refined at the processing plant south of Safi. The project is now producing more than half a million tonnes of potash annually making Jordan one of the world's largest producers but with world prices failing to reach the levels predicted in feasibility studies, the project has not been the money spinner that had been hoped for. In fact the Arab Potash Company has yet to turn a profit since production began in 1983 and is saddled with debts of about US$170 million, although full production has yet to be reached.

### Suweimeh

There is only one resort on the east bank of the Dead Sea – the government-owned *Dead Sea Rest House* at Suweimeh – and this provides day-trippers with showers, changing rooms and an air-conditioned restaurant. Entry to the resort costs 250 fils and it's another 250 fils for a shower – bring your own soap. The prices in the restaurant are high so bring something to eat if you are staying for the day. The resort gets crowded on Fridays and Sundays.

If you have your own vehicle there is a better place to swim about 10 km south of Suweimeh. Here there are hot, freshwater springs gushing out by the shore, so you can have a swim and then sit under a hot waterfall or in the tepid pools.

### Getting There

The Dead Sea is not served at all by public transport so you have to take a service-taxi from Abdali station in Amman to South Shuneh (Shuneh Nimrin in Arabic) and hitch or take a taxi from there. Fridays and Sundays are the best days for hitching as families head down to the sea on their day off, although many of the cars are full.

If you are going to be visiting Israel, the resorts on the western side at Ein Feshka (Occupied West Bank) and Ein Gedi (Israel) are far more accessible.

# East of Amman

To the east of Amman, the stony desert plain rolls on to Iraq and Saudia Arabia. It is cut by the Trans Arabia Pipeline and the highway to Iraq, and if not for these, east Jordan would be left alone to the Bedouin. Apart from Azraq there are no towns to speak of and no points of interest except for the desert castles.

## THE DESERT CASTLES

A string of castles lies in the desert east of Amman. Most of them were built by the 7th-century Omayyed rulers from Damascus. These early Arab rulers were still Bedouin at heart and their love of the desert led them to build these pleasure palaces. Here they pursued their habitual pastimes of hawking, hunting and horse-racing for a few weeks each year. The evenings were spent being entertained by poets and musicians. Two of the castles, Azraq and Hallabat, date back to Roman times and there is even evidence of Nabataean occupation.

The castles can be visited in a loop from Amman via Azraq and are never more than a couple of km off the road. However, they are not served by regular public transport, with the exception of Qasr al Mushatta (see the Around Amman section), and the only way to see them all is by private vehicle. The castles can be visited in one day with a hire-car, if you set out early. It would be possible to hitch it in a couple of days, but the hassle involved makes this an option for committed castle-lovers only.

### The Desert Loop

From Amman take the road for Zarqa and then turn off to Azraq. Qasr al Hallabat and Hamaam al Sarah are signposted off to the left after 25 km; Azraq is a further 75 km. From here an excellent new road heads back to Amman going right past the castles of Qasr al Amra and Qasr al Kharanah before joining the Desert Highway on the southern outskirts of Amman. At one stage this road widens out and has runway markings on it! Don't panic – you haven't got yourself onto the airport, it's just an emergency strip should the Amman airport be put out of action at any time. This road is incredibly busy and it was built to carry the enormous trucks that ply this back-door route into Iraq from Aqaba, allowing them to by-pass Amman. Because of the Gulf War, most of Iraq's imports and oil exports go by this route.

### Qasr al Hallabat

This was originally a Roman fort built during the reign of Caracalla (198-217 AD) as a defence post against raiding desert tribes. During the 7th century it became a monastery and then the Omayyeds further fortified it and also converted it to a pleasure palace.

Today it is a jumble of fallen stone, and many of them bear Greek inscriptions. The site is kept locked but the custodian of the key will wander over if you wait by the gate. He will also point out the sites of interest among the ruins.

### Hamaam al Sarah

On the same road as the Qasr al Hallabat is this bath-house and hunting lodge built by the Omayyeds. It has been almost completely reconstructed over the years and you can see the channels that were used for the hot water and steam.

This site is fenced off but not locked. Just use a bit of force on the stiff gate.

### AZRAQ

The oasis of Azraq is about 90 km east of Amman and is the junction of the roads heading north-east to a place called H5 and on to Iraq, and the road south-east into Saudi Arabia.

To the south the wide shallow valley of the Wadi Sirhan stretches away to Saudi Arabia. This was a major caravan route and was used by T E Lawrence on his trips between Aqaba and his headquarters in the castle here.

Azraq has the only water in the whole of the eastern desert and used to be one of the most important oases in the Middle East for birds migrating between Africa and Europe. In the last five years or so, the water level in the swamps has fallen drastically due to the large-scale pumping of water from wells to supply Amman with drinking water. In the 1960s the swamp in and around Azraq covered some 10 square km; today it has been reduced to little more than a pool. The number of birds stopping here has been reduced by 95% – they now settle on the shores of the Sea of Galilee in Israel – and it has been suggested that it will cease to be an oasis if pumping is not reduced dramatically. The water that gives the oasis life originates in Syria, filters slowly through underground streams and surfaces at Azraq. It is estimated that this process takes 10,000 years. It is not being replenished at anything like the rate that it is being used.

The area also used to be home to various species of deer, bear, cheetah, ibex and gazelle but hunting in recent years has virtually wiped out the wildlife.

### Qasr al Azraq

The large castle here is built out of black basalt and in its present form dates back to the beginning of the 13th century. Greek and Latin inscriptions date earlier constructions on the site to around 300 AD.

After the 12th century, the only other recorded use of the castle was during WW I when T E Lawrence used it as his desert headquarters in the final stages of the Arab Revolt against the Turks. He set up his quarters in the room immediately above the southern entrance. His men used other areas of the fort, and covered the gaping holes in the roof with palm branches and clay. They were holed up here for an entire winter and more than one man died from the bitter cold.

The southern door is a single massive slab of basalt and Lawrence describes how it 'went shut with a clang and crash that made tremble the west wall of the castle'. Some of the paving stones inside the door have small indentations. These were carved by former gatekeepers, who played an old board game using pebbles to pass the time.

There is a caretaker in attendance who will show you around the few points of interest. The site is open daily and entrance is free.

**Places to Stay & Eat** The one hotel in Azraq is just before the castle on the left. This is the *Hunter Hotel* and it has a beautiful position on a high point among fruit trees, but at JD9 for a double, rooms are not cheap. It is up behind the *Al Sayyam Rest House* which sells drinks and food.

For a really cheap meal with absolutely no frills, there's the Iraqi truck-stop café, the *Baghdadi Restaurant*, between the main junction in Azraq and the castle. For 500 fils you can get an omelette, bread and unlimited tea, and they have other meat dishes as well. Only recommended for the uncritical eater.

### Qasr al Amra

Heading back towards Amman on the new road, the Qasr al Amra, built during the reign of Caliph Walid 1 (705-715 AD), appears on the right after about 25 km. This is the most interesting and best preserved of the desert castles and the walls of the three halls are covered with frescoes. The plain exterior belies the beauty that lies within.

These frescoes are some of the earliest surviving examples but have suffered over the years from the smoke of squatters' fires, and vandalism. There has been an attempt at restoration in

Top: Hiking in the desert – Wadi Rum, Jordan
Left: The Gulf of Aqaba with Eilat in the distance – Aqaba, Jordan
Right: Bedouin camp – Wadi Rum, Jordan

Top: Sea-level marker in the Jordan Valley
Left: Sixth-century mosaic in St Georges Church – Madaba, Jordan
Right: Walking the streets – Amman, Jordan

recent years and some of the frescoes have been cleaned. The paintings depict various scenes, from nude women to the enemies of Islam – the Byzantine emperor, the Visigoth king Roderick, the Persian emperor Chosroes, and the Negus of Abyssinia. The small room with the dome was the steam room and had benches at either end. The dome is of special interest because it has a map of the heavens on it.

The two rooms at the back of the main hall have fine mosaic floors.

## Qasr al Kharanah

This castle is a further 15 km along the road to Amman, stuck in the middle of an absolutely treeless plain. It seems it was the only one of the castles built solely for defensive purposes. The date of construction is uncertain but a painted inscription above one of the doors on the upper floor puts it at 711 AD. The presence of stones with Greek inscriptions in the main entrance frame suggest that it was built on the site of a Roman or Byzantine building.

The Bedouin caretaker will wander over from his hut and show you around. The long rooms either side of the entrance were used as stables. It is built around a central courtyard and in it are pillars which used to support a balcony. Right in the centre of the courtyard is a permanent damp patch which provides the only clue as to where the residents may have got their water from.

The castle is remarkably well preserved and most of the rooms, particularly those of the upper level, are decorated with carved plaster medallions set around the top of the walls.

From Qasr al Kharanah it is also possible to visit Qasr al Mushatta (see the Around Amman section). There are tracks from the main road that cut across the desert to the airport, but these should not be attempted without a guide. The other alternative is to take the highway to the outskirts of Amman and then take the road to the airport.

# South of Amman

There are two routes south of Amman to Aqaba: the Desert Highway and the King's Highway.

The Desert Highway is exactly that – a strip of bitumen running through the monotonous desert for the 300 km to Ras an Naqab where it then winds down off the plateau to Aqaba. Although it is gradually being made into dual carriageway, the sections closest to Amman and Aqaba are a real nightmare. The road is choked day and night with massive semi-trailers from Iraq carrying sixty tonnes of fuel or freight. The drivers, mostly Filipinos and Thais, have little regard for safety and drive like maniacs overtaking whenever they please, regardless of what might be coming the other way. The charred wrecks of the ones that didn't make it litter the road.

If you only have limited time this is the road to use, but by far the more interesting route is the picturesque King's Highway which twists and winds its way south, connecting the historic centres of Madaba, Kerak, Shobak and Petra. Transport along the route is reliable but infrequent. Hitching is the quickest way to go as you don't have to wait for the minibus to fill up, but be prepared for waits of an hour or two on deserted stretches.

There's also a road running along the Wadi Araba from South Shuneh to Aqaba but south of Safi it is only open to military traffic.

## MADABA

This small easygoing little town 30 km south of Amman has some fine mosaics

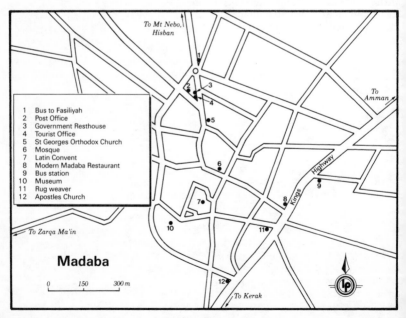

1  Bus to Fasiliyah
2  Post Office
3  Government Resthouse
4  Tourist Office
5  St Georges Orthodox Church
6  Mosque
7  Latin Convent
8  Modern Madaba Restaurant
9  Bus station
10 Museum
11 Rug weaver
12 Apostles Church

To Mt Nebo, Hisban

To Amman

To Zarqa Ma'in

To Kerak

**Madaba**

0    150    300 m

including the famous 6th-century map of Palestine.

The **tourist office** is right opposite St Georges Church and the staff here are extremely helpful. It is open daily from 8 am to 1.30 pm. Next door is the Government Rest House which sells food and drink.

### History

Madaba is the Moabite town of Medeba of the Bible (Isaiah 15:2, Joshua 13:9,16) and it was one of the towns divided among the 12 tribes of Israel. It is also mentioned on the famous Mesha stele, or Moabite Stone, an inscribed stone dating from 850 BC that details the battles of the Moab king Mesha with the kings of Israel.

The Ammonites had retaken Madaba by 165 BC but it was taken by Hyrcanus I of Israel in about 110 BC. It was promised to the Nabataeans by Hyrcanus II if they would help him recover Jerusalem. Under the Romans it became a prosperous provincial town with the usual colonnaded streets and impressive public buildings.

During the Byzantine period up until the Persian invasion in 614 AD, Madaba continued to prosper and most of the mosaics are from this time.

Further damage was inflicted after the Persians by a devastating earthquake in the middle of the 8th century which led to the town's abandonment. It wasn't until the late 19th century that the mosaics were uncovered when 2000 Christians from Kerak migrated here and started digging foundations for houses.

### Things to See

The best and most interesting **mosaic** is in the Greek Orthodox Church of St George. It is a clear map of Palestine and lower Egypt and although it is now far from complete, many features can still be made out, including the Nile River, the Dead Sea and the map of Jerusalem showing the Church of the Holy Sepulchre. It was made around 560 AD and originally measured a staggering 25 by five metres and was made from over two million pieces.

The **museum** is tucked away at the end of a small alley and houses a number of fine mosaics as well as a small section with local jewellery and costumes. It is open from 9 am to 5 pm daily except Tuesday and entry is 250 fils.

In the Church of the Apostles down by the King's Highway is an enormous mosaic dedicated to the 12 Apostles. The church looks like it would be better suited for use as a vegetable market. You can use the same ticket from the museum to get in here.

Madaba is also famous for its colourful rugs and in a couple of small shops in town you can see them being woven on large hand looms.

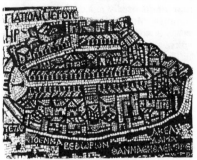
Mosaic map of Jerusalem, Madaba

### Places to Stay & Eat

There's nowhere to stay so it's a case of making a day trip from Amman or seeing Madaba en route between Amman and Kerak.

Along the King's Highway there are a few cheap restaurants. The *Madaba Modern Restaurant* does a half chicken and salad for 550 fils.

### Getting There

Madaba is served by Amman town buses. The bus station is just off the King's Highway, a few minutes walk from the main intersection. Buses to Amman cost 200 fils and the last one leaves at 7.30 pm. In Amman they leave from near the Church of the Saviour.

Service-taxis to Wahadat station in Amman go from the highway just outside the bus station for 300 fils.

Minibuses for Mt Nebo can be flagged down at the roundabout just past the tourist office.

Transport to the south along the King's Highway is irregular – hitching is the most reliable way to go.

## AROUND MADABA
### Mt Nebo
This is an area about 10 km west of Madaba on the edge of the plateau. There are actually three peaks, the first is called Nebo and the last is Siyagha, which is right on the edge of the eastern plateau and is supposedly one of the sites of the tomb of Moses. On a clear day it is possible to see the Dead Sea and the spires of the churches in Jerusalem.

The ruins at Siyagha consist of a church and monastery which have been excavated over the years by the Franciscan Fathers. The existence of the church was reported by a Roman nun, Etheria, in 390 AD, and by the 6th century it had expanded to a large Byzantine church and baptistry. It is the mosaics from this period which can be seen today.

The main mosaic is stunning. Measuring some three by nine metres, it is very well preserved and depicts animals, hunters and vegetation. The animals in it look more African than anything.

When you arrive you may have to hunt around to find someone to open the place up for you.

**Getting There** Take a minibus from the traffic roundabout near the tourist office in Madaba heading for Fasaliyah for 100 fils. From there it's about a four-km, 45-minute walk. Just past the stone marker on the left indicating Mt Nebo it's possible to see the church at Siyagha out on the end of the ridge to the left. There are a few vehicles along this section so it may be possible to hitch.

Mosaic floor, Siyagha

### Zarqa Ma'in
The hot springs of Zarqa Ma'in, the Callirhoe of the Bible, are about 14 km south-west of Madaba down a steep and winding road. The hot therapeutic waters were enjoyed by many in ancient times, including figures such as Herod the Great.

At the time of writing the road was closed and the springs themselves were being developed, which in this part of the world usually means it is getting covered with concrete-block buildings.

## KERAK
The town of Kerak can be reached from the Desert Highway but if you went this way you'd miss one of the most spectacular sights in Jordan – the canyon of Wadi Mujib about 20 km north of Kerak on the King's Highway. It is over 1000 metres deep and the road winds precariously down one side and up the other. At the bottom, there is only a bridge over the wadi and a post office looking totally out of place. This canyon is the Arnon of the Bible and formed a

natural boundary between the Moabites in the south and the Amorites in the north.

The greater part of the town of Kerak lies within the walls of the old Crusader town and is dominated by the fort – one in a long line built by the Crusaders which stretched from Aqaba in the south right up into Turkey in the north.

## History

Kerak lies on the routes of the ancient caravans that used to travel from Egypt to Syria in the time of the Biblical kings and were also used by the Greeks and Romans.

The Crusader king, Baldwin I of Jerusalem, had the castle built in 1132 AD. This site was chosen because it was strategically placed mid-way between Shobak and Jerusalem and had a commanding position. It became the capital of the Crusader district of Oultre Jordan and, with the taxes levied on the passing caravans and the food grown in the district, helped Jerusalem prosper.

After holding out for years against the attacking Arab armies, it finally fell to the forces of Saladin in 1188 AD. The governor of the fort at the time, Renauld de Chatillon, who was killed by Saladin shortly after the Crusaders' defeat at the Battle of Hittin, had the charming habit of throwing his enemies over the battlements of the castle into the valley 450 metres below. He even went to the trouble of fastening a wooden box over their heads so they wouldn't lose consciousness before hitting the bottom!

## Fort

The fort itself has been partially restored and is a jumble of rooms and vaulted passages. It is still possible to see the cisterns where water was stored, but not much else. A torch would be useful for poking around some of the darker places, but watch your step as there are gaping

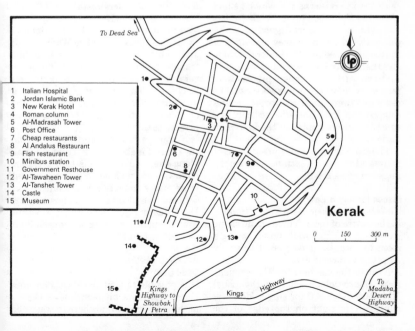

1  Italian Hospital
2  Jordan Islamic Bank
3  New Kerak Hotel
4  Roman column
5  Al-Madrasah Tower
6  Post Office
7  Cheap restaurants
8  Al Andalus Restaurant
9  Fish restaurant
10  Minibus station
11  Government Resthouse
12  Al-Tawaheen Tower
13  Al-Tanshet Tower
14  Castle
15  Museum

Kerak

To Dead Sea

Kings Highway to Showbak, Petra

Kings Highway

To Madaba, Desert Highway

0    150    300 m

light shafts and collapsed ceilings all over the place.

## Museum

The museum is down a flight of stairs on the right as you enter the castle. Apart from a selection of Neolithic tools and Bronze and Iron Age pottery, it also has one of the many copies of the Mesha stele and a translation of its text.

The original stele was found by a missionary at Dhiban, just north of Wadi Mujib, in 1868. It was a major discovery because, not only did it give historical detail of the battles between the Moabites and the kings of Israel, but it was also the earliest example of Hebrew script to be found. After surviving intact from about 850 BC to 1868 AD, it came to a rather unfortunate end. After finding it, the missionary reported it to Charles Clermont-Ganneau at the French Consulate in Jerusalem who then saw it, made a mould of it and went back to Jerusalem to raise the £60 which he had offered to the locals for it. While he was away the local families argued over who was going to get the money and some of the discontented lit a fire under the stone and then poured water on it causing it to shatter. Although most pieces were recovered, inevitably some were lost. The remnants were gathered together and shipped off to France and the reconstructed stone is now on display in the Louvre in Paris.

The castle is open daily during daylight hours and there is no entrance charge; the museum costs 250 fils.

## Places to Stay & Eat

The clean but basic *Kerak New Hotel* is in the centre of town. There are no single rooms but you may well end up having a room to yourself anyway as it's usually empty; a bed costs JD2.

Next to the castle is the *Government Rest House* which charges the usual JD4.950/7.700/9.900 for singles/doubles/triples. It is right on the edge of the escarpment and from the restaurant there are great views over the Dead Sea on a clear day. If you want to eat here, expect to pay over the odds. A can of beer is 750 fils and tea is 220 fils.

Apart from the rest house there are a few other cheap eateries around but after 8 pm it can be difficult to find one that's open. The *Al Andalus Restaurant* has kebabs and other meat dishes but closes around 6 pm.

Opposite Grindlays Bank is a collection of three or four restaurants with chicken and kebabs. A couple of doors along from the bank is a large bakery which has all sorts of sweet buns as well as the usual *khobz*.

For a change, there's a small restaurant in the same street that sells whole roasted fish with hummus, salad and bread for 600 fils.

## Getting There

From the bus station there are minibuses (800 fils) and service-taxis (JD1) for Amman along the Desert Highway. They also run north along the King's Highway as far as Ariha (just before Wadi Mujib) and south to Tafila although public transport along the King's Highway is very infrequent and you're better off hitching. That way you can jump on a minibus if one comes and also have the chance of getting a lift with a truck or private car.

If you are heading north to Madaba, the turn off is about five km east of Kerak along the road that runs to the Desert Highway, so you have to get yourself out there either on foot or by hitching.

Minibuses also run to Safi down by the Dead Sea but you need to get a permit from the police in Kerak before setting off (see below for details).

## AROUND KERAK
### Dead Sea

It is possible to visit the Dead Sea from Kerak but it's a bit pointless as there's nothing to see and nowhere to wash the salt off after a swim. If you still want to do it, it's necessary to get a permit in Kerak. The office that issues them is not, as you might expect, on the road to the Dead Sea but is in fact about two km back along the road towards Amman. There is a sign pointing off the road to the right about one km past the King's Highway turn off to the south.

Once you've got the permit find a minibus heading for the phosphate-mining town of Safi. This will drop you at a road junction in the Wadi Araba from where it's about a five-km walk to the water. The whole bloody trip is more hassle than it's worth.

## SHOBAK

This is yet another Crusader fort in the chain and, like Kerak, has a commanding position over some incredibly desolate land. The fortress, called Mons Realis (Montreal), was built by Baldwin I in 1115 and suffered numerous attacks from Saladin before it finally fell to him in 1189. Its present form is actually the Mameluke restoration from the 14th century.

Today the place looks more impressive from the outside as it is built on a small knoll right on the edge of the plateau. The inside is in a very decrepit state and somewhere in the ruins is a well with 375 steps cut into the rock.

### Getting There

A side road leads to the castle from the King's Highway, about two km north of the small village. It is marked by a white stone post but is easy to miss. From there it is another four km to the fort, although it comes into view on the right after about 2½ km. If you are on foot head straight for it as soon as you sight it and you'll cut off a km or so.

## PETRA

If you are only going to see one place in Jordan, or the whole Middle East for that matter, make it Petra. It's worth going a

long way to see and is certainly the number one attraction in Jordan. It is the ruined capital of the Nabataeans – Arabs who dominated the Transjordan area in pre-Roman times – and they carved elaborate buildings and tombs out of the solid rock.

So many words have been written about Petra (which means 'rock' in Greek), including the much over-worked 'rose-red city half as old as time', but these can hardly do the place justice. You have to spend at least a couple of days walking around in the silence and getting the feel of the place.

Much of Petra's fascination comes from its setting on the edge of the Wadi Araba. The sheer and rugged sandstone hills form a deep canyon easily protected from all directions. The easiest access is through the *Siq*, a narrow winding cleft in the rock that is anything from five to 200 metres deep. Although the sandstone could hardly be called rose-red, it is still a deep rust colour and is banded with grey and yellow and every shade in between.

There is only one free-standing building in Petra, the rest are all cut into the rock, and there are hundreds of them. Up until a few years ago many of these caves were home to the local Bedouin, but they have now been moved to a 'new village' to the north – an arrangement which they are less than happy with. There are still a few families who have the black tents set up and live in the caves. They make their money from Pepsi stands and selling potshards and other artefacts – usually scraps of the distinctive pottery and 'old' coins – to the tourists.

Not so long ago it was an arduous journey from Amman to Petra, only affordable by the lucky few. Now it is connected to Amman and Aqaba by good bitumen roads and can be reached in only three hours via the Desert Highway and Shobak or five hours down the historic King's Highway. When you arrive, there is accommodation ranging from the five-star Forum Hotel to a Bedouin cave.

Most people rush Petra. They spend a couple of hours taking happy snaps and then zoom off to the next place on their itinerary, which is great because it means that for the best parts of the day, early morning and late afternoon, the place is almost deserted. Spend a couple of days exploring, stay in a cave and soak up the atmosphere.

## History

Excavations carried out in the 1950s in the region unearthed a Neolithic village just to the north of Petra at Beidha which dates back to about 7000 BC. This puts it in the same league as Jericho on the West Bank as one of the earliest known farming communities in the Middle East.

Between that period and the Iron Age (*circa* 1200 BC) when it was the home of the Edomites, nothing is known. The Edomite capital Sela in the Bible (II Kings 14:7, Isaiah 16:1) is often thought to have been the massif Umm el Biyara – the Mother of Cisterns – which is part of the western wall of the canyon. If this in fact was Sela (which also means 'rock'), then it was from here that the Judaean king Amaziah, who ruled from 796 to 781 BC, threw 10,000 prisoners to their death over the precipice.

The Nabataeans were a nomadic tribe from western Arabia who settled in the area somewhere around the 6th century BC and became rich, first by plundering and then by levying tolls on the trade caravans for safe passage through the area under their control. The Seleucid ruler Antigonus, who had come to power in Babylonia when Alexander the Great's empire was parcelled up, rode against the Nabataeans in 312 BC and attacked one day when the men were all absent. He killed many of the women and children and made off with valuable silver and spices. The Arabs retaliated immediately killing all but 50 of the 4000 raiders. Antigonus tried once more to storm Petra but his forces led by his son Demetrius were driven off.

Petra then became the sophisticated capital of a flourishing empire which extended well into Syria. As the Nabataeans expanded their territory, more caravan routes came under their control and their wealth increased accordingly.

The Roman emperor Pompey, having conquered Syria and Palestine in 63 BC, tried to exert control over the Nabataean territory but the Nabataean king Aretas III was able to buy off the Roman forces and remain independent. Nonetheless, Rome exerted a cultural influence and the buildings and coinage of the period reflect the Graeco-Roman style.

The Nabataeans weren't so lucky when they chose to side with the Parthians in the latter's war with the Romans. Petra had to pay tribute to Rome after the defeat of the Parthians. When the Nabataeans fell behind in paying this tribute, they were invaded twice by Herod the Great. The second attack, in 31 BC, saw him gain control of a large slice of territory. Finally in 106 AD the Romans took the city and set about transforming it with the usual plan of a colonnaded street, baths, a theatre and all the rest of the trappings of modern Roman life.

With the rise of Palmyra in the north and the opening up of the sea-trade routes, Petra's importance started to decline. During the Christian era there was a Bishopric of Petra and a number of Nabataean buildings were altered for Christian use. By the time of the Muslim invasion in the 7th century Petra had passed into obscurity and the only activity in the next 500 years was when the Crusaders moved in briefly in the 12th century and constructed a fort.

From then until the early 19th century, Petra was a forgotten city known only to the local Bedouin inhabitants. These descendants of the Nabataeans were not inclined to reveal its existence because they feared the influx of foreigners might interfere with their livelihood.

Finally in 1812, a young European explorer and convert to Islam, Johann

Louis Burckhardt, while en route from Damascus to Cairo, heard the locals tell of some fantastic ruins hidden in the mountains of Wadi Musa. In order to make the detour to Wadi Musa without arousing local suspicions, he had to think of a ploy. As he says:

I, therefore, pretended to have made a vow to have slaughtered a goat in honour of Haroun (Aaron), whose tomb I knew was situated at the extremity of the valley, and by this stratagem I thought that I should have the means of seeing the valley on the way to the tomb.

This is exactly what happened and he was able to examine very briefly only a couple of sites, including the Khazneh (Treasury) and the Urn Tomb, which aroused the suspicions of his guide. He managed to bluff his way through and report to the outside world that 'it seems very probable that the ruins at Wadi Musa are those of the ancient Petra'.

## Information

For **tourist information** the Visitors Centre down at the entrance to the site has a wide range of guide books in many languages as well as tacky souvenirs and film. The centre also has the only facilities for changing money in Wadi Musa but as the rate is terrible, bring whatever you need with you. It's also possible to get a permit to stay in the site overnight, despite what the sign at the entrance says about having to contact the Ministry of Antiquities in Amman.

In the village of Wadi Musa there's a small **post office** and **medical centre**.

## Ain Musa (Moses' Spring)

The first thing you come across as you enter Wadi Musa from Amman or Aqaba is a small building on the right with three white domes. This is not a mosque but Ain Musa (Moses' Spring) where Moses supposedly struck the rock and water gushed forth. The road then winds down the two km to the village of Elji, which has now taken on the name of Wadi Musa,

and a further three km to the site entrance at the Government Rest House.

## The Ruins

From the entrance, where you pay your JD1 entry, the track leads down to the Siq – the narrow winding wadi that leads in to Petra. The gate here is supposedly only open from 6 am to 6 pm but these hours are flexible. There are dozens of Bedouin with horses eager to take you the three km or so to the Khazneh for JD2. It's more interesting to walk and this gives you time to look at the first of the monuments – two square free-standing tombs on the right, and the **Obelisk Tomb** a bit further down on the left.

After a party of 23 tourists were drowned in a flash-flood in the Siq in 1963, the entrance was blocked by a dam which diverts the intermittent flow of water into an ancient tunnel on the right and into Petra the long way. During construction, engineers working on the project found the foundations of a Nabataean dam and used them as the base for the new one.

Once inside the Siq, the path narrows to about five metres and the walls tower up to 200 metres overhead. The original channels cut in the walls to bring water into Petra are visible and in some places the 2000-year-old terracotta pipes are still in place. In Roman times the path was paved and one section is still intact. The niches in the walls used to hold figures of the Nabataean god Dushara.

The walls close in still further and at times almost meet overhead, shutting out the light and seemingly the sound as well. Just as you start to think that there's no end to the Siq, you catch glimpses ahead of the most impressive of all Petra's monuments – the *Khazneh*.

**Khazneh (Treasury)** Being in such a confined space, the Khazneh is well protected and has not suffered the ravages of the elements and it must be from here that Petra gained its 'rose-red'

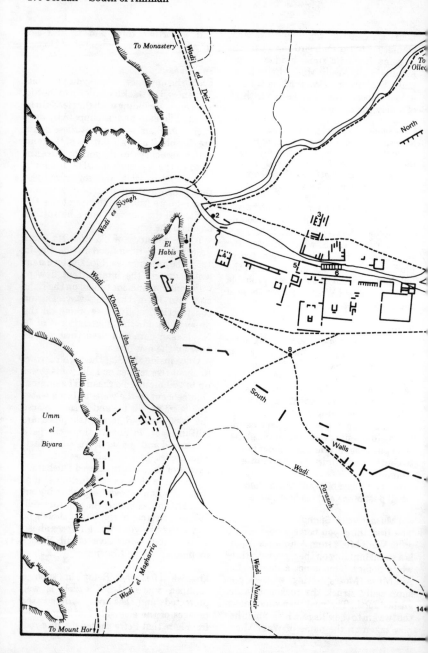

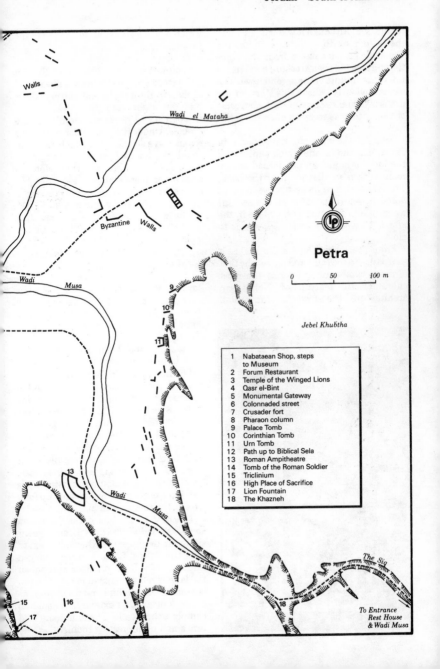

Walls

Wadi el Mataha

Byzantine Walls

Wadi Musa

**Petra**

0        50        100 m

Jebel Khubtha

1   Nabataean Shop, steps
    to Museum
2   Forum Restaurant
3   Temple of the Winged Lions
4   Qasr el-Bint
5   Monumental Gateway
6   Colonnaded street
7   Crusader fort
8   Pharaon column
9   Palace Tomb
10  Corinthian Tomb
11  Urn Tomb
12  Path up to Biblical Sela
13  Roman Ampitheatre
14  Tomb of the Roman Soldier
15  Triclinium
16  High Place of Sacrifice
17  Lion Fountain
18  The Khazneh

Wadi Musa

The Siq

To Entrance
Rest House
& Wadi Musa

reputation. Although it was carved out of the solid rock to serve as a tomb, the Treasury gets its name from the story that pirates hid their treasure here, in the urn in the middle of the second level. The locals obviously believe this story for the urn is pockmarked by rifle shot, the result of vain attempts to break open the solid-rock urn.

Like all the rock-cut monuments in Petra, it is the facade which captivates; the interior is just an unadorned square room with a smaller room at the back. The Khazneh is at its best between about 9 and 11 am (depending on the season) when it is in full sunlight, or late in the afternoon when the rock itself seems to glow.

From the Khazneh, the Siq makes a sharp turn to the right and passes the first of many tombs, often bearing the most characteristic feature of Nabataean architecture – the 'crow-step' decoration,

Khazneh (Treasury), Petra

which is like a staircase on the top of the facade.

**Amphitheatre** The 3000-seat Roman amphitheatre comes into view ahead and to the left. Built in the 2nd century AD, it was cut right into the rock, slicing through many caves and tombs in the process. Under the stage floor were store rooms and a slot through which a curtain could be lowered at the start of a performance. Through this slot an almost-complete statue of Hercules was recovered. The area around the theatre is riddled with caves, some of which were tombs while others were houses. Just before the theatre on the left is a staircase leading up to the High Place of Sacrifice – an interesting 1½-hour climb (detailed in the High Places section below).

**Royal Tombs** The wadi widens right out after the theatre and after passing a few Pepsi-and-souvenir stalls you come to the main city area covering about three square km. Up to the right, carved into the face of Jebel Kubtha, are the three most impressive Royal Tombs.

The first is the **Urn Tomb** with its open terrace built over a double layer of vaults. The room inside is enormous, measuring 20 by 18 metres, and the patterns in the rock are striking. It's hard to imagine how the smooth walls and sharp corners were carved out with such precision. A Greek inscription on the back wall details how it was used as a church in Byzantine times. An enterprising Bedouin has painted his own signs urging visitors to come up for a look at the tomb – and his souvenirs.

The next in the line is the **Corinthian Tomb**, a badly weathered monument similar in design to the Khazneh. Next to it is the **Palace Tomb**, a three-storeyed imitation of a Roman palace and one of the largest monuments in Petra. The top left-hand corner is built out of cut stone as the rock face didn't extend far enough to complete the facade. The four doors lead into small uninteresting rooms.

**The Colonnaded Street** with a few of its columns re-erected, runs alongside the wadi and the slopes of the hills either side are littered with the debris of the ancient city. As yet, little excavation has been done. The street finishes at the **Temenos Gateway** which was originally fitted with wooden doors and marked the entrance to the *temenos*, or courtyard, of the Qasr el Bint.

**Qasr el Bint** This is Nabataean and dates from around 30 BC. The Qasr el Bint (Castle of the Pharaoh's Daughter) is also known as the Temple of Dushara, after the god who was worshipped there. It is the only free-standing structure in Petra and is at present supported by massive wooden scaffolding until it is restored. Much of it has already fallen and the rest looks as though it's ready to follow.

**Temple of the Winged Lions** Up on the rise to the east of the Temenos Gate is the recently excavated Temple of Al-'Uzza-Atargatis or Temple of the Winged Lions, named after the carved lions that topped the capitals of the columns. The temple was dedicated to the fertility goddess, Atargatis, who was the partner to the main male god, Dushara. The excavation of the temple, started in 1975 by an American group and still continuing, soon revealed that this was a building of great importance and had a colonnaded entry with arches and porticoes that extended right down to and across the wadi at the bottom. Fragments of decorative stone and plaster found on the site and now on display in the small museum suggest that both the temple and entry were handsomely decorated.

**El Habis** Just beyond the Qasr el Bint is the small massif of El Habis (The Prison). In the old cave dwellings at the base are a couple more of the small souvenir-and-Pepsi shops found dotted around the whole city. Steps to the left of the Nabataean Shop lead up the face of El

Temple of the Winged Lions, Petra

Habis to the small **museum** which has a collection of artefacts found here over the years. A track to the right leads across the wadi past the fancy Forum Restaurant and up to the Monastery (or Deir), another 'High Place' that takes a good hour to slog your way up to but shouldn't be missed.

### High Places

There are a number of things well worth seeing which require a bit of hard sweat to reach but the effort is repaid by the spectacular views. As well as the climbs following, if you're keen you can do the six-hour climb to the top of **Mt Hor** and **Aaron's Tomb**. Collect the keys from the Bedouin in the tent at the bottom.

**Crusader Castle** The easiest of these climbs is up to the Crusader Castle on top of El Habis. With so many other fine monuments around, the ruins of the castle itself are of little interest. The steps leading to the top start from the base of the hill on the rise behind the Qasr el Bint.

**Monastery** The climb to the monastery is quite long but the ancient rock-cut path is easy to follow and not steep. Not far along the path, a sign points the way left to the **Lion Tomb** set in a small gully. The monastery itself is similar in design to the Khazneh but, at 50 metres wide and 45 metres high, it is far bigger. You don't really appreciate the size until you see someone standing in the eight-metre-high doorway. As usual, the inside is very plain. It was built in the 3rd century BC and crosses carved on the walls inside suggest that it was later used as a church. On the left of the facade, through a small gap in the rock where a lone tree grows, is a staircase that takes you right up to the rim of the urn on top.

Opposite the monastery, there's a strategically placed stall in a cave with a row of seats outside where you can sit and contemplate the monastery. The views from here are stunning. The village of Wadi Musa can be seen right over the top of the Siq to the south-east; to the west and about 1500 metres below is the Wadi Araba which stretches from the Dead Sea to Aqaba; and 500 metres to the south-west is the peak of Jebel Haroun (Mt Hor) topped by the small white dome which marks the traditional site of the tomb of Aaron, the brother of Moses.

**High Place of Sacrifice** The third climb is up to the High Place of Sacrifice near the Siq. This 1½-hour climb is best done in the early morning so you have the sun behind you. The steps head up to the left just as the theatre comes into view as you enter from the Khazneh. At the top the track cuts sharply back to the right. The top of the ridge has been quarried flat to make a platform and large depressions with drains show where the blood of the sacrificial animals flowed out. There are

also altars cut into the rock and just to the south are obelisks and the remains of buildings, probably used to house the priests. Once again the views over the ruined city to the west and Wadi Musa to the east are excellent.

The path then continues down the other side between the obelisk and the ramshackle souvenir-and-Pepsi stall and leads to the **Lion Fountain** where the water used to run down the rock from above and out of the lion's mouth. The steps wind further down the side of the cliff to the **Garden Tomb** and then a little further on is the **Tomb of the Roman Soldier**, so named because of the statue over the door. Opposite this is the **Triclinium** (feast hall) which is unique in Petra for its decorations on the interior walls. The path then flattens out and follows the Wadi Farasa, the site of the ancient rubbish dumps, and ends up at the **Pharaon Column**, the only surviving column of another temple; its mates lie neatly next to it exactly as they fell.

**Umm el Biyara** The hike up to the top of Umm el Biyara, the Biblical Sela, is tough going and takes two to three hours. It is certainly not for the faint-hearted or vertigo sufferers! The path up the face starts from next to the largest of the rock-cut tombs at the base. Climb up the rock-strewn gully to the left of this tomb for 50 metres or so and you'll find the original path cut into the rocks; just keep following it. At times the steps are indistinct and have been almost completely eroded. Once on top there is not much to see on the site itself, other than some 8000-year-old piles of stones and some rock-cut cisterns, but the views over Petra and the surrounding area are the best you'll get from anywhere.

**Beidha**
About four km north of the Forum Hotel are the ruins of the ancient village of Beidha. These date back some 9000 years and along with Jericho it is one of the

oldest archaeological sites in the Middle East. It was excavated by Diana Kirkbride from 1958 to 1983 and the excavations have shown that it was occupied for at least 500 years during the 7th century BC. On the various levels are the ruins of houses of different design, fireplaces and workshops.

## Places to Stay & Eat

**Wadi Musa** The *New Petra Student House*, right up above Wadi Musa, is not a bad place to stay. The only problem is that it is a full hour's walk from the entrance to Petra, although the owner, Khaled, will usually give you a lift down there. Beds are JD2 although a bit of bargaining will get it down to JD1.500. Meals are expensive at JD1.200 for a plate of meat, an omelette, salad and bread; breakfast is eggs, yoghurt, bread and tea for 500 fils.

The building next to Moses' Spring is the *Al Khalil Tea House* (no sign) which has one room with four beds; JD1 each. Despite the fact that it's right next to the spring this place has no water!

There are a couple of very unhealthy looking restaurants in Wadi Musa but there are a couple of shops selling bread, cheese and vegetables so you can stock up and put your own food together. There's no bread available after 5 pm so if you're preparing for the next day's lunch in the ruins, buy it early.

**Petra** The *Government Rest House* right by the entrance gate has excellent single/double/triple rooms for JD4.900/7.700/9.900 with bathroom and hot water. The central part of the restaurant has been set up in an old Nabataean tomb. The food is institutionalised and none too cheap.

The *Petra Forum Hotel* has only opened up in the last few years and has been specially designed and built to blend in with the environment. Rooms cost JD19/23 for air-con singles/doubles. There is a terrace with pool and a top-class restaurant.

The *Forum* also has a gravel *camping area* which is designed more for vehicles than tents. There is a shower block and the tents set up on the site can be rented for JD2 per person.

Really the best place to stay in Petra is a cave inside the site. Find yourself one or try asking some of the local Bedouin. Although the signs say that staying in the site overnight without a permit is prohibited, no-one seems to bat an eyelid if you walk in with what is obviously not just a camera bag. The permits can be obtained from the Visitors Centre in Petra or the Ministry of Antiquities in Amman. By staying in the site you also save yourself the expense of paying the entry fee twice – a worthwhile consideration when it is JD1 a time.

## Getting There

**JETT Bus** There is one JETT bus daily from Amman, leaving at 6.30 am. It is mainly for day trippers who don't have the time to spare for a longer stay and the JD13 price reflects this. The fare includes lunch at the Government Rest House and entry to the site. As the drive from Amman is three hours each way, it doesn't leave much time for exploring the ruins. To take the bus one-way without lunch or entry fee is still JD6 – a blatant rip-off.

**Minibus/Service-Taxi** Public transport connections to Petra are irregular. Daily at 6 am (Arab time!) there are two minibuses leaving from the Visitors Centre; one for Amman (JD1.500) and one for Aqaba (900 fils).

There are service-taxis from Wadi Musa to Amman (JD2.500) but don't expect anything in the afternoon. The most frequent connection is by minibus to Ma'an, but even these only run a few times daily.

Coming from Amman, get to Wahadat station early in the morning for buses and service-taxis for Wadi Musa as things quieten down in the afternoon.

**Hitching** Hitching is easy enough if you get yourself up to the junction by Moses' Spring. Allow five hours to get to Kerak and three to Aqaba.

A lot of the traffic coming out of Wadi Musa is only going as far as Ma'an, 50 km to the south-east on the Desert Highway, but from here there's plenty of traffic in both directions.

## MA'AN

There's nothing of interest in Ma'an, the biggest town in southern Jordan and the administrative centre of the region, but you may find yourself coming through here en route from Amman to Aqaba and Petra.

The Desert Highway skirts the town so if you are hitching through there's no need to go into Ma'an itself.

### Places to Stay & Eat

Petra and Aqaba offer far better accommodation alternatives but there is a hotel here if you get stuck; JD1.500 for a bed.

For a change in diet there's a good truck-stop restaurant on the Desert Highway at the junction of the southern access road from Ma'an. It caters for the tastes of the Asian truck drivers doing the run to Iraq so you'll find all sorts of Asian goods and the restaurant specialises in Filipino food, which makes a great change from the ubiquitous felafel and shawarma.

### QUWEIRA

From Ma'an the Desert Highway continues to Ras en Naqab and then descends tortuously down through the hills. It's one of the most dangerous sections of road and tankers frequently get out of control and explode. The antics of the trucks as they jockey for position makes for some hairraising entertainment.

Quweira is the only town between Ma'an and Aqaba and is the nearest town to Wadi Rum, 35 km to the south-east. The turn-off for Wadi Rum is five km south of town; a sign just says Rum and

there's a couple of little restaurants at the intersection.

### WADI RUM

Many people are put off going to Wadi Rum because it takes some effort to get there and there is no hotel, but it has some of the most spectacular desert scenery you'll ever see and is well worth a visit. Along with Petra, this is a 'must' in Jordan.

During the Arab Revolt in 1917 it was one of the stamping grounds of the enigmatic T E Lawrence, and the desert shots in the film *Lawrence of Arabia* were taken here. In his book, *Seven Pillars of Wisdom*, he describes his approach by camel from the south:

The hills drew together until only two miles divided them, and then, towering gradually until their parallel parapets must have been a thousand feet above us, ran forward in an avenue for miles ... The Arab armies would have been lost in the length and breadth of it, and within the walls a squadron of planes could have wheeled in formation. Our little caravan grew self-conscious, and fell dead quiet, ashamed and afraid to flaunt its smallness in the presence of the stupendous hills.

Lawrence can't have had much of a head for heights because Jebel Rum is in fact closer to 6000 feet (5788 feet or 1754 metres to be exact).

The rusty *jebels* of Wadi Rum rise sheer from the two-km-wide valley floor and are capped with smooth, pale sandstone. They completely dominate the tiny settlement of Rum, which is a collection of about 20 Bedouin families in their black goat-hair tents, a school, a shop and the 'Beau Geste' fort, headquarters of the much-photographed Desert Patrol Corps.

The camel-mounted Desert Patrol was originally set up to keep dissident tribes in order and patrol the border. Today their role is more as a tourist attraction, and they rescue the occasional tourist who gets lost. The men of the patrol are quite a sight in their full-length khaki

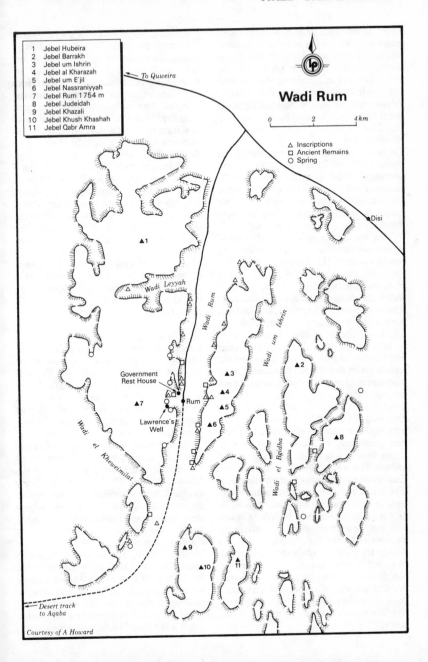

1  Jebel Hubeira
2  Jebel Barrakh
3  Jebel um Ishrin
4  Jebel al Kharazah
5  Jebel um E'jil
6  Jebel Nassraniyyah
7  Jebel Rum 1754 m
8  Jebel Judeidah
9  Jebel Khazali
10 Jebel Khush Khashah
11 Jebel Qabr Amra

To Quweira

Wadi Rum

0        2        4 km

△ Inscriptions
□ Ancient Remains
○ Spring

Disi

▲1

Wadi Leyyah

Wadi Rum

Wadi um Ishrin

Government
Rest House

▲3

▲2

▲7

Rum

▲4

▲5

Lawrence's
Well

▲6

Wadi el Bgidha

▲8

Wadi el Kheweimilat

▲9

▲10

▲11

Desert track
to Aqaba

Courtesy of A Howard

robes, bandolier, dagger at the waist, pistol and rifle slung over the shoulder. Inside the compound under the shady eucalypt trees, the officer on duty whiles away the time entertaining visitors with the traditional Arabic coffee heavily spiced with cardamom followed by sickly sweet tea.

## Things to See

There are a few things of interest in the immediate vicinity of the village. **Lawrence's Well** is a spring about 500 metres south-west of the fort, tucked right in at the base of Jebel Rum – just follow the white paint on the rocks which the army has splashed everywhere while playing war games. This is the largest of many springs in the area and until recently, when the Government laid a water pipeline from Disi 10 km to the east, it supplied the settlement with water. By the spring are many Nabataean inscriptions, and Thamudic inscriptions, written by the camel drivers from the Thamud tribe in Saudia Arabia.

Between the Government Rest House and the face of Jebel Rum are the ruins of a 1st-century **Nabataean temple** which was a square courtyard surrounded by rooms on three sides.

## Exploring the Desert

The main attraction of a visit to Wadi Rum, however, is the desert, and to fully appreciate it you need to get out of the village. There are a few alternatives here: Land Rover, camel and your own two feet. The local Bedouin population have the monopoly on the first two and know it. To hire a Land Rover for a couple of hours will cost you about JD10 and although you get out into the desert, you don't escape the noise. Camels are a better way to go but here too you are at the mercy of the Bedouin. They charge JD7 per camel per day and will take you out for as many days as you like, staying on the way with the Bedouin families camped in the desert.

The best way to do it is on your own, although care must be taken as this is inhospitable country and it is easy to get lost. It should not be attempted in summer as the temperatures are extreme and dehydration and exhaustion are real dangers. The only gear you need is a sleeping bag, hat, good shoes and adequate food and water. Five-litre water containers can be bought at the shop in Rum for 350 fils and this should be enough water for one person for two days. Once you're prepared, just head off south down the wadi and camp the night somewhere. There is enough small dead wood around for a fire and the experience of a sunset in the desert is unbeatable. At night the silence is so strong that it rings in your ears. There are the occasional Bedouin camps dotted around and you'll always be welcomed, but don't just waltz in – wait for an invitation. The Bedouin are incredibly hospitable people and will never turn away a stranger.

## Rock-Climbing

If rock-climbing is your thing, Wadi Rum offers some very challenging routes equal to just about anything in Europe. Nothing has been done towards catering to the climber so you need to have your own gear, but recently the Ministry of Tourism commissioned a British climber, Tony Howard, to explore the area and map the climbs he did. The result after over two years of research is the excellent and detailed book *Treks & Climbs in the Mountains of Wadi Rum & Petra* available from the Ministry of Tourism. It describes about 140 walks, four-wheel-drive routes, camel treks and rock climbs.

## Places to Stay & Eat

There's nothing in the way of hotels or hostels in Wadi Rum. The Government Rest House at the entrance to the village is never open and even if it was, there's nothing in it. Out the back are a few ugly fibreglass shelters where you can throw down a sleeping bag for a few nights.

The only other alternative is to head out into the desert and stay in a Bedouin tent or under the stars.

It's the same story with food here – bring your own. There is a small shop which sells all sorts of things that you are never likely to need. In the way of food it only has basics such as processed cheese spread and tins of fish and occasionally bread. You can also get the traditional *kafiyeh* headgear for JD2 if you need something to keep the sun off.

### Getting There

Public transport into Wadi Rum is non-existent so it's a matter of sticking out your thumb. The turn off for Wadi Rum is five km south of Quweira and the 30-km road from there is all surfaced. A minibus from Aqaba to the turn off is 600 fils.

Traffic along the Rum road is infrequent and you may well have to wait a couple of hours. When leaving Wadi Rum, be by the road early in the morning as nothing much goes out after 9 am. Some drivers ask for ridiculous payments – like JD5 – but 500 fils is reasonable for the ride to Quweira.

The only other possibility is to ask the drivers of the JETT buses which come in regularly at about 5 pm and stay for an hour or so – just long enough for the tourists to ride a camel and take a few snaps – and then head back to Amman or Aqaba.

### AQABA

The balmy winter climate and idyllic setting on the Gulf of Aqaba make this Jordan's aquatic playground. While Amman shivers with temperatures around 5°C and the occasional snowfall, the mercury hovers steadily around 25°C in Aqaba. The water is clear and warm and as an added bonus, offers some excellent diving for the underwater enthusiast. In summer the weather is uncomfortably hot with daytime temperatures around 35°C and higher.

The town itself is of little interest but with the beaches, good cheap hotels and restaurants that offer something a bit different, it's not a bad place to stay for a few days.

The port to the south of town gives Jordan an outlet for its exports and since the start of the Gulf war between Iran and Iraq it has become the main port for Iraq. Day and night there's a steady stream of road tankers bringing Iraqi oil down to Aqaba and semi-trailers loaded with imports make the trip back. Fortunately the trucks are kept out of the town centre and their activities centre around the enormous truck park three km north of town.

On the western side of the gulf, just across the border fence from Aqaba, is the Israeli resort of Eilat and despite the hostilities between the two countries since 1948, the two towns have managed to co-exist peacefully. Depending on which side of the fence you're on, the gulf is known as either the Gulf of Aqaba or the Gulf of Eilat.

The airports serving the two towns lie close to each other either side of the border, which has led to the occasional stuff up. In 1986 a plane carrying Israeli tourists to Eilat landed. The pilot confirmed with the traffic controller that he had landed but was somewhat startled when the reply came back: 'Where? You're not on my strip'. He had in fact managed to land at the Aqaba airfield. A Jordanian official came on board, wished the passengers a happy flight and the plane took off for the two-minute flight to Eilat.

### History

And King Solomon made a navy of ships in Ezion Geber, which is beside Eloth, on the shore of the Red Sea, in the land of Edom.

This is a verse from the Old Testament (I Kings 9:26) and probably refers to the present-day Aqaba. The name Eloth is a reference to the Israeli town of Eilat. Excavations at Tell al Khalifa to the west of Aqaba right on the Jordan-Israel border have revealed copper smelters, held to be the site of Solomon's Ezion Geber. Smelting was carried out here from the 10th to the 5th centuries BC with the ore coming from mines in the Wadi Araba.

With the development of trade with Southern Arabia and Sheba (present-day Yemen) it became a thriving settlement. In Roman times the great road from Damascus came through here via Amman and Petra and then headed off west to Egypt and Palestine.

At the time of the Muslim invasion in the 7th century there was a church and even a Bishop of Aqaba. The Crusaders occupied the area in the 12th century and fortified the small island of Ile de Graye, now known as Pharaoh's Island, seven km offshore. The small fort in the town was built sometime around the 14th century and today it houses the useless Visitors Centre.

For the next 500 years or so Aqaba remained an insignificant fishing village until the Arab Revolt during WW I. The Ottomans occupied the town but were forced to withdraw after a raid by T E Lawrence and the Arab forces. From then on the British used it as a supply centre from Egypt for the push up through Transjordan and Palestine.

After the war the Transjordan-Saudi Arabian border was never defined but Britain arbitrarily drew a line a few km south of Aqaba. The Saudis disputed the claim but took no action. As the port of Aqaba expanded, the limited coastline proved insufficient and in 1965 King Hussein traded 6000 square km of Jordanian desert for another 12 km of coastline. This gave the port room to expand and saw a fine coral reef, the Yamanieh Reef, become Jordanian territory.

## Information

**Tourist Office** This is housed in the Visitors Centre in part of the old fort by the waterfront. There is absolutely no reason to visit it though as they seem to regard visitors as something of a nuisance and are unhelpful in the extreme.

**Post & Telecommunications** The post office is right in the centre of town and is open every day. You can also make international telephone calls from here.

**Money** For changing money there are numerous banks around as well as moneychangers, who usually give good rates and some are open on Friday.

The American Express agent is International Traders on Municipality Square just along from the Ali Baba Restaurant and is open from 8 am to 1 pm and 3 to 6 pm – or that's what the sign on the door says anyway.

**Egyptian Visas** The Egyptian consulate is in the new part of town, about 20 minutes walk from the centre. Tourist visas are issued on the spot for JD7 with a minimum of fuss and the place is deserted – a great contrast to the shambles at the consulate in Amman. The visa office is open from 8 am to 12 noon daily except Friday. A taxi from Municipality Square will cost 350 fils with bargaining.

**Other** The Yamani bookshop opposite the post office has a good range of books on Jordan and the Middle East as well as current local and international newspapers.

The Princess Haya hospital is well-equipped, even to the extent of having decompression chambers, and the staff are trained to deal with diving accidents.

If you have an FM radio there's a good music station broadcasting from Eilat, and Radio Jordan is on the dial at 99 kHz.

## Fort

The small fort down on the waterfront is worth a quick look. The Hashemite Coat of Arms are above the main entrance to this 14th-century Arab construction. The old caretaker takes great pleasure in showing people the few points of interest

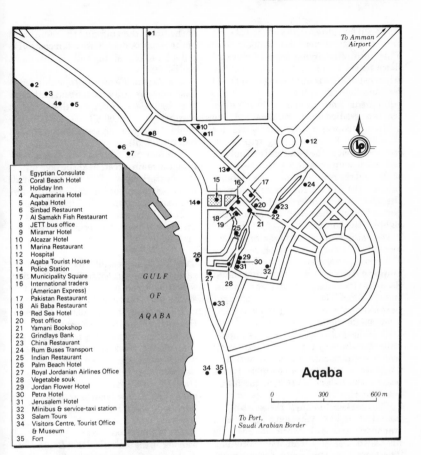

1   Egyptian Consulate
2   Coral Beach Hotel
3   Holiday Inn
4   Aquamarina Hotel
5   Aqaba Hotel
6   Sinbad Restaurant
7   Al Samakh Fish Restaurant
8   JETT bus office
9   Miramar Hotel
10  Alcazar Hotel
11  Marina Restaurant
12  Hospital
13  Aqaba Tourist House
14  Police Station
15  Municipality Square
16  International traders
    (American Express)
17  Pakistan Restaurant
18  Ali Baba Restaurant
19  Red Sea Hotel
20  Post office
21  Yamani Bookshop
22  Grindlays Bank
23  China Restaurant
24  Rum Buses Transport
25  Indian Restaurant
26  Palm Beach Hotel
27  Royal Jordanian Airlines Office
28  Vegetable souk
29  Jordan Flower Hotel
30  Petra Hotel
31  Jerusalem Hotel
32  Minibus & service-taxi station
33  Salam Tours
34  Visitors Centre, Tourist Office
    & Museum
35  Fort

GULF
OF
AQABA

**Aqaba**

0          300          600 m

To Port,
Saudi Arabian Border

around the old courtyard including the prison cells and a tunnel which used to give access to the sea. His pride and joy, however, is the two eucalyptus trees in the centre which he planted in 1963.

## Museum

The museum, next to the fort in the Visitors Centre, is locked most of the time but if you bash on the door someone will come and open up. Apart from some old photos of Sherif Hussein, Emir Faisal and King Abdullah with Winston Churchill there's little to see.

## Beaches & Diving

The big hotels tend to have a monopoly on the beach and charge through the nose for the privilege of sitting on their strip. The Aqaba Hotel charges JD1 to use the beach for the day and another JD1 for a deck chair. A bit of bluff usually gets you through the gate – just act as though you own the place. It is the best bit of beach as there are sun shelters along the water's edge.

Next door to the Aqaba Hotel is the Aquamarina Hotel & Diving Centre which has a pool and restaurant built out over the water. This place is the best equipped for watersports and for a fee you can go waterskiing and sailboarding. They also offer diving trips to the reef down by the Saudi border. The half-day trips cost JD5 for scuba diving or JD2.500 for snorkelling. This price includes equipment and transport but unless you're a certified diver, you'll have to take a diving course (JD20) or settle for snorkelling. The snorkelling trip is not really worth it as the best coral can only be seen with scuba gear.

Beyond the Aquamarina is the Holiday Inn and the Coral Beach Hotel and past them, a beach reserved for military personnel and then King Hussein's villa right by the border.

Depending on your bargaining skill and how much you spend in the restaurant, you can rent or borrow a crappy old mask and snorkel from the Al Samakh Fish Restaurant right on the water's edge. The section of beach right next to the Al Samakh is not bad and has a few shade shelters.

There are glass-bottomed boats continually buzzing up and down the beach which a group can rent for about JD5. There are a few small shipwrecks in the water which are a haven for some colourful fish.

The best beaches are to the south of the port but unless you have your own transport access is difficult and the unshaded beaches can be scorching. There are a few sun shelters at one point between the main port and the potash-loading terminal – not as bad as it sounds. The government is also making some attempt to develop a small area here to provide a few facilities, including a camping ground, but until this happens the town beaches are the best bet.

### Places to Stay – bottom end

Three of the cheapest places are all next to each other on the main street. The *Petra Hotel* in the middle is the best of them. Rooms at the front on the 3rd and 4th floors have balconies with a great view

of the town, the gulf, and the mountains of the Sinai. A double with fan costs JD3 but a bit of bargaining will get this down to JD2.500.

The *Jordan Flower Hotel* on one side has rooms for JD3 with fan and bath, and the *Jerusalem Hotel* on the other is cheaper at JD1.500/2.500 for singles/doubles and you can sleep on the shaded roof for 700 fils.

The *Red Sea Hotel* is one block back from the main street, near the post office. It's overpriced at JD2.500/4 for small rooms with fan but has the cheapest air-con rooms in town at JD6 for a double.

The *Al Samakh Fish Restaurant* on the beach has a few crummy beds for JD1.500 each.

**Camping** It is possible to camp in the garden of the *Aqaba Hotel* for JD1.500, which isn't too bad and gives you free access to their beach. You can also camp in the squalid little garden of the *Palm Beach Hotel* for JD2 per person.

If you want to get away from things and camp on the beach south of the port, get a permit from the police station on the waterfront near Municipality Square. Until the new government camping area opens up the only facilities out here are a few shade shelters.

### Places to Stay – top end

Moving up the scale, the *Palm Beach Hotel* on the waterfront has air-con double rooms for JD8 but you may be able to bargain this down a bit if the place is empty.

Of the big hotels on the beach strip, the *Aqaba Hotel* is the cheapest at JD8/9.200 for singles/doubles and it also has bungalows in amongst the palm trees for JD10/13 and newer ones with air-con for JD13/16.

The *Aquamarina Hotel* next door has air-con singles/doubles for JD11.700/14.560. It has all facilities, including a beach shared with the Holiday Inn next door, which they charge non-residents an outrageous JD2.500 to use.

Others in this bracket include the friendly *Alcazar Hotel* with a swimming pool where air-con singles/doubles go for JD11/13, and the *Aqaba Tourist House* which charges JD14.300/16.500 including breakfast.

## Places to Eat

Aqaba has quite a few choices when it comes to food. The *Ali Baba Restaurant* is the most up-market in town and has tables set up outside. An excellent meal of soup (250 fils) and spaghetti (770 fils) can be accompanied by a bottle of local wine from the West Bank, available for 800 fils from one of the liquor stores.

For fresh fish, there are two somewhat grotty restaurants close to the water's edge – so close in fact that the water laps at your feet if you sit at the tables out the front. The *Sinbad Restaurant* and the *Al Samakh Fish Restaurant* have similar food and prices; JD1.500 for a whole fish with salad, hummus and potatoes.

The *Indian Restaurant* has good food and a pleasant balcony with views of the water. A large vegetable curry with rice is only 380 fils and other dishes include chicken biryani (490 fils), samosas (200 fils), yoghurt (80 fils), kebabs (660 fils) and kofta (770 fils). They even add a bit of Indian authenticity by insisting that the menu on the wall is the old one and that the prices have actually gone up – believe them or not as you like. Around the back of the post office, the *Pakistan Restaurant* has a more limited range and the food is not as good.

Up by Grindlays Bank the *Chinese Restaurant* does some pretty good meat and rice dishes and great soups for 450 fils.

If you want a reasonable hamburger, the *Marina Restaurant* just up from the Alcazar Hotel doesn't do a bad job for 330 fils and they have other western dishes including spaghetti and fish. The sign at the front of the place just says Fast Food.

Then of course there's the restaurants with all the old favourites like chicken,

kebabs and felafel. There's a group of three or four one block back from the main street down the steps towards the Indian Restaurant. The *Jerusalem Restaurant* on the street level of the Jerusalem Hotel does a half chicken with salad and hummus for 800 fils.

The shops along the main street are well stocked with all sorts of food so if you are heading for Wadi Rum, stock up with goodies like dates, cheese and bread. The vegetable souk also has plenty of fruit and fresh vegetables.

## Getting There

**Air** Royal Jordanian have nine flights a week to Amman for JD13 one-way and JD18 return.

**Boat to/from Egypt** There is a whole stack of travel agents along the waterfront road selling ferry tickets to Nuweiba and Suez. The Salam Tours office deals only in these tickets and they seem to have their finger on what's going on. The ferry terminal is south of the port, about 10 km from the centre. The only way to get there is to walk, or more sensibly, take a taxi which should cost about JD1 with fierce bargaining.

There are two car-ferry services operating out of Aqaba – to Nuweiba on the Sinai Peninsula and to Suez. The Nuweiba service is relatively new and makes it possible to see the Sinai without backtracking to or from Suez. The two daily departures are at 12 noon and 4 pm and the three-hour trip costs JD7. Tickets can be bought on the day of departure and you only need to be at the dock about one hour before sailing.

The connections to Suez are a little less reliable but run every second day from Aqaba at 11 am. Tickets for the 15-hour trip vary from JD17 for a dorm up to JD27 for a 1st-class cabin.

**Boat/Bus to Egypt** There is a daily JETT bus from Aqaba at 7.30 am to Cairo. The trip takes a total of 16 hours and the fare of JD15 includes the ferry ride. Where the bus actually goes between 7.30 am and the 12 noon departure of the Nuweiba ferry is anyone's guess.

**JETT Bus** The JETT office is on the waterfront road near the Al Samakh Fish Restaurant. The smooth and fast air-con buses run five-times daily between Aqaba and Amman at 7, 8 and 9 am and 2.15 and 4 pm. The five-hour trip costs JD3.

**Bus/Minibus** The Rum Buses Transport company runs air-con buses to Amman for JD2.500.

The bus station for minibuses is just a couple of minutes walk from the main street. Buses for Ma'an leave irregularly when full for 600 fils. There is one minibus daily for Petra which leaves at about 10 am and costs 900 fils although you'll probably be asked for a lot more. There's very little transport leaving Aqaba after about 10 am.

**Service-taxi** The *servees* use the same station as the minibuses. There are departures for Amman throughout the day but you may have to wait for an hour

or so for one to fill up. As they cost the same as the JETT bus (JD3) you may as well take the bus and have some air-conditioned comfort.

**Hitching** If you arrive in Aqaba by truck you'll probably be dropped off at the truck park about three km north of town. A taxi into the centre shouldn't cost more than 500 fils as you can usually find other people going into town.

For hitching north from Aqaba the truck park is also a good place to start.

### Getting Around
**Airport Transport** The Aqaba airport is about 10 km north of town and a taxi costs about JD2.

**Taxi** Other than walking, taxi is the only way to get around Aqaba but the only time you should need to catch one is if you want to go to the port (JD1) or airport.

**Car Rental** If you want to rent a car there are agencies in the big hotels. The Kada Rent-a-Car company, with its office in the lobby of the Aqaba Tourist House, is one of the cheapest.

# West Bank

With the loss of the West Bank to Israel in the 1967 war, Jordan lost its two most important sources of revenue – agriculture, from the Jordan Valley; and tourism, from the Old City of Jerusalem.

Naturally Jordan has never recognised the Israeli occupation of the West Bank but with Israel's military superiority, it is hardly in a position to do anything about it. So if you come from the East Bank you are in the rather curious position of being in two countries at once. The Israelis have not officially annexed the area but with the constant growth of more and more Jewish settlements it obviously plans to hang on to it and it appears that King Hussein has privately accepted this.

Most of the Palestinians on the West Bank are fiercely anti-Israel and violent clashes are common. Frustration amongst Palestinians has been heightened recently by what is seen by many to be King Hussein's co-operation with the Israeli authorities in the administration of the West Bank. Hussein's attempts to cultivate an alternative Palestinian leadership to the PLO has also been cause for dissension and his plans to spend US$1 billion on West Bank development in the next five years are seen as a part of this. Hussein can't afford to alienate the Palestinians as they account for 60% of Jordan's population, and if he is seen to be making no effort towards ending the Israeli occupation of the West Bank, the Palestinians there will exercise their right of Jordanian citizenship and move to the East Bank.

# Jerusalem

Known as Al Khodz in Arabic and Yerushalayim in Hebrew, Jerusalem is a holy city for the three great monotheistic religions of the world – Christianity, Islam and Judaism.

For Christians it is the site of the crucifixion and resurrection of Jesus Christ, for Muslims it is the place where Mohammed made his final flight to heaven and for the Jews it is the site of the first and second Temples and is the seat of government of Israel.

It takes at least a week to see most of what Jerusalem has to offer and a good deal longer to know the city well. The Old City has a fascination and appeal that just keeps you coming back for more.

### History

The city of Urusalim was one of the strongholds of southern Palestine as early as 1400 BC but was taken in about 1000 BC by the Israelites led by the shepherd king David.

It was established as the capital of a united Israelite kingdom. His son Solomon succeeded him and during his reign palaces and walls were built, including a lavish temple on Mt Moriah (described in I Kings 6 & 7).

On the death of Solomon in 922 BC, the kingdom split into the separate kingdoms of Israel in the north and the southern kingdom of Judah with Jerusalem as its capital. After 400 years of unstable rule when Jerusalem was attacked from all sides by the Egyptians, the Philistines and the Arabians, it finally fell to the Assyrians who were in turn overpowered by Nebuchadnezzar, king of Babylon, in 587 BC. He sacked the city, destroyed the temple and exiled many of the citizens to the Euphrates.

Babylonian rule was short-lived however, and they were defeated by Cyrus I of Persia in 539 BC. The Jews were allowed to return to Jerusalem and under the prophet Nehemiah, the walls of Jerusalem were rebuilt.

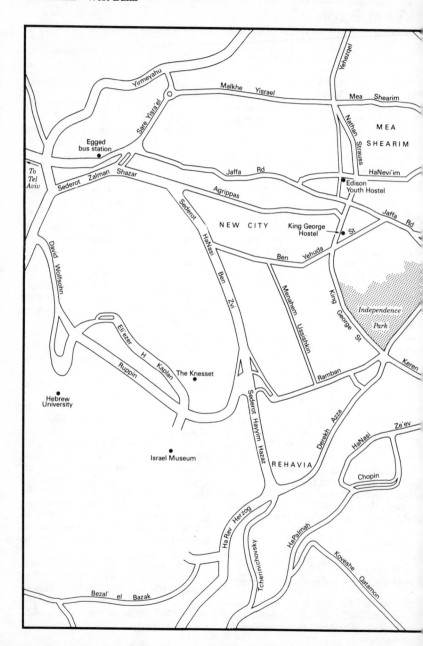

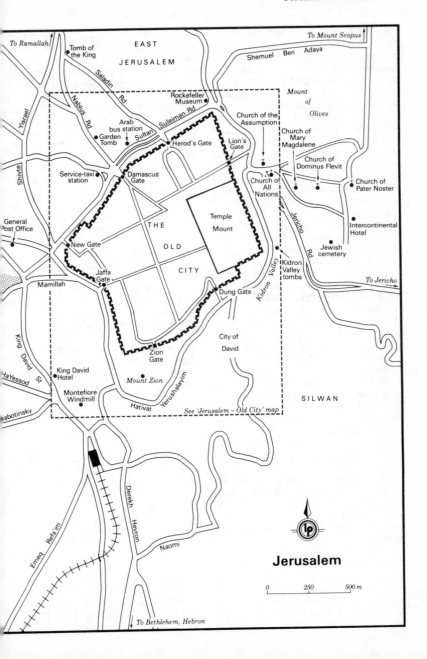

**Jerusalem**

0    250    500 m

Alexander the Great took the city in 332 BC without violence, but in 170 BC under the Seleucids led by Antiochus IV, Jerusalem was sacked once again. The Jews led by the rebel Judas Maccabeus revolted and regained the city, purified the temple and rebuilt the fortifications. In 64 BC Rome was forced to intervene to settle internal rivalry between Hyrcanus and Aristobolus and the kingdom came under Roman control. Herod was appointed king by the Roman senate and the period of his rule from 37 BC to 4 AD saw the construction of magnificent public buildings and palaces and the restoration of the temple.

Herod's son Archelaus was deposed after only nine years and Judaea became a Roman province governed by a procurator. It was the fifth procurator, Pontius Pilate, who had Jesus crucified. In later years Pilate became tyrannical and was forced out of office. The oppressive rule of the procurators led the Jews to revolt in 66 AD and the Roman army was forced to withdraw. Such was the extent of the rebellion that the commander Vespasian was despatched with 60,000 men to quash it. Vespasian's son Titus took Jerusalem in 70 AD after a siege lasting more then four months. Despite orders from Titus that the Temple should not be destroyed, it was burned to the ground along with the greater part of the city.

The emperor Hadrian set about building a new city called Aelia Capitolina in 130 AD and there followed a second revolt by the Jews which was also put down. Captive Jews were sold into slavery, the Temple was destroyed and those Jews who remained were restricted in their religious practices. The Old City that survives today is on Hadrian's plan.

With the conversion of the emperor Constantine to Christianity, he and his Christian successors set about building churches and basilicas over the sites sacred to Christians, including the Church of the Holy Sepulchre over the site determined by Constantine's mother

as Golgotha, the place of the crucifixion and burial of Jesus. The Jews were given permission to return to the city and rebuild the Temple, a task they were unable to achieve because of their small numbers.

Early in the 7th century the Persians moved in but were forced to surrender to the Caliph Omar in 637 who showed remarkable tolerance towards both Jews and Christians. Jerusalem became a sacred Muslim city and the Dome of the Rock was built on the site of the Jewish Temple in 688.

The Fatimid rulers of Egypt were the next to take over and their persecution of the Christians, continued by their successors the Seljuk Turks in 1077, caused outrage in Europe and led to the mounting of the Crusades. The invading armies captured Jerusalem in 1098 and a Latin kingdom was established. Churches, hospices and hospitals were built for the pilgrims.

The city fell to Saladin in 1187 and, apart from a couple of short intervals, remained in Muslim hands for the next three centuries. It was ruled by the Omayyeds in Damascus and then from Egypt by the Mamelukes.

Syria and Palestine fell to the Ottoman Turks in 1517 and in 1542 the walls of Jerusalem were rebuilt by Suleiman the Magnificent. They still stand today.

In 1856 the Sultan of Turkey issued the Edict of Toleration for all religions in the empire and non-Muslims were allowed into the Temple of the Mount and were encouraged to settle in the city. Churches and synagogues rapidly sprang up both within and outside the city walls.

Four hundred years of Ottoman rule were brought to an end when General Allenby led the British forces into Jerusalem in 1917. In July 1920 Sir Herbert Samuel became His Majesty's High Commissioner for Palestine and with the approval of the British Mandate by the League of Nations in 1922 a civil administration was established. The

British, unable to honour pledges made separately to both Arabs and Jews which implied that each would end up in control of the city, were faced with increasing outbreaks of violence between the two communities.

British plans to establish a Palestinian state run by both Jews and Arabs were blocked by the Zionist movement and Britain referred the whole problem to the United Nations in 1947. War broke out in 1948 when the UN voted in favour of partition and the end result saw the Arabs in control of the Old City and East Jerusalem while the Jews had the northern and western suburbs. The city was divided by a strip of no-man's-land and Jerusalem became the capital of the newly proclaimed state of Israel.

In the Six-Day War of 1967 Israel annexed the Old City and occupied the Jordanian territory known as the West Bank.

## Orientation

Jerusalem is hilly and confusing. Most of the historical sites and cheap hostels are within the walled Old City in the east. The Old City is still divided into four quarters as it was laid out by the emperor Hadrian in the 2nd century. The Muslim Quarter is in the north-east; the Christian Quarter is in the north-west; the Jewish Quarter is in the south-east; and the Armenian Quarter is in the south-west. The Temple Mount occupies most of the eastern side of the Old City.

East Jerusalem is directly north of the Old City and its main attractions are the cheap hostels and hotels, the *sherut* (service-taxi) station and the Arab Bus Station – all close to the Damascus Gate in the north wall.

To the east and overlooking the Old City is the Hebrew University (Mt Scopus) and the Mount of Olives.

The New City is Jerusalem's commercial and administrative centre. The main street is Jaffa Rd (Rehov Yafo) which runs from Jaffa Gate to the Central (or Egged) Bus Station. The main downtown area where the tourist office, restaurants and cinemas are located is in the area bounded by Ben Yehuda St (a pedestrian precinct), Yaffa Rd and King George St (HaMelekh George).

## Information

**Tourist Office** The main tourist office (tel 241281) is at 24 King George St near the corner of Ben Yehuda St. It is open Sunday to Thursday from 8.30 am to 6 pm, Friday from 8.30 am to 2.30 pm. They only have a limited amount of information here although there is an up-to-date Egged Bus schedule displayed.

The staff in the branch office (tel 282295) just inside Jaffa Gate are much more helpful and they have good free handout maps. It is open the same hours as the main office as well as on Saturday from 10 am to 2 pm. The free weekly booklet *This Week in Jerusalem* has comprehensive listings of what's on as well as handy phone numbers and a list of the major hotels.

The Christian Information Centre just inside Jaffa Gate has some useful maps for sale. It is open Monday to Saturday from 8.30 am to 12.30 pm and from 3 to 6 pm.

**Post & Telecommunications** The main post office is at 23 Yaffa Rd and is open from 8 am to 6 pm Sunday to Thursday, 8 am to 1 pm Friday, and is closed Saturdays. The poste restante counter is well organised and you need to show some form of identification.

The international telephone office is down the stairs and around the back. It's open from 6 am to 10 pm Sunday to Thursday, 6.30 am to 3.30 pm Friday, closed Saturday. International connections are quick and easy. It's also possible to make international collect calls from many public phones – just dial 18 for the international operator. Public telephones take tokens which are available from any post office.

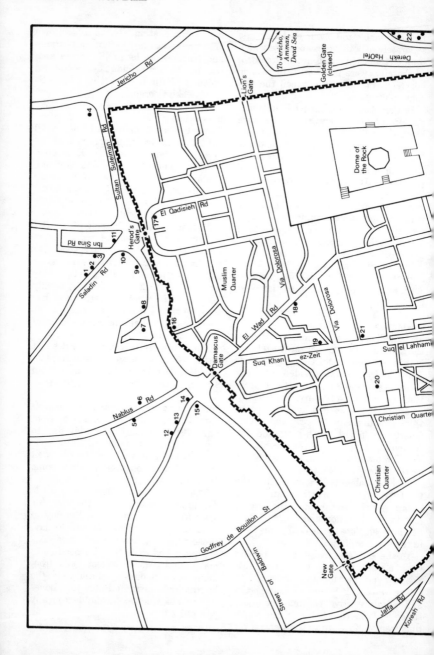

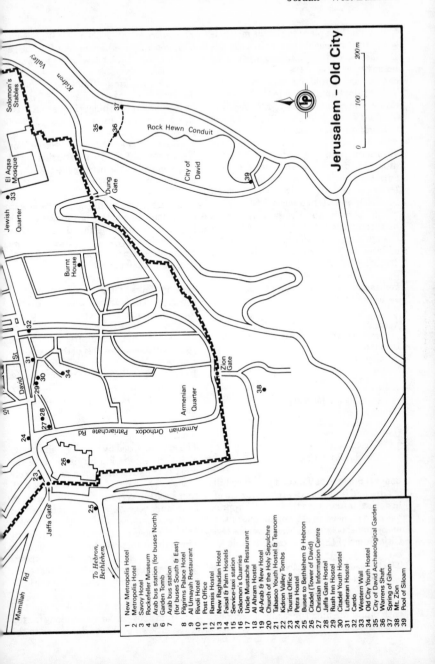

# Jerusalem – Old City

0    100    200 m

Solomon's Stables

Kidron Valley

El Aqsa Mosque 33

Jewish Quarter

Dung Gate

35 • 37
36
Rock Hewn Conduit

City of David

39

Burnt House

32
31
David St
St
30
29
28
27 34
24
26
23
Jaffa Gate
25

Mamillah Rd

To Hebron, Bethlehem

Armenian Orthodox Patriarchate Rd

Armenian Quarter

Zion Gate

38

1    New Metropolis Hotel
2    Metropolis Hotel
3    Savoy Hotel
4    Rockefeller Museum
5    Arab bus station (for buses North)
6    Garden Tomb
7    Arab bus station
     (for buses South & East)
8    Pilgrims Palace Hotel
9    Al Umayah Restaurant
10   Rivoli Hotel
11   Post Office
12   Ramsis Hostel
13   New Raghadan Hotel
14   Faisal & Palm Hostels
15   Service-taxi station
16   Solomon's Quarries
17   Uncle Mustache Restaurant
18   Al Ahram Hostel
19   Al-Arab & New Hotel
20   Church of the Holy Sepulchre
21   Tabasco Youth Hostel & Tearoom
22   Kidron Valley Tombs
23   Tourist Office
24   Petra Hostel
25   Buses to Bethlehem & Hebron
26   Citadel (Tower of David)
27   Christian Information Centre
28   Jaffa Gate Hostel
29   Rush Inn Hostel
30   Citadel Youth Hostel
31   Lutheran Hostel
32   Cardo
33   Western Wall
34   Old City Youth Hostel
35   City of David Archaeological Garden
36   Warrens Shaft
37   Spring of Gihon
38   Mt. Zion
39   Pool of Siloam

**Money** The best place to change money is with the moneychangers just inside Damascus Gate. They are open long hours but as most of them are Muslims it can be hard to find one open on Fridays. The regular banks are all in the New City and are open on Sunday, Monday and Thursday from 8.30 am to 12.30 pm and 4 to 5 pm; on Wednesday and Friday from 8.30 am to 12 noon, closed Monday afternoon and Saturday. Jordanian dinars and US dollars are the best currencies to have. The rates for cash are: US$1 equals 1.5 NIS (New Israeli Shekels), and JD1 equals 4.8 NIS.

The American Express agent is Meditrad Ltd (tel 222211), 27 King George St in the New City. The postal address is PO Box 2345, New City, Jerusalem 91022.

**Embassies** Some of the embassies in Jerusalem are:

Austria
    8 Hoveve Zion St, tel 631291
Denmark
    5 Beni Brit St, tel 228083
Italy
    November St, tel 631236
Sweden
    58 Nablus Rd, tel 284117
United Kingdom
    19 Nashashibi St, tel 717724
USA
    18 Agron St, tel 234271
    27 Nablus Rd, tel 272681

**Books & Bookshops** The Old City is so full of sites and buildings of archaeological or historical importance that to fully appreciate it you need to get hold of one of the many guidebooks available all over the Old City. Some of the better ones include:

*The Jerusalem Guide* by Gloria Shamis and Diana Shalem, 8 NIS; guided walks through Old City and Mount of Olives, places of interest in New City; complete with maps, opening times and directions to each place.

*This is Jerusalem – A Complete Walkabout Guidebook* by Herbert Bishka, 7.5 NIS; a well put together book with guided walks in the Old City.

*Marty's Walking Tours of Biblical Jerusalem* by Marty Isaacs, 8 NIS; a humorous guide to places in the Old City, the Mount of Olives and the City of David.

*Footloose in Jerusalem* by Sarah Fox Kaminker, 10 NIS; illustrations and maps as well as the usual guided walks in the Old and New Cities.

There are a number of good bookshops in Jerusalem. One of the best places to look for books is along Jaffa Rd in the New City. Steimatzky's at 39 Jaffa Rd, has an extensive selection of English-language books and magazines.

**Walking Tours** There are a number of accompanied walking tours available, some of which are free. The Sheraton Jerusalem Plaza Hotel (tel 228133) at 47 King George St conducts free tours where you have to share the cost of the taxi to the starting point. Others which cost from 10 NIS to 15 NIS start from outside the Tower of David by Jaffa Gate. *This Week in Jerusalem* has a day by day list of what tours are available.

### Old City

The area enclosed by the city walls is only about one square km but it is one of the most fascinating areas you're ever likely to visit. The narrow alleys are thick with shops selling every imaginable souvenir, fruit and vegetable stalls, meat shops with whole carcasses hanging on hooks, and little hole-in-the-wall shoe repairers. Through all this are the tourists in their thousands. Every day during daylight hours the streets are packed with visitors of all ages and sizes from all over the world.

**The Walls** To get a good look at the Old City from above, take a walk along the top of the city walls. These date back to the

Top: The desert castle of Qasr al Kharanah – near Azraq, Jordan
Left: Dusk at the mosque in Ajlun, Jordan
Right: The Golan Heights as seen from Umm Qais, Jordan

Top: Intensive farming on the West Bank near Jericho, Jordan
Left: Israelis near the Western Wall in the Old City of Jerusalem
Right: The Dome of the Rock in Jerusalem's Old City

16th century and are pierced by eight gates, only one of which is not in use today. The Damascus Gate is the main gate in the northern wall and at the base of it, below the present ground level, can be seen the foundations of the original gate dating to the time of Hadrian. East of here is Herod's Gate, named after a house in the Muslim Quarter reputed to have belonged to Herod Antipas. In Arabic the gate is called Bab ez-Zahireh – the Flowery Gate.

Of the two gates in the eastern wall, only Lion's Gate (also called St Stephen's Gate) is open. The name comes from the lions decorating it. The Golden Gate further south has been blocked since 1530, and is believed to be the site of the Closed Gate of the First Temple and the entrance which the Messiah will pass through (Ezekiel 44, 1-3).

The southern wall is pierced by Dung Gate, which opens on to the Western Wall, and Zion Gate, which is where Mt Zion is cut in half leaving David's Tomb and the Church of the Dormition outside.

The only gate in the west wall is Jaffa Gate which is the busiest today. The wall was breached in the 19th century to give vehicle access. The last gate is New Gate in the western corner, built in 1887. It costs 1.5 NIS to get on the ramparts, which are open from 9 am to 5 pm daily, and you can walk from Lion's Gate around to Jaffa Gate, and from Zion Gate along to Dung Gate.

**Temple Mount & Western Wall** Occupying almost 20% of the area of the Old City is Temple Mount, sacred to Jews, Christians and Muslims. Although the site had been used for pagan worship as early as 3000 BC, it was during Solomon's reign from 970 to 930 BC that the first Temple was built. Nebuchadnezzar destroyed it in 586 BC and carted the Jews off to Babylon. The Jews returned from exile and built the Second Temple later the same century.

Herod the Great decided to enlarge the platform and rebuilt the Temple in lavish style. Some of the walls he built around the platform still stand – the Western Wall is today the most sacred for the Jewish people. In 70 AD during the Jewish Revolt the Temple was destroyed by the Romans. From then until the Muslim conquest in 638 the site was neglected. The Muslims identified the rock (Al Sakhra) as the site of Mohammed's ascent to heaven and the exquisite monument, the Dome of the Rock, was built in 688.

Jews were banned from the Temple during the years from partition in 1948 until they annexed the Old City and East Jerusalem after the 1967 war. The Dome of the Rock is still held by the Muslims and although they have the sole right of worship, by Israeli law it is open to people of any faith.

The entrance for non-Muslims is through the Moors Gate by the Western Wall and as you ascend the ramp to the entrance, down to the right you can see excavations which have yielded discoveries from all stages of the city's history. Temple Mount is open to visitors from 8 am to 4 pm daily except Fridays and during Muslim prayer times and holidays. All bags are searched as you go in – something you'll get thoroughly sick of if you spend any time in Jerusalem. Tickets are sold from the booth inside the gate. It costs 5.2 NIS to visit the Islamic Museum, the Al Aqsa Mosque and the Dome of the Rock. The tickets still have the price printed in Jordanian dinars (JD1.200).

The Western Wall of the Temple Mount is part of the retaining wall built by Herod and is where the Jews come to mourn the destruction of the First and Second Temples, hence its more common name – the Wailing Wall. The large blocks of the lower courses are the original Herodian wall; the smaller blocks higher up belong to the Roman, Byzantine, Arab and Turkish periods. More than 20 metres of the wall is buried below the present ground level. As prescribed by Jewish law, the prayer sections for men

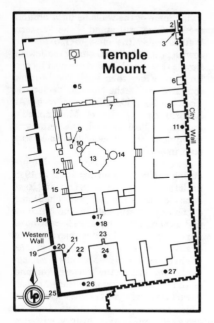

| | |
|---|---|
| 1 | Throne of Jesus |
| 2 | Tourist entrance |
| 3 | Gate of the Tribes |
| 4 | Herodian tower |
| 5 | Herodian Pavement of Temple Courtyard |
| 6 | Solomon's Throne |
| 7 | The Scales |
| 8 | Muslim Cemetery |
| 9 | Dome of the Ascension |
| 10 | Dome of the Prophet |
| 11 | Golden Gate |
| 12 | Medressa Sultaniyya |
| 13 | Dome of the Rock |
| 14 | Dome of the Chain |
| 15 | Medressa Shrafiya |
| 16 | Wisons Arch |
| 17 | Olive Tree of the Prophet |
| 18 | El Kas (The Cup) |
| 19 | Tourist entrance |
| 20 | Moors Gate |
| 21 | Islamic Museum |
| 22 | Dome of Joseph |
| 23 | Steps to Ancient Aqsa |
| 24 | El Aqsa Mosque |
| 25 | Robinson's Arch |
| 26 | Women's Mosque |
| 27 | Solomon's Stables |

and women are separate. The best time for a visit to the wall is at sunset on Friday afternoon – the beginning of *shabbat* (Sabbath) – when thousands of Jews come down to make their devotions. It is important to note that smoking and photography in the vicinity of the wall are prohibited during the Sabbath, which lasts from sunset Friday to sunset on Saturday.

The Torahs are kept in the vault at the northern end of the wall known as Wilson's Arch, named after the British archaeologist who discovered it.

**The Via Dolorosa** This is the Path of Sorrow that follows the route of Jesus from his condemnation to his tomb. It starts at Lion's Gate and finishes inside the Church of the Holy Sepulchre. The 14 stations of the Cross are marked, usually indistinctly, along the route. Every day hundreds of Christian tourists trace the route, sometimes bearing crosses, and

stop at each station to pray. It's easy to tag along with a group if you hear one speaking your language and you want the full details.

Inside the Lion's Gate on the right is the Church of Anne, the traditional site of the birthplace of Mary. The church dates back to Crusader times and is open daily from 8 am to 12 noon and 2 to 5 pm.

Further up on the left is a ramp leading up to the Al Omariya School – the site of the trial of Jesus and the 1st Station of the Cross. Some Christians believe that the true site is under the Convent of the Sisters of Zion, just across the road. Every Friday at 3 pm a group of priests and dozens of tourists assemble in the school courtyard and follow the Via Dolorosa – it's an interesting procession to join.

Next on the right are the Convents of the Flagellation & Condemnation, the 2nd station where Jesus received the Cross (open during the mornings only).

Stations three to eight are marked along the route. At the 3rd, on the corner of El Wad Rd, Jesus fell for the first time; at the 4th, just past the Armenian Catholic Church, he met Mary.

The Via Dolorosa then turns up the steps to the right to the 5th Station where Simon of Cyrene wiped the face of Jesus; the 6th Station is marked by the Church of St Veronica, where Veronica wiped Jesus' face. At the 7th station he fell for the second time. The 8th is marked by a cross on the wall of a Greek Monastery and marks the site where Christ spoke to the 'Daughters of Jerusalem' – women who were mourning along the route. To get to the rest of the stations, return along Suq Khan ez-Zeit and take a right turn. At the ninth station Jesus fell for the third time. The last five stations of the Cross are inside the Church of the Holy Sepulchre.

**The Church of the Holy Sepulchre** is built on the site that traditionally marks the place

where Jesus was Crucified and buried, first identified by the emperor Constantine's mother, Helena, on a pilgrimage to Jerusalem in the 4th century. Constantine had a magnificent church built on the site in 335 AD which was destroyed by the Persians in 614 and later rebuilt on a more modest scale, only to be destroyed by the Turks in 1010.

The Crusaders again rebuilt the church in the 12th century and it is this building that stands today.

The Ottoman Turks then divided the church between six communities: Greek Orthodox, Armenian Orthodox, Franciscans, Syrian, Coptic and Ethiopian Churches. Each community has the rights to certain parts of the church and so the cavernous interior is a mixture of different styles. The division of the church has also meant that no co-ordinated restoration has been carried out and only bits and pieces get done.

The Via Dolorosa continues inside, and

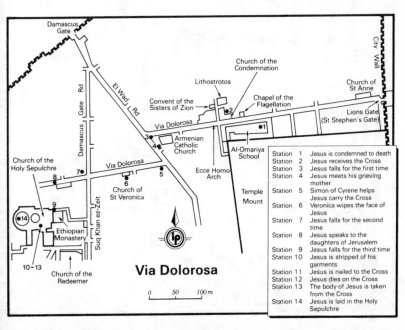

|  | |
|---|---|
| Station 1 | Jesus is condemned to death |
| Station 2 | Jesus receives the Cross |
| Station 3 | Jesus falls for the first time |
| Station 4 | Jesus meets his grieving mother |
| Station 5 | Simon of Cyrene helps Jesus carry the Cross |
| Station 6 | Veronica wipes the face of Jesus |
| Station 7 | Jesus falls for the second time |
| Station 8 | Jesus speaks to the daughters of Jerusalem |
| Station 9 | Jesus falls for the third time |
| Station 10 | Jesus is stripped of his garments |
| Station 11 | Jesus is nailed to the Cross |
| Station 12 | Jesus dies on the Cross |
| Station 13 | The body of Jesus is taken from the Cross |
| Station 14 | Jesus is laid in the Holy Sepulchre |

**Via Dolorosa**

0      50      100 m

# Church of the Holy Sepulchre

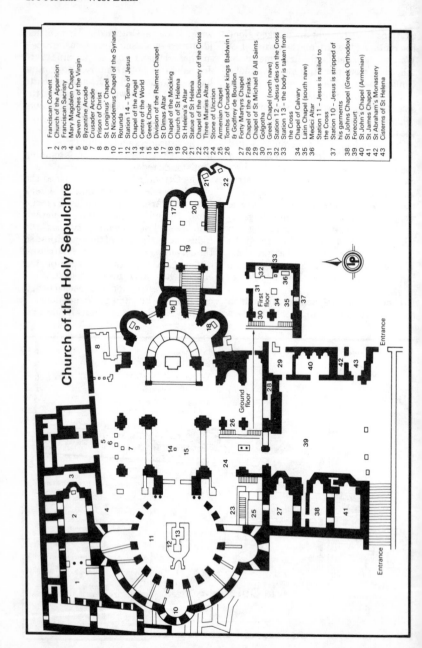

1   Franciscan Convent
2   Church of the Apparition
3   Franciscan Sacristy
4   Mary Magdalen Chapel
5   Seven Arches of the Virgin
6   Byzantine Arcade
7   Crusader Arcade
8   Prison of Christ
9   St Longinus' Chapel
10  St Nicodemus Chapel of the Syrians
11  Rotunda
12  Station 14 – Tomb of Jesus
13  Chapel of the Angel
14  Centre of the World
15  Greek Choir
16  Division of the Raiment Chapel
17  St Dimas Altar
18  Chapel of the Mocking
19  Church of St Helena
20  St Helena's Altar
21  Statue of St Helena
22  Chapel of the Discovery of the Cross
23  Three Maries Altar
24  Stone of Unction
25  Armenian Chapel
26  Tombs of Crusader kings Baldwin I
     & Godfrey de Bouillon
27  Forty Martyrs Chapel
28  Chapel of the Franks
29  Chapel of St Michael & All Saints
30  Golgotha
31  Greek Chapel (north nave)
32  Station 12 – Jesus dies on the Cross
33  Station 13 – the body is taken from
     the Cross
34  Chapel of Calvary
35  Latin Chapel (south nave)
36  Medici Altar
37  Station 11 – Jesus is nailed to
     the Cross
     Station 10 – Jesus is stripped of
     his garments
38  St Johns Chapel (Greek Orthodox)
39  Forecourt
40  St John's Chapel (Armenian)
41  St James Chapel
42  St Abraham's Monastery
43  Cisterns of St Helena

up the stairs to the right are two chapels. The southern one belongs to the Franciscans and marks the 10th and 11th stations of the Cross where Jesus was stripped of his clothes and nailed to the Cross. The northern chapel belongs to the Greek Orthodox Church and they venerate the 12th Station where Jesus died on the Cross – the site is marked by a silver disc on the floor under the altar. In between the two chapels is the 13th station where Mary received Jesus' body and it is marked by a statue of Mary surrounded by all manner of offerings.

The 14th station is in the marble structure in the rotunda and marks the site where Jesus was laid in the Holy Sepulchre. No more than four people can enter the tomb at once so the queue outside it is often 50 metres long! Inside are two chambers; the first is the Chapel of the Angel where the Resurrection was supposedly announced from, and the second is the sepulchre itself, dimly lit by candles and guarded over by a priest.

The rest of the church is a jumble of various chapels and shrines belonging to the different faiths. At the eastern end steps lead down to the Church of St Helena and another flight lead further down to the Chapel of the Discovery of the Cross.

Try to visit in the early morning or late in the evening when there are likely to be fewer crowds – this place gets packed out. It is open daily from early in the morning until 8 pm and modest dress is necessary, which means long pants for men and dresses for women.

**The Citadel** Right by Jaffa Gate is the Citadel, the only surviving example of the towers built to protect the city in the 1st century. The upper sections were built by the Crusaders. From the top of the Tower of Phaesal there are excellent views across the Old City to the Mount of Olives in the distance.

Excavations in the Citadel have revealed finds from all periods and the Tower of Phaesal is a good vantage point to see the layout. The enormous model of Jerusalem as it was in 1873 is also worth seeing.

The site is open daily from 8.30 am to 4.30 pm in summer and 8.30 am to 7 pm in winter. There is an impressive, eight-screen audio visual show introducing Jerusalem in different languages. English screenings are on weekdays at 8.30 and 10.30 am, 12 noon, 12.30, 2.30, 4, 6 and 6.30 pm. French screenings at 10 am, 2 and 5 pm; German at 8.30 am, 12.30 and 6 pm.

**The Jewish Quarter** was virtually destroyed in the war of 1948 and has been rebuilt since 1967. The new buildings give it a very modern, almost sterile feel in places and the trendy boutiques look out of place. Fortunately, Jerusalem's building laws require that all buildings use local sandstone in their construction which means something of the old character has been preserved.

The Jewish Quarter starts off to the right of David St which leads down into the heart of the Old City from Jaffa Gate. The Cardo Maximus, the main street in ancient times, continues on from Suq al Attarin. It has now been covered over and houses very up-market shops. At one point you can descend some stairs on the right and see remains of the Hasmonean city walls from the First Temple period.

Dotted throughout the quarter are historical synagogues and *yeshivas* (places of religious study) and all the sites of interest are well signposted.

The Burnt House near the eastern edge is the well-displayed ruins of the house belonging to a priest in the Second Temple period. It was destroyed by the Romans during the Jewish Revolt in 70 AD and the excavations here yielded some of the first evidence of the destruction of the city. Furniture and household items were found beneath the collapsed walls and these remain in position. In one corner the remains of an arm were found gripping a stairway, and a spear, half melted by the heat of the fire, was stuck to one wall. The ruins are now in the basement of a private house and are only open during the sound-and-light show which is in English daily at 11.30 am, 1.30 and 3.30 pm; entry is 2 NIS.

Outside the Burnt House are the Seven Arches, the remains of the Jewish bazaar of the old city, which have been incorporated into the modern reconstruction.

## Mount Zion

Mount Zion lies outside the walled city to the south although at some stages since the Second Temple era it has been within the walls. According to tradition, Suleiman's engineers forgot to include it when the present walls were being built in the 16th century and they were executed for this omission.

It was long believed that David was buried here but it is now thought that the Tombs of David are at Silwan, further to the east.

Christians revere Mount Zion as the place of the Last Supper, the Dormition of Mary and the resting place of St Stephen. For Jews it was important as a substitute place of worship during the periods when they were banned from Temple Mount because, according to the Bible, it was here that David placed the Ark of the Covenant before Solomon built the Temple.

Sites to visit here include the Church of the Dormition, built when the German Emperor acquired the land in 1898 to commemorate the last sleep of the Virgin Mary; the Tomb of the House of David (very little to see); and the Convent of the Cenacle, which contains the room of the Last Supper (open 7 am to 12 noon and 3 to 6 pm weekdays).

## City of David

The City of David lies on the ridge called Ophel directly south of the Temple Mount. This was Canaanite Jerusalem, conquered by King David when his army poured through the underground course of the Spring of Gihon, the city's water supply. Excavations have just been completed and the new City of David Archaeological Garden is conveniently small to look through and the points of interest are well marked. The stairs leading down to it are 200 metres east of Dung Gate where the road curves around the south-east corner of Temple Mount; entry is 1.5 NIS.

From the Archaeological Garden, take the exit on the downhill side and you come to the new building built over Warren's Shaft, a water shaft named after the archaeologist who discovered it. This is where the residents of Canaanite Jerusalem used to come to draw water from the Spring of Gihon. The tunnel winds down through the rock for 50 metres or so and ends in a 20-metre drop to the spring. You can hear the voices of people down below.

In 701 BC, King Hezekiah built a 540-metre tunnel to bring the water from the spring to a place within the city walls, denying the attacking Assyrians access to water. Known as Hezekiah's Tunnel, it was built by labourers who started at either end and only joined the two tunnels hours before the arrival of the Assyrians. It's still possible to walk through the tunnel today if you have shorts and a flashlight. The entrance is through the Spring Of Gihon right at the bottom of the steps down from Ophel. The spring is also known as the Fountain of the Virgin because the story goes that Mary once drew water here.

## Kidron Valley

From the Spring of Gihon, you can walk up through the Kidron Valley to the burial monuments known collectively as the Tomb of Absalom. They date from the Second Temple period and are the best preserved Hasmonean monuments in the city. The first is the Tomb of Zachariah, a priest at the time. Next is the Tomb of Beni Hezir with its Greek portico cut into the face of the rock. It belongs to a priestly family from the 2nd century BC.

The most impressive of the four tombs here is the Pillar of Absalom, which traditionally is the tomb of David's son (II Samuel 15-19), but he is in fact buried elsewhere. It is over 20 metres tall and has been carved out of the solid rock. Behind it is the Cavern of Jehoshaphat with eight burial chambers.

### East Jerusalem

**The Mount of Olives** to the east of the Old City is revered by Christians as the site of Jesus' arrest after his betrayal by Judas at Gethsemane, and as the place of his ascension to heaven. The southern slope is an enormous Jewish cemetery and to

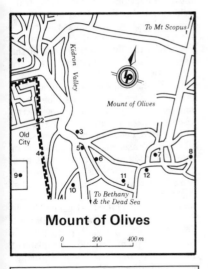

**Mount of Olives**

```
0        200      400 m
```

| 1 | Rockefeller Museum |
| 2 | Lion's Gate |
| 3 | Church of the Assumption & Grotto |
| 4 | Golden Gate |
| 5 | Church of All Nations |
| 6 | Church of Mary Magdalene |
| 7 | Chapel of the Ascension |
| 8 | Russian Orthodox Church |
| 9 | Dome of the Rock |
| 10 | Tombs of Absalom |
| 11 | Church of Dominus Flevit |
| 12 | Church of the Pater Noster |

the north of this are a number of churches, the most impressive being the Russian Orthodox with its bell tower – the highest point in Jerusalem. The northern peak of the Mount is the site of the Mount Scopus campus of the Hebrew University.

At the bottom of the hill, the first of the churches is the Church of the Assumption or the Tomb of the Virgin Mary. This gloomy underground church is lit only by candles and whatever daylight can find its way in from the entrance. Upkeep is shared by the Greek Orthodox, Armenian, Syrian and Coptic churches. It is open from 6 to 11.30 am and 2 to 5 pm. The grotto to the right of the entrance courtyard is said to be where Jesus was betrayed – one of the three supposed sites of the Garden of Gethsemane.

The Church of All Nations or the Basilica of the Agony is next on the right and is easily recognised by the colourful mosaic of Christ above the entrance. The entrance is up the side road through another Garden of Gethsemane with eight ancient olive trees. The interior of the church has some original Byzantine mosaics on the floors; the ones on the walls are exact replicas. The coats of arms of the countries which contributed to its building in 1924 also adorn the interior. It is open from 8.30 am to 12 noon and summer afternoons from 2 to 5 pm, winter afternoons 3 to 7 pm. Long trousers must be worn by men visiting this church.

Up behind the Church of All Nations on the path leading off to the right is the decorative, Russian Church of Mary Magdalene with its gilded, onion domes. It was built by Tsar Alexander III in 1885 and the crypt contains the body of the Grand Duchess Elizabeth killed in the Russian Revolution.

Next up the hill is the Basilica of Dominus Flevit, the 'Lord Wept'. Built in 1891, it marks the site where Jesus wept for Jerusalem. Up towards the top of the hill on the right are the rock-cut tombs known as the Tombs of the Prophets – Haggai, Zachariah and Malachi.

On the top are the Church of the Pater Noster and Basilica of Eleona, where Christ is said to have taught his disciples the Lord's Prayer; the Chapel of the Ascension, where Christ ascended to Heaven; and the Russian Orthodox Church with its bell-tower which you need permission to enter, only available from the Russian Mission in the Old City.

**The Rockefeller Museum** right opposite the north-east corner of the Old City has finds on display from prehistory to the present. Of greatest interest is the beautiful stucco work found in the Hisham Palace (Khirbat al Mafjar) near Jericho dating back to the time of the Omayyed Caliphs of Damascus.

It is open from 10 am to 5 pm Sunday to Thursday and 10 am to 2 pm Friday and Saturday; entry is 4.5 NIS.

**The Garden Tomb** is on the right up Nablus Rd just before the second Arab Bus Station. This is believed by some to be the true site of Christ's crucifixion at Golgotha (which means 'skull' in Hebrew) because of the skull-shaped rock here identified by General Gordon (of Khartoum fame) in 1883.

The garden is a cool escape from the traffic and bustle outside and you can be entertained by the tourist groups who come in and fervently sing gospel songs.

It is open from 8 am to 12.15 pm and 2.15 to 5.15 pm and the building at the entrance has an amazing array of souvenirs with a religious theme – most of them tacky – and a good selection of books.

**The Tomb of the Kings** is further up Nablus Rd on the right. It was so named because it was originally thought that the Kings of Judaea were buried here. It is in fact the family tomb of a queen from Mesopotamia who came to Jerusalem in the first century AD.

The enormous staircase leads down to a forecourt and in the tombs here you can still see the stone in place that was rolled across in front of the entrance. Bring a torch if you want to have a poke around in some of the 30 tombs.

It is open daily from 8 am to 12.30 and 2 to 5 pm; entry is 1 NIS, 50 agorot for students.

### New City

Despite the fact that the new city is built of the same golden limestone as the Old City, it has none of the fascination of the latter and is just a modern, bustling capital city reminiscent of many European cities.

**The Israel Museum** This has one of the finest collections of artefacts from prehistoric times. Even if you are normally bored shitless by museums, this one is worth a visit. The free guided tours which leave from the information desk in the main building at 11 am are very informative.

The Shrine of the Book is the building housing the Dead Sea Scrolls. The scrolls were written by the members of the obscure Jewish Essene sect in the 2nd century BC. They are the oldest known Biblical manuscripts and lay stashed in the caves at Qumran by the Dead Sea for almost 2000 years before being discovered by a couple of Bedouin boys in the 1940s. The curious shape of the Shrine of the Book is modelled after the upended bowls that covered the pots that the scrolls were found in. Unfortunately there is little in the way of explanation and description of the scrolls and the poor lighting, presumably designed to stop any deterioration of the originals, makes it difficult to see. There are guided tours in English at 1.30 pm on Sunday and 3 pm on Tuesday.

The museum is open from 10 am to 5 pm on Sunday, Monday, Wednesday and Thursday; 10 am to 10 pm Tuesday; and 10 am to 2 pm Friday and Saturday. The Shrine of the Book is closed on Friday and Saturday. Entry is 4.50 NIS for the museum only, 6.50 for the museum and the shrine; 3 NIS for students. To get there take bus No 9 from outside the Central Bus Station.

**The Knesset** is Israel's parliament building and is open during public sessions from 4 to 9 pm on Monday and Tuesday and from 11 am to 1 pm on Wednesday. Free guided tours on Sunday and Thursday from 8.30 am to 2.30 pm – bring your passport.

The building is just across the road from the Israel Museum; bus No 9 from the Central Bus Station.

**Yad VaShem** is a massive memorial and museum to the Jews who died in Europe. There are photographs, videos and commentaries arranged chronologically which document Hitler's rise to power and the suppression and extermination of the Jewish people. It's designed to shock.

It is open from 9 am to 5 pm Sunday to Thursday and on Friday from 8 am to 1 pm. Take bus No 20 from Jaffa Gate, bus 27 from Damascus Gate or buses 17, 18, 20, 23 or 27 from the Central Bus Station and get off at the Mt Herzl park on the right. Yad VaShem is down the road to the left of the park.

For a complete guide to the New City (and the rest of Israel) see the Lonely Planet guidebook *Israel – a travel survival kit*.

**Places to Stay**
As you might expect in a place with as many tourists as Jerusalem, there are almost endless accommodation possibilities from the US$2 fleapit to the US$100 five-star.

Cheap hostels abound, mostly in and around the Old City and as competition is fierce, the standard in most places is quite acceptable. Many have curfews and are closed for a few hours during the day so it's a matter of finding one that suits your habits. Theft can be a problem in these places so be careful with valuables. Usual charges are 4 to 5 NIS.

Next up the scale are the Christian Hospices in the Old City run by the various churches. These offer safe, clean accommodation, often with breakfast thrown in, but are usually heavily booked and have an air of austerity about them. Prices in the range of US$6 for a dorm and US$25 to US$50 a double.

There's a cluster of mid-range hotels in East Jerusalem in the US$15/30 range for singles/doubles. From here on up the sky is the limit with the Hilton, Sheraton and Intercontinental type place.

**Places to Stay - bottom end**
**Around Damascus Gate** The Old City offers the most atmosphere and colour but also the most noise. Accommodation centres around Damascus and Jaffa Gates.

Just outside Damascus Gate opposite the *sherut* station are two of the best hostels in Jerusalem. The *Palm Hostel* at 6 HaNevi'im St has dorms which are not too crowded, a great lounge and a friendly atmosphere. There are cooking facilities and a fridge for guests' use. The only hassle is the 10.30 am to 2.30 pm lock-out and the 11 pm (flexible) curfew, although you can check in at any time during the day. They charge 5 NIS for a dorm bed.

Right next door is the *Faisal Hostel* (tel 282189) at 4 HaNevi'im St. It has the cavernous air of a railway station but is certainly spacious and has good views of Damascus Gate from the balcony. Free tea and coffee; kitchen and fridge; closed from 10.30 am to 1.30 during the day; midnight curfew; 5 NIS in a dorm.

Just up the road a bit is the *New Raghadan Hotel* (tel 282725) at No 10 and the *Ramsis Hostel* (tel 283733) at No 20. Both places are quite OK and the Raghadan has double rooms for US$10 and a midnight curfew.

Inside the Old City, the *Al Ahram Youth Hostel* on El Wad St near the corner of the Via Dolorosa is a very friendly, easygoing place run by Arabs.

There is a tiny kitchen, fridge and the graffiti walls in the lounge makes for some interesting reading! They really pack 'em in here, especially on the roof on the 5th floor. Good views from the top bunks but the loudspeaker from the mosque is only a couple of metres above your head which makes for an extremely loud awakening at 5 am – you have been warned. There's no curfew during the day and the midnight curfew is very flexible – just knock on the door if you're late. A bed on the roof is 4 NIS; or in a room downstairs for 5 NIS; doubles for 10 NIS per person.

The *Tabasco Youth Hostel & Tea Room* on Aqabat Al Takiyeh St is a bit of a strange place but is friendly enough. The rooms are dingy and feel damp and the music from the bar downstairs blares away till all hours. Dorm beds for 5 NIS.

The *New Hotel* on Khan Ez Zeit has reasonable doubles for 15 NIS with bath but as the place has absolutely zilch in the way of atmosphere it is usually empty and bargaining is possible. The same applies to the *El Arab Hotel*, a couple of doors down, where dirty doubles cost 10 NIS.

**Around Jaffa Gate** The management in the *Petra Hostel* just inside Jaffa Gate on the left are a bit stern and the rooms are crowded, but the ones at the front have balconies where you can sit out and watch the passing parade. Open all day and a flexible 11 pm curfew; 5 NIS.

In a lane by the Christian Information Centre is the *Jaffa Gate Hostel* where you can get an idea of what it must be like to be a sardine. It's cheap at 4.5 NIS for a bed and 13 NIS for a double. It is open all day and has a late curfew of 12.30 am.

At 42 St Marks Rd the *Rush Inn Hostel* is the last place you would want to rush in to. Two tiny, claustrophobic dorms which the manageress describes as 'cosy' – what an imagination! The kitchen would serve better as a cupboard. Open all day with an 11 pm curfew. At 5 NIS it's only for the desperate.

A bit further along St Marks Rd, the

*Citadel Youth Hostel* is friendly and well run but the dungeon-like rooms are crowded. There's a small kitchen for guests to use. It's open all day; midnight curfew; 5 NIS for a bed.

The *Lutheran Hostel* (tel 282120), also on St Marks Rd, is very well appointed but you get the feeling that you're likely to be shot (or worse) if you put a foot wrong. Curfew from 9 am to 12 noon, and at 11 pm. A dorm bed is 7 NIS and a double is a hefty US$50 including breakfast.

The *Old City Youth Hostel* (tel 288611) is an IYHA hostel just off St Marks Rd – follow the signs from the Lutheran Hostel. It's closed from 9 am to 5 pm and the curfew is at 10 pm sharp!

Opposite the Citadel is the *Christ Church Hospice* (tel 282082) staffed by Englishmen. It is usually booked out by groups but beds cost US$6 in segregated dorms; the price includes breakfast. Closed from 10 am to 4 pm; 11 pm curfew.

**New City** If you want the night life, the New City is the place to stay as nothing much goes on in the Old City after 9 pm.

The *King George Hostel* at 15 King George St near the corner of Ben Yehuda St is a real rabbit warren and is full of budding guitar strummers and faded hippies. There's no evening curfew and the place is open all day. Dorm beds cost 5 NIS; doubles 13 NIS.

A little more sane is the *Edison Youth Hostel* on Yeshayahu St opposite the Edison Cinema. The atmosphere is friendly but the dorms are packed. A bed is 4.50 NIS and if you pay for six nights you get the seventh free.

The *Geffen Hostel* (tel 224075) in HaHavatselet St, just off Jaffa Rd near Zion Square, is bright and airy and has singles/doubles/triples for US$7/14/20. There's a kitchen, TV lounge and a helpful manager.

**Places to Stay – middle**
**Around Damascus Gate** The mid-range hotels on and around Saladin Rd north of

Herod's Gate all require payment in foreign currency. The *Savoy Hotel* (tel 283366) on Ibn Sina Rd charges US$12/20 for rather gloomy singles/doubles with breakfast. The *Metropole Hotel* (tel 282507) is better at US$15/30, also including breakfast.

The *Jerusalem Hotel* (tel 283282) at 4 Antara Ben-Shaddad St is just off Nablus Rd north of the bus station, near the last stop for the No 27 Egged bus. Good value in this quiet, comfortable, friendly hotel. If it's empty, bargain for around US$10 per person with breakfast.

On Sultan Suleiman Rd near the Arab Bus Station, the three-star *Pilgrims Palace Hotel* (tel 284831) is popular with tour groups and charges US$26/38 including breakfast for air-con rooms.

Other three-star and above places around Saladin St include the *National Palace* (tel 282246), the *Ritz* (tel 284853), the *St George* (tel 282571), and the *Capitol* (tel 282561).

**Around Jaffa Gate** The *Knights Palace Hotel* (tel 282537) 4 Jawalden St is in the Old City. It is basic but good and it is a grand old building. Singles/doubles are US$18/32 with breakfast. From Jaffa Gate take the first left and follow it around the bend; it is on the left.

*Lark Hotel* (tel 283431/2), Latin Patriarchate Rd, near Jaffa Gate is quiet and well run. Singles/doubles are US$15/28 with breakfast.

**The Mount of Olives** has a number of places with excellent views over the Old City but they are all of the three-star-plus variety. They include the *Palace Hotel* (tel 284981), the *Commodore Hotel* (tel 284845), and the *Astoria Hotel* (tel 284965) which at US$15/30 is the cheapest of the bunch.

**Places to Stay – top end**
Jerusalem's luxury hotels are almost all in the New City. Top-end hotels include the *Tirat Bat-Sheva* (tel 232121), King George St and the *Jerusalem Plaza* (tel 228133), King George St, which is part of the Sheraton chain and is centrally located. The *Intercontinental Jerusalem* (tel 282551) is on top of the Mount of Olives with views over the whole city.

The *American Colony Hotel* (tel 282421) is at 1 Louis Vincent St, Nablus Rd, East Jerusalem. This grand old place was once the home of a Turkish pasha. Rooms vary in quality and price from US$26 to US$70 for singles, US$50 to US$100 for doubles.

Jerusalem's most famous hotel is the *King David* (tel 221111) on King David St. Singles are US$72 to US$137, doubles US$84 to US$149.

**Places to Eat**
If you are on a tight budget then the only way to go is to find a hostel with a kitchen and do your own cooking. Shops, stalls and carts in the Old City sell everything you're likely to need. Once you start buying prepared food your costs will rocket enormously.

**Old City & East Jerusalem** The cheapest staple are the felafels – pitta bread stuffed with fried chickpeas, hummus and salad. Next up the scale are shawarma – pitta stuffed with meat and salad. These are Arabic foods so are most readily available in the Old City and East Jerusalem. Use some discretion about which stalls you patronise as the standards of hygiene often leave a lot to be desired. Felafels cost about 1 NIS, shawarmas 2.50 NIS. Some of the best felafel stalls set up just inside Damascus Gate in the early evening. There are also restaurants all through the Old City where you can sit down and eat this food as well.

The restaurants just inside Jaffa Gate cater for international tastes; main courses are around 8 NIS.

Just inside Herod's Gate is the *Uncle Moustache Restaurant* where you can get a half chicken or kebabs for 5 NIS. Opposite the same gate on Sultan

Suleiman Rd, the *Al Umayah Restaurant* charges about 10 NIS for main courses and the emphasis is on European food.

**New City** Fast food is the all the rage in the New City and there are a couple of chains. *McDavids* (good grief!) is Israel's answer to you-know-who and they serve the same bland processed garbage. They have even gone as far as naming their hamburgers 'McDavid' (2.40 NIS) and 'Big MacD' (3.60 NIS). Their Jerusalem outlet is at 40 Jaffa Rd near Zion Square.

*Bagel Nash* in the Ben Yehuda pedestrian mall is another American-style chain and offers bagels with various fillings. Set breakfasts for 3.30 NIS and a 7 NIS lunch.

Other places in the mall include the *Liber Vegetarian* with main courses around 5 NIS, blintzes 4 NIS and salads for 3 NIS, and the *Café Sinai* which offers a good breakfast for 3.50 NIS. There are plenty of others in the mall, most of them with tables out on the footpath and they are pleasant places to while away a couple of hours on a warm evening – but check out the prices before you order as they vary widely.

King George Rd between Ben Yehuda St and Jaffa Rd is another good street to go hunting for food. Here there are take-away pizza places, felafel joints where you can stuff your pitta with as much as will fit, and plenty of other sit-down places.

For excellent Italian food try *Mamma Mia's* at 18 Rabbi Kiva St near the Jerusalem Towers Hotel. Their home-made dishes take a lot of beating and you can sit inside or out. Main courses are around 10 NIS; open 12 noon to 12 midnight.

At the entrance to the Central Bus Station there is a fast-food place which does a reasonable burger and chips for 2.40 NIS.

### Getting There

**Egged Bus** The Central (or Egged) Bus Station (tel 528231) is right up at the western end of Jaffa Rd. A No 20 or 23 bus from Jaffa Gate along Jaffa Rd gets you there, or a No 12 from Damascus Gate goes up Saladin St.

The station is well set out with the platforms and timetables listed inside. The staff at the information office are harassed but helpful. Only the buses to Eilat can be booked in advance (window 4 or 5); for all the others you just turn up and stand in the queue. Demand on all routes is usually high so get there at least 30 minutes before your departure and get in the queue.

Due to nervousness about bomb blasts, it is illegal to leave any baggage unattended here. There is a left-luggage service across the road from the station.

Buses stop running about 4 pm on Fridays and nothing at all runs on Saturday. For a complete list of destinations and times, check the board in the tourist office in King George St. The major departures are:

**Tel Aviv**, No 402; nine daily, first at 6.20 am, last at 7.50 pm; 3.50 NIS

**Eilat**, No 444; four daily, first at 7 am, last at 5 pm; 13.50 NIS

**Masada**, No 486; five daily, first at 8.30 am, last at 1 pm; 6.20 NIS.

**Tiberias**, No 961; 10 daily, first at 6.40 am; 6.80 NIS

**Ein Gedi**, No 487; nine daily, first at 7.20 am; 3.50 NIS; last bus returns at 5 pm, 3.20 pm on Fridays.

**Arab Bus** The Arab Bus Station is on Sultan Suleiman Rd in East Jerusalem, about 100 metres from Damascus Gate. Arab buses run to places on the West Bank and are usually cheaper than the Egged buses as they not air-conditioned. There is supposedly a schedule but it's not adhered to. Services are limited on Fridays and Saturdays. There is another station about 100 metres up Nablus Rd for buses to the north of the West Bank (Ramallah and Nablus).

If you are travelling to places on the West Bank you'll get a much better reception from the mainly Arab population if you use the Arab buses.

The only services you are likely to need are to Bethlehem, Jericho and Hebron:

**Bethlehem**, No 22; every 15 minutes or so; 0.50 NIS; you can get on at Jaffa Gate.
**Hebron**, No 23; every half hour; 1.50 NIS; also runs past Jaffa Gate.
**Jericho**, No 28; every hour; 1.30 NIS.

**Train** The railway station is about one km south of Jaffa Gate at the end of King David St. Take a bus No 5, 6, 8, 21 or 30 to get to Jaffa Rd in the New City.

There's a daily service to Tel Aviv, and another to Haifa daily except Friday and Saturday.

**Service-taxi** *(sherut)* The main *sherut* station for West Bank taxis is right outside Damascus Gate. If you are heading for Jordan, be there by about 7 am to be assured of getting one, or ring 223223 the night before and book a seat. It costs 10 NIS to the immigration post, from where you catch a Jordanian JETT bus for the trip to Amman; JD2.500, or JD1.500 just to get to the checkpoint on the East Bank, from where it's an easy hitch to Amman.

For *sheruts* to Tel Aviv, there is a station behind the Central Bus Station.

### Getting Around

**Bus** Jerusalem has an efficient local bus system. The brown map which the tourist office hands out has a list of bus routes on the back.

Jaffa Gate to Central Bus Station – Nos 20, 23
Damascus Gate to Central Bus Station – Nos 12, 27
City Centre to Central Bus Station – Nos 5, 6, 12, 18, 20, 23
Central Bus Station to Knesset & Museum – No 9
Railway Station to centre – Nos 5, 6, 8, 21, 30

Damascus Gate to top of Mt of Olives – No 75

**Taxi** Taxis hang around Jaffa and Damascus Gates and run all over town.

## BETHLEHEM

Lying only about 17 km to the south, Bethlehem is virtually a suburb of Jerusalem. Its setting in the hills make it one of the most beautiful towns on the West Bank.

It is of course famous as being the birth place of Jesus, but it is also the place where King David was anointed by Samuel and where Rachel, the wife of Jacob, died while giving birth to Benjamin.

Today it is on the itinerary of every tour group and the centre of town, Manger Square by the Basilica of the Nativity, is nothing more than a crowded car park for the masses of tour buses which disgorge their loads daily.

### Information

The **tourist office** (tel 742591) on the western edge of Manger Square has a good map of Bethlehem and very little else. It is open Monday to Friday from 8 am to 5 pm and Saturday from 8 am to 1 pm.

The **post office** is just south of the tourist office.

### Basilica of the Nativity

This is certainly not the most beautiful church in the world but is one of the most revered and oldest still in use.

The first church was built on the site during the reign of Constantine in 336 AD under the supervision of his mother. It was destroyed by fire and rebuilt by Justinian in 531. When the Persians invaded in the 7th century and destroyed all the churches in the Holy Land, the Basilica of the Nativity was spared because of the mosaic depicting three wise men in Persian dress. Under Crusader rule, the church was extensively restored and improved.

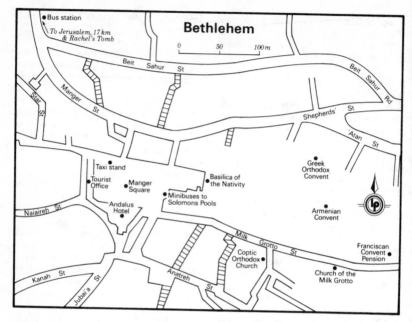

By the 15th century the church was virtually derelict after centuries of neglect by the Mameluke rulers and in 1646 the Ottoman Turks removed the lead roof and melted it down for ammunition. It was finally restored in the 19th century.

Its fortress-like appearance is heightened by the monasteries surrounding it on three sides and by the fact that, apart from the tiny Door of Humility, all the windows and doors have been blocked off.

Once inside the Door of Humility, the imposing rows of red limestone pillars dating back to the time of Justinian dominate the interior. Traces of mosaics on the walls depicting scenes from the New Testament can be seen and beneath the wooden trap-doors in the floors are the impressive mosaics of Constantine's original church floor.

The font in the right nave dates from the Justinian Basilica.

Of the altars in the church, the Main Altar and the Altar of the Circumcision belong to the Greek Orthodox, while the Altar of the Virgin and the Altar of the Three Kings (traditionally where the three kings dismounted) are for the Armenian Orthodox.

The Grotto of the Nativity is reached by stairs either side of the Main Altar. This is supposedly the site where Jesus was born and is the major destination of many pilgrims on a tour of Israel. Below the small altar is a silver star bearing the Latin inscription *Hic de Virgine Maria Jesus Christus natus est* (Here Christ was born of the Virgin Mary). The star that is in place now is a replica of the 1717 original which was stolen in 1847 – one of the events which contributed to the outbreak of the Crimean War. If you want to you can reach down and touch it, or even kiss it, as do many of the devout.

Other altars in the Grotto mark the site of the manger and where the three wise kings worshipped the baby Jesus.

The other grottoes beneath the Basilica are accessible from the bright and airy St Catherine's Church which adjoins the Basilica and was built by the Franciscans in 1881. The Chapel of St Joseph commemorates Joseph's vision of the angel advising him to flee with his family (Matthew 2:13); the Chapel of the Holy Innocents is for the children who died on Herod's orders (Matthew 2:16) – the burial cave can be seen through a grill beneath the altar; other rooms contain the tombs of St Paula and her daughter (St Eusebius) and St Heironymus.

The Basilica is open daily from 6 am to 7 pm; men must wear long pants and women long skirts and long sleeves.

### Church of the Milk Grotto

The cellar of this church is where the Holy Family are said to have hidden while fleeing Herod. It takes its name from the story that the white rocks here are coloured by drops of the nursing Virgin's

| 1 | Cloisters |
|---|---|
| 2 | St Catherine's Church |
| 3 | Altar of the Virgin |
| 4 | Altar of the Three Kings |
| 5 | Door of Humility |
| 6 | Forecourt |
| 7 | Justinian Narthex |
| 8 | Inner room |
| 9 | Choir |
| 10 | Main altar |
| 11 | Font |
| 12 | Altar of the Circumcision |
| 13 | St George's Chapel |
| 14 | Stairs |
| 15 | Chapel of St Heironymus |
| 16 | Tomb of St Eusebius |
| 17 | Tomb of St Paula & Her Daughter |
| 18 | Tomb of St Heironymus |
| 19 | Chapel of the Holy Innocents |
| 20 | Chapel of St Joseph |
| 21 | Christ's birthplace |
| 22 | Altar of the Manger |
| 23 | Altar of the Three Kings |

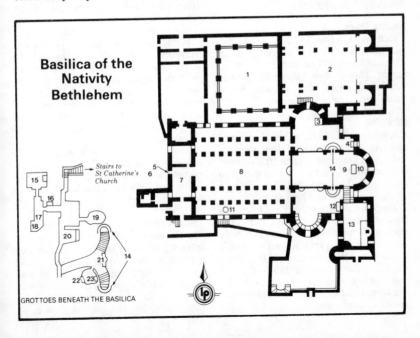

**Basilica of the Nativity Bethlehem**

GROTTOES BENEATH THE BASILICA

milk which spilt onto them. If you are really keen you can buy packets of white powder supposedly made from the rocks.

## Rachel's Tomb

This is about one km north of the town. Rachel died in childbirth and the tomb is sacred to Jews as the place to pray for a safe delivery, despite Rachel's misfortune. It was built by the British Jew, Montefiore, in 1860. Men must don a paper *yarmulkah* (skull-cap) before entering.

It is open Sunday to Thursday from 8 am to 5 pm, Friday 8 am to 1 pm, and closed Saturday.

## Places to Stay & Eat

Bethlehem is an easy half-day excursion from Jerusalem but there are a few expensive hotels around Manger Square if you want to stay the night.

Cafés around Manger Square sell food and snacks. Although it doesn't look too promising, the one opposite Rachel's Tomb serves the best felafel in the Middle East.

## Getting There

Catch an Arab bus No 22 from the Arab Bus Station or pick it up at Jaffa Gate. The trip takes half an hour and costs 50 agorot. There is also a stop right outside Rachel's Tomb. There are also Egged buses operating to Bethlehem.

## HEBRON

Known as Al Khalil in Arabic, the town of Hebron, 45 km south of Jerusalem, is unique in that it has a shrine (the Tomb of the Patriarchs) that is not only sacred to Jews and Muslims but has both a synagogue and a mosque in it.

Despite this rare example of tolerance (from both sides) in the West Bank, the town itself has been the scene of bloody fighting in the years since the Israeli occupation. Although outbreaks of violence are not common today, they still occur and it is not a bad idea to check on the situation at the tourist office in Jerusalem before visiting.

Hebron is also famous for its glass-blowers and examples of their art are for sale all over town.

## History

In ancient times Hebron was known as Kiryat Arba (The Town of Four). Some say this is because of the four hills it is built upon, while legend has it that it was because of the four giants who fell to earth here after a revolt against God. When Moses sent scouts to spy out the area they came back with a bunch of grapes so big that they had to 'bare it between two upon a staff', (Numbers 13:23).

Abraham bought the Cave of Machpelah from a Hittite and buried his wife Sarah there (Genesis 23:17-19), and was later buried there himself. Later, Isaac and his wife Rebecca, and Jacob and his wife Leah were also buried in the cave. King David also lived here for seven years before the capture of Jerusalem.

The town became sacred to Muslims after their conquest because of its association with Abraham, who built the first shrine to Allah in Mecca.

Hebron has remained predominantly Muslim since then, although there was an influx of Russian Jewish immigrants in the 19th century, followed by more in the early 1920s. The local Arab population revolted and in 1929 the Jews were set upon. Many were massacred and the British forces evacuated the survivors to Jerusalem.

After the 1967 war a new Jewish settlement was established in the north-east of the town and clashes between the Arabs and Jews have continued sporadically since then.

## Things to See

The Haram al-Khalil is the main point of interest, but other things in the town to see include the *souk* and Abraham's Oak, where Abraham supposedly rested and was visited by three angels – it is now in the grounds of a Russian Orthodox Monastery. You can also see glass being

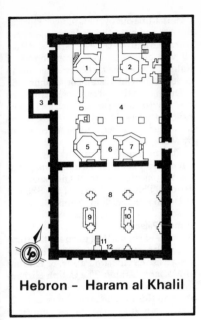

## Hebron – Haram al Khalil

| | |
|---|---|
| 1 | Cenotaph of Jacob |
| 2 | Cenotaph of Leah |
| 3 | Tomb of Joseph |
| 4 | Forecourt |
| 5 | Cenotaph of Abraham |
| 6 | Forecourt |
| 7 | Cenotaph of Sarah |
| 8 | Mosque |
| 9 | Cenotaph of Isaac |
| 10 | Cenotaph of Rebecca |
| 11 | Minbar (pulpit) |
| 12 | Mihrab (prayer niche) |

Crusader church, apart from the minarets which were built by the Mamelukes.

On entering the usually crowded mosque, the empty cenotaphs of Abraham and Sarah are draped with green velvet donated by a Turkish Sultan in the 19th century. The *mihrab* (prayer niche) in the southern wall is finely decorated and the wooden *minbar* (pulpit) dates from the 11th century and was built on the orders of the Fatimid Caliph of Egypt. In front of the minbar are the marble cenotaphs of Isaac and Rebecca and across the courtyard lie the cenotaphs of Jacob and Leah. The cenotaphs are all empty and the bodies are actually in the cave below, which is inaccessible although you can look through a grill in the floor down a shaft where a small oil lamp burns at the bottom.

Another small room contains the cenotaph of Joseph who, according to tradition, is also buried in Hebron.

Visiting hours are 7.30 to 11.30 am and 1.30 to 4.30 pm Sunday to Thursday. During Ramadan and at prayer times it is not possible to enter the mosque.

### Getting There

Hebron is only an hour or so from Jerusalem on a No 23 bus from the Arab bus station near Damascus Gate; 1.50 NIS.

There are also Egged buses (No 060) but these only run to the new Jewish Quarter in the north-east of town.

### JERICHO

Yep, this is where Joshua fit de battle and de walls came tumblin' down! It's the only town of any size on either side of the Jordan River.

The road from Jerusalem winds down through the barren hills into the scorched Jordan Valley and the oasis town of Jericho, which is one of the oldest in the world. The greenery and shady trees are in stark contrast to the blinding glare of the surrounding desert.

Apart from being the site of Joshua's tumbling walls, it was also on a street in

blown at the workshops in the Harat el Qazzazin (the New Glass Blowers Quarter) north of town.

### Haram al-Khalil

The Haram al-Khalil, built over the Cave of Machpelah, dominates the central area of town. The foundations of the building date back to Herodian times; the rest of the construction used to be a

Jericho that Jesus healed a blind beggar and stayed at the house of the publican Zaccheus.

Today Jericho, called Ariha in Arabic, is an agricultural centre and on its outskirts towards Jerusalem is the large expanse of one of the many Palestinian refugee camps.

If you need to change money, there are a few moneychangers around the shady town square, which also has plenty of small felafel shops on it.

## History

The finds from archaeological excavations at Tell es Sultan, on a hill overlooking the town, indicate that Jericho was inhabited as early as 10,000 years ago. The remains of a 7000-year-old fortified village have been unearthed which lend credence to the claim that Jericho is the oldest continuously inhabited village in the world.

Jericho was taken by the Jews around 1250 BC, when the famous wall-tumbling incident is alleged to have happened. Joshua sent two spies into Jericho, where they stayed in the house of the harlot, Rahab. For sheltering the spies, her house and family would be spared if she draped

Neolithic skull, Jericho

a scarlet line out of the window. This she did and when the priests blew the trumpets and the tribes of Israel shouted, all was destroyed except the house of Rahab. The whole attack is described in detail in the Old Testament, Joshua 2-6.

During the time of the Romans Jericho was moved to its present site and was a haven of orchards and palm trees. It was presented to Queen Cleopatra of Egypt by Mark Antony.

The town reached its peak during the reign of Herod and his winter palace was located in the Wadi al-Qilt south of Jericho. This is the Valley of the Shadow of Death referred to in Psalm 23.

## Hisham Palace

A couple of km north of town are the ruins of an 8th-century Omayyed residence known as the Hisham Palace, or Khirbat al-Mafjar in Arabic. The Caliph Hisham Ibn Abdul Malik had a love of the desert and had this luxurious residence built. It was destroyed by an earthquake only four years after its completion.

The palace buildings include baths, a mosque, colonnaded forecourt and an ornamental pool. They are fine examples of Islamic architecture. The rooms were richly decorated with carved stucco, much of it now on display in the Rockefeller Museum in Jerusalem, and the 30-metre-square floor of the baths revealed one of the largest areas of ancient mosaics known. Apart from a couple of small areas, these mosaics have been covered with a layer of sand to preserve them from further deterioration. In the north-west corner of the baths is a small retiring room which contains one of the most beautiful and well-preserved mosaics in the world. Entitled the Tree of Life, it depicts an orange tree complete with fruit and there are three gazelles at its base, one of them being brought down by a lion. The size of the tiles in this mosaic are extremely small so the fine detail and shading are far more delicate than in most mosaics of this era. The rest

Tree of Life, Jericho

of the mosaic floor has the design of a Persian rug.

The palace is four km north of town on the road which runs off the town square, to the right of the police station – a 45-minute walk. It is open daily from 8 am to 4 pm; entry is 2.30 NIS. There's a small kiosk and museum inside the entrance where you can buy a much-needed drink or top up your water container.

### Tell es Sultan

The ruins of ancient Jericho at Tell es Sultan are also four km from town, but to the north-west. From the top of the site you get a good view of the surrounding valley with the Dead Sea shimmering in the distance. It is open daily from 8 am to 5 pm; entry is 2.30 NIS.

Across the road from the foot of Tell es Sultan is Elisha's Spring, where tradition has it that the prophet purified the undrinkable water by throwing a handful of salt in it (II Kings 2:21).

### Mount of Temptation

A km or so further on from Tell es Sultan is a monastery built on a cliff, believed to be the Biblical Mount of Temptation where Jesus fasted for 40 days and nights and was tempted by Satan (Matthew 4:8-9). The monastery belongs to the Greek

Orthodox Church and the monks there will show you around. It is open from 7 am to 2 pm and 3 to 4 pm in winter; longer hours in summer but these are very flexible.

### Getting There

The buses for Jerusalem leave from the street to the left of the police station on the town square, and the *sheruts* go from the street leading off it towards Jerusalem.

To get to Jericho from Jerusalem, take a No 28 bus from the Arab Bus Station for the half-hour, 1.30 NIS ride, or a *sherut* for 2.5 NIS from the station outside Damascus Gate and ask for Ariha – the Arabic name for Jericho.

## QUMRAN

In 1947 in the caves at Qumran, 20 km south of Jericho, the now-famous Dead Sea Scrolls were found in earthenware pots by a couple of Bedouin boys looking for lost goats. In the years immediately following, all the caves in the surrounding hills were scoured and the finds were sensational. Over 4000 scrolls were discovered, some of them Biblical manuscripts written in Hebrew representing almost all of the Old Testament books.

The ancient village of Qumran at the foot of the hills was then excavated and it was revealed that this was the village of the Essenes, an obscure Jewish sect who had moved to this barren site in the 2nd century BC to pursue their unorthodox religious practices undisturbed.

Only the ruins of the ancient village exist today along with a small visitors centre selling cold drinks and food. The site is easy to visit as it's only 100 metres or so off the busy highway which runs along the western shore of the Dead Sea to Ein Gedi and Masada and on to Eilat on the Red Sea.

### History

Originally a fortress in about the 8th century BC, the site was deserted until the Essenes came along and built small

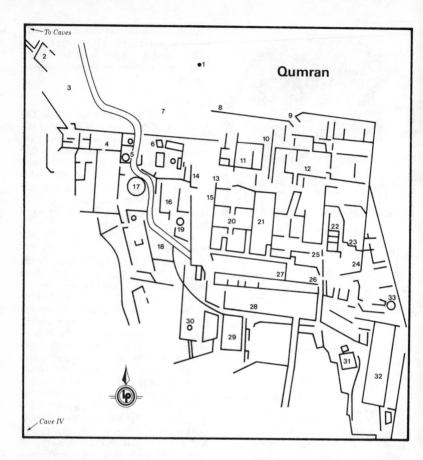

houses around the older ruins. One of their main concerns was obviously obtaining water in such a desolate area, attested to by the number of cisterns they built. These were fed by a water channel from the waterfalls at nearby Wadi Qumran.

They lived a peaceful existence here for almost 300 years, although they were forced to abandon it for some years after a disastrous earthquake in about 31 BC. In 66 AD when the first Jewish revolt started, the Roman army moved throughout the country to suppress it and the Essenes

copped it, although it is not known whether they were actually part of the revolt. They must have had advance warning of the attack, however, as they had time to stash their precious scrolls in the nearby caves and flee. Apart from being used briefly as a hideout by rebels during the second Jewish revolt in the 2nd century AD, the site was totally abandoned.

## The Ruins

The ruins have been excavated and labelled and a fenced path, which is a bit of an obstacle course, leads through them

| | |
|---|---|
| 1 | Visitors Centre |
| 2 | Stepped cistern |
| 3 | Settling pool |
| 4 | Divided room |
| 5 | Grain storage bins |
| 6 | Cistern |
| 7 | Open courtyard |
| 8 | Tower |
| 9 | Roman door |
| 10 | Room with shattered lintel |
| 11 | Doorless room |
| 12 | Kitchen |
| 13 | Door |
| 14 | Open courtyard |
| 15 | Door |
| 16 | Cistern |
| 17 | Cistern |
| 18 | Flour mill |
| 19 | Bread oven |
| 20 | Assembly room |
| 21 | Room |
| 22 | Stepped cistern |
| 23 | Bathroom |
| 24 | Cracked cistern |
| 25 | Bathroom |
| 26 | Divided cistern |
| 27 | Divided cistern |
| 28 | Room of worship |
| 29 | Pottery store |
| 30 | Cistern with steps |
| 31 | Clay-working area |
| 32 | Stepped cistern |
| 33 | Pottery kilns |

so that nothing is disturbed. In the long, narrow room (21 on the plan) a bench was found with two inkwells set in it and it was concluded that this was the room where the Essenes wrote the scrolls. Other finds include a pottery kiln (33), bread oven (19) and many cisterns. The steps leading to one of the cisterns (22) are split by an enormous crack, which shows the devastation of the earthquake in 31 BC.

**Cave IV**, where some of the major finds were made, can be seen across a gully at the south of the site. Other caves further up are accessible from a path on the north of the site.

The site is open daily from 8 am to 5 pm; entry is 2.50 NIS. The flash tourist shop has flash prices to match, but there are water tanks at the back of the entrance booth if you want a reasonably priced drink.

### Ein Feshka
A few km further south along the main road are the freshwater springs and beach at Ein Feshka. This is a very low-key resort and doesn't have the crowds of Ein Gedi. It is open daily from 8 am to 4 pm.

### Getting There
Egged buses to Ein Gedi and Masada pass by the turn-off for Qumran so you have to keep your eyes peeled and ring the bell when you see it. There are red bus shelters on either side of the road, right where the road comes in close to the cliffs for the first time. The bus services along this route are inadequate and you need to get to the Central Bus Station at least half an hour before the listed departure time to be assured of a seat. The trip to Qumran takes about 40 minutes and costs 3.50 NIS.

It is not too difficult to hitch back to Jerusalem or Jericho from Qumran, and as the turn-off also serves a nearby kibbutz, there are often young people driving into Jerusalem.

# Index

## Temperature

To convert °C to °F multiply by 1.8 and add 32

To convert °F to °C subtract 32 and multiply by ·55

## Length, Distance & Area

| | *multiply by* |
|---|---|
| inches to centimetres | 2.54 |
| centimetres to inches | 0.39 |
| feet to metres | 0.30 |
| metres to feet | 3.28 |
| yards to metres | 0.91 |
| metres to yards | 1.09 |
| miles to kilometres | 1.61 |
| kilometres to miles | 0.62 |
| acres to hectares | 0.40 |
| hectares to acres | 2.47 |

## Weight

| | *multiply by* |
|---|---|
| ounces to grams | 28.35 |
| grams to ounces | 0.035 |
| pounds to kilograms | 0.45 |
| kilograms to pounds | 2.21 |
| British tons to kilograms | 1016 |
| US tons to kilograms | 907 |

A British ton is 2240 lbs, a US ton is 2000 lbs

## Volume

| | *multiply by* |
|---|---|
| Imperial gallons to litres | 4.55 |
| litres to imperial gallons | 0.22 |
| US gallons to litres | 3.79 |
| litres to US gallons | 0.26 |

5 imperial gallons equals 6 US gallons
a litre is slightly more than a US quart, slightly less
than a British one

Dear traveller

Prices go up, good places go bad, bad places go bankrupt ... and every guide book is inevitably outdated in places. Fortunately, many travellers write to us about their experiences, telling us when things have changed. If we reprint a book between editions, we try to include as much of this information as possible in a Stop Press section. Most of this information has not been verified by our own writers.

We really enjoy hearing from people out on the road, and apart from guaranteeing that others will benefit from your good and bad experiences, we're prepared to bribe you with the offer of a free book for sending us substantial useful information.

Thank you to everyone who has written, and to those who haven't, I hope you do find this book useful – and that you let us know when it isn't.

Tony Wheeler

---

While Jordan is a popular tourist destination, Syria is a country that few travellers manage to visit, however, those who do get to Syria are not disappointed. The locals are said to be very friendly and hospitable.

The following section was compiled using information sent to us by these travellers: Ivo Breukers (Nl), M & M Clark (Aus), J Clayburn (UK), Martin Dichtl (D), Janice Flaherty (USA), Ruth Jaeger (USA), H & H Pearman (UK), John Rice (USA), N Shillcock (Aus), Victor Sadilek (D) and Eric van Kempen (Nl).

## JORDAN
### Visas
Australians and some other nationalities can obtain visas on arrival at Queen Alia Airport. One traveller told us that when he entered Jordan, his passport was stamped telling him to report to a police station within a certain number of days. At the police station he was given a card, written in Arabic, which was to be presented to officials as he left Jordan. When Tony Wheeler visited Jordan early this year, there was no mention at all of having to report to the police.

West Bank permits can be easily obtained in Amman. Ask taxi drivers for the Marriot or Plaza Hotels, useful landmarks near the Ministry of the Interior. The passes are issued from the small building outside and to one side of the Ministry of the Interior compound. When you come to collect your pass it is now simply handed over the counter to you without any waiting around or shuffling from place to place.

### Money & Costs
All the currency exchange offices were closed in early '89 and a year later there was no sign of them reopening. Exchange rates vary widely from bank to bank and hotel to hotel although, curiously, large hotels sometimes offer better exchange rates than the banks. The dinar is in decline and the exchange rate is getting more favourable for foreigners. The current exchange rate is about US$1 to JD0.670.

It's important to note is that prices are often quoted in piastres. There are 10 fils to one piastre and 1000 fils to one dinar. When someone gives you a price, check whether they are talking about fils or piastres.

When travelling from Amman's airport into town by taxi it will cost about JD5 to JD6. Note that these taxis are quite different from the regular ones and their meters show fares in piastres. Regular taxis' meters show fares in fils. So when an airport taxi meter says 150 it means 150 piastres, which is JD1.500. When a regular taxi meter says 150 it means JD0.150. This causes considerable confusion when you first get into a regular taxi and find the meter spinning round at an incredible rate, compared to the airport taxi.

### Getting There & Away

You cannot take food, not even tinned, into Israel from Jordan. It is not true that people entering from Jordan must remove film from their cameras at the border.

For those going to Iraq, the Cliff Hotel (tel 624 273) in Amman has a travellers' notebook with excellent information in it.

### Travellers' Tips & Comments

There are now several hotels in Petra, including the *Sun Set Hotel & Restaurant* (tel (03) 83579) which is near the entrance gate and has neat, clean singles/doubles for JD6/10.

Other new hotels include the *Al Ambat Hotel & Restaurant* in Wadi Musa and the *Mussa Spring Hotel & Restaurant* (tel (03) 83310) right on the outskirts. Singles/doubles at the *Rest House* are now JD14.400/19.600 and at the *Forum Hotel* they are JD50/60, a big price jump.

If you are driving down to Petra from Amman you should leave as early as possible in winter in order to have time to see the attractions en route and arrive before it gets dark at 5 pm.

Tony Wheeler – Australia

The Hejaz railway line resumed service in October last year after seven years' interruption. The 80-year-old narrow gauge cars run over the very tracks once raided by T E Lawrence. It costs around US$3.50 in 1st class and US$2.10 in 2nd class. There is also a JD4 departure tax.

John Rice – Jordan

### SYRIA
### Visas

It is no longer possible for ordinary British citizens to get into Syria. Two British travellers failed after enquiring at both the British and Syrian embassies in Amman. This was due to the severance of all diplomatic contacts. There is also a Syrian national in jail in the UK who apparently attempted to plant a bomb on an El Al plane.

As Syria has no diplomatic representation in Australia, Australians can obtain Syrian visas at the border or the airport. Visas cost JD5.500 per person. They are cheaper at the Turkish border. We've heard that the Syrian Embassy in Istanbul, Turkey, insists on seeing a letter of recommendation from your own embassy. You won't be asked for a letter of recommendation if you wait and get your visa at the border with Turkey.

### Money & Costs

The official exchange rate is around US$1 to S£20. There is a black market but beware – there are secret police everywhere and the punishment for those caught using the black market is up to 15 years' imprisonment!

Apparently, the Syrian government now lets you bring in as much Syrian currency as you like. You can buy it in Jordan or Turkey. One traveller bought some Syrian pounds from the Midland Bank of England at a fantastic rate of exchange.

It's no longer necessary to pay for most hotels in US dollars. Generally, hotel prices have increased 100% or more since this edition was first published.

Hitching is easy, although some people ask for money. If you say to a driver, *Ana maffi fluus*, which means something like 'I don't have money', they will normally just laugh and, with a invite you into the car.

### Getting Around

If you want to take day trips from Aleppo, you should go down to the Karnak Bus Station early in the morning to buy your tickets two days in advance.

### Travellers' Tips & Comments

In Aleppo, a nice thing for women to do on a Thursday or Saturday is go to a *hammam* (Turkish bath). When you leave the citadel, turn left and walk down the right-hand side of the street to the Al Nasri Turkish Bath, renovated in 1440. Women will steam you, wash your hair, scrub you with a loofa sponge, and massage you for approximately US$3. You can then have tea (costs extra) and relax on the couches.

Janice Flaherty – USA

# Guides to the Middle East

### Egypt & the Sudan – a travel survival kit
The sights of Egypt and the Sudan have impressed visitors for more than 50 centuries. This guide takes you beyond the spectacular pyramids to discover the villages of the Nile, diving in the Red Sea and many other attractions.

### Israel – a travel survival kit
This is a comprehensive guidebook to a small, fascinating country that is packed with things to see and do. This guide will help you unravel its political and religious significance – and enjoy your stay.

### Turkey – a travel survival kit
Unspoilt by tourism, Turkey is a travellers' paradise, whether you want to lie on a beach or explore the ancient cities that are the legacy of a rich and varied past. This acclaimed guide will help you to make the most of your stay.

### West Asia on a shoestring
A complete guide to the overland trip from Bangladesh to Turkey. Information for budget travellers to Afghanistan, Bangladesh, Bhutan, India, Iran, Maldives, Nepal, Pakistan, Sri Lanka, Turkey and the Middle East.

### Yemen – a travel survival kit
One of the oldest inhabited regions in the world, the Yemen is a beautiful mountainous region with a unique architecture. This book covers both North and South Yemen in detail.

# Guides to the Indian Sub-continent

### Bangladesh – a travel survival kit
The adventurous traveller in Bangladesh can explore tropical forests and beaches, superb hill country, and ancient Buddhist ruins. This guide covers all these alternatives – and many more.

### India – a travel survival kit
An award-winning guidebook that is recognised as the outstanding contemporary guide to the subcontinent. Looking for a houseboat in Kashmir? Trying to post a parcel? This definitive guidebook has all the facts.

### Karakoram Highway, the high road to China – a travel survival kit
Travelling the Karakoram Highway is one of the greatest adventures. Travellers can now follow the Silk Road in the footsteps of Alexander the Great and Marco Polo. As well as information about the route, this guide covers treks and places away from the highway.

### Kashmir, Ladakh & Zanskar – a travel survival kit
This book contains detailed information on three contrasting Himalayan regions in the Indian state of Jammu and Kashmir – the narrow valley of Zanskar, reclusive Ladakh, and the beautiful Vale of Kashmir.

### Kathmandu & the Kingdom of Nepal – a travel survival kit
Few travellers can resist the lure of magical Kathmandu and its surrounding mountains. This guidebook takes you round the temples, to the foothills of the Himalaya, and to the Terai.

### Pakistan – a travel survival kit
Pakistan has been called 'the unknown land of the Indus' and many people don't realise the great variety of experiences it offers – from bustling Karachi, to ancient cities and tranquil mountain valleys.

### Sri Lanka – a travel survival kit
This guide takes a complete look at the island Marco Polo described as 'the finest in the world'. In one handy package you'll find ancient cities, superb countryside, and beautiful beaches.

# Lonely Planet Guidebooks

Lonely Planet guidebooks cover virtually every accessible part of Asia as well as Australia, the Pacific, Central and South America, Africa, the Middle East and parts of North America. There are four main series: 'travel survival kits', covering a single country for a range of budgets; 'shoestring' guides with compact information for low-budget travel in a major region; trekking guides; and 'phrasebooks'.

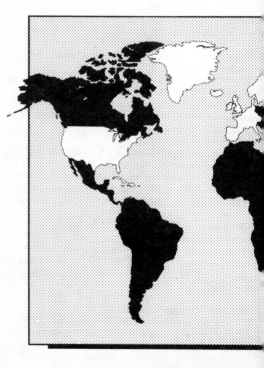

# Mail Order

Lonely Planet guidebooks are distributed worldwide and are sold by good bookshops everywhere. They are also available by mail order from Lonely Planet, so if you have difficulty finding a title please write to us. US and Canadian residents should write to Embarcadero West, 112 Linden St, Oakland CA 94607, USA and residents of other countries to PO Box 617, Hawthorn, Victoria 3122, Australia.

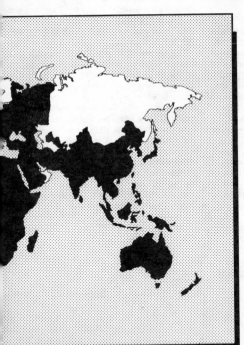

## Eastern Europe
Eastern Europe

## Indian Subcontinent
India
Hindi/Urdu phrasebook
Kashmir, Ladakh & Zanskar
Trekking in the Indian Himalaya
Pakistan
Kathmandu & the Kingdom of Nepal
Trekking in the Nepal Himalaya
Nepal phrasebook
Sri Lanka
Sri Lanka phrasebook
Bangladesh
Karakoram Highway

## Africa
Africa on a shoestring
East Africa
Swahili phrasebook
West Africa
Central Africa
Morocco, Algeria & Tunisia

## North America
Canada
Alaska

## Mexico
Mexico
Baja California

## South America
South America on a shoestring
Ecuador & the Galapagos Islands
Colombia
Chile & Easter Island
Bolivia
Brazil
Brazilian phrasebook
Peru
Argentina
Quechua phrasebook

## Middle East
Israel
Egypt & the Sudan
Jordan & Syria
Yemen

## Lonely Planet

Lonely Planet published its first book in 1973. Tony and Maureen Wheeler had made a lengthy overland trip from England to Australia and, in response to numerous 'how do you do it?' questions, Tony wrote and they published *Across Asia on the Cheap*. It became an instant local best-seller and inspired thoughts of a second travel guide. A year and a half in South-East Asia resulted in their second book, *South-East Asia on a Shoestring*, which they put together in a backstreet Chinese hotel in Singapore in 1975. The 'yellow book', as it quickly became known, soon became *the* guide to the region and has gone through five editions, always with its familiar yellow cover.

Soon other writers came to them with ideas for similar books – books that went off the beaten track with an adventurous approach to travel, books that 'assumed you knew how to get your luggage off the carousel,' as one reviewer put it. Lonely Planet grew from a kitchen table operation to a spare room and then to its own office. Its international reputation began to grow as the Lonely Planet logo began to appear in more and more countries. In 1982 *India – a travel survival kit* won the Thomas Cook award for the best guidebook of the year.

These days there are over 70 Lonely Planet titles. Over 40 people work at our office in Melbourne, Australia and another half dozen at our US office in Oakland, California.

At first Lonely Planet specialised in the Asia region but these days we are also developing major ranges of guidebooks to the Pacific region, to South America and to Africa. The list of walking guides is growing and Lonely Planet now has a unique series of phrasebooks to 'unusual' languages. The emphasis continues to be on travel for travellers and Tony and Maureen still manage to fit in a number of trips each year and play a very active part in the writing and updating of Lonely Planet's guides.

Keeping guidebooks up to date is a constant battle which requires an ear to the ground and lots of walking, but technology also plays its part. All Lonely Planet guidebooks are now stored and updated on computer, and some authors even take lap-top computers into the field. Lonely Planet is also using computers to draw maps and eventually many of the maps will be stored on disk.

The people at Lonely Planet strongly feel that travellers can make a positive contribution to the countries they visit both by better appreciation of cultures and by the money they spend. In addition the company tries to make a direct contribution to the countries and regions it covers. Since 1986 a percentage of the income from each book has gone to aid groups and associations. This has included donations to famine relief in Africa, to aid projects in India, to agricultural projects in Central America, to Greenpeace's efforts to halt French nuclear testing in the Pacific and to Amnesty International. In 1989 $41,000 was donated by Lonely Planet to these projects.